STAR WARS®
EMPIRE

VOLUME FIVE: ALLIES AND ADVERSARIES

DARK HORSE BOOKS™

STAR WARS: EMPIRE VOLUME 5

THIS VOLUME COLLECTS ISSUES #23-27 OF
THE DARK HORSE COMIC-BOOK SERIES
STAR WARS: EMPIRE.

PUBLISHED BY
DARK HORSE BOOKS
A DIVISION OF DARK HORSE COMICS, INC.
10956 SE MAIN STREET
MILWAUKIE, OR 97222

DARKHORSE.COM
STARWARS.COM

TO FIND A COMICS SHOP IN YOUR
AREA, CALL THE COMIC SHOP
LOCATOR SERVICE TOLL-FREE
AT 1-888-266-4226

FIRST EDITION: FEBRUARY 2006
ISBN: 1-59307-466-2

1 3 5 7 9 10 8 6 4 2

VOLUME FIVE:
ALLIES AND ADVERSARIES

WRITERS RON MARZ
JEREMY BARLOW

ARTISTS NICOLA SCOTT
BRANDON BADEAUX
JEFF JOHNSON
JOE CORRONEY
ADRIANA MELO

COLORIST MICHAEL ATIYEH

LETTERER MICHAEL DAVID THOMAS

FRONT COVER TOMMY LEE EDWARDS

BACK COVER DAVID MICHAEL BECK

PUBLISHER
MIKE RICHARDSON

COLLECTION DESIGNER
DEBRA BAILEY

ART DIRECTOR
LIA RIBACCHI

ASSISTANT EDITOR
DAVE MARSHALL

ASSOCIATE EDITOR
JEREMY BARLOW

EDITOR
RANDY STRADLEY

SPECIAL THANKS TO
LELAND CHEE, SUE ROSTONI
AND AMY GARY AT LUCAS LICENSING

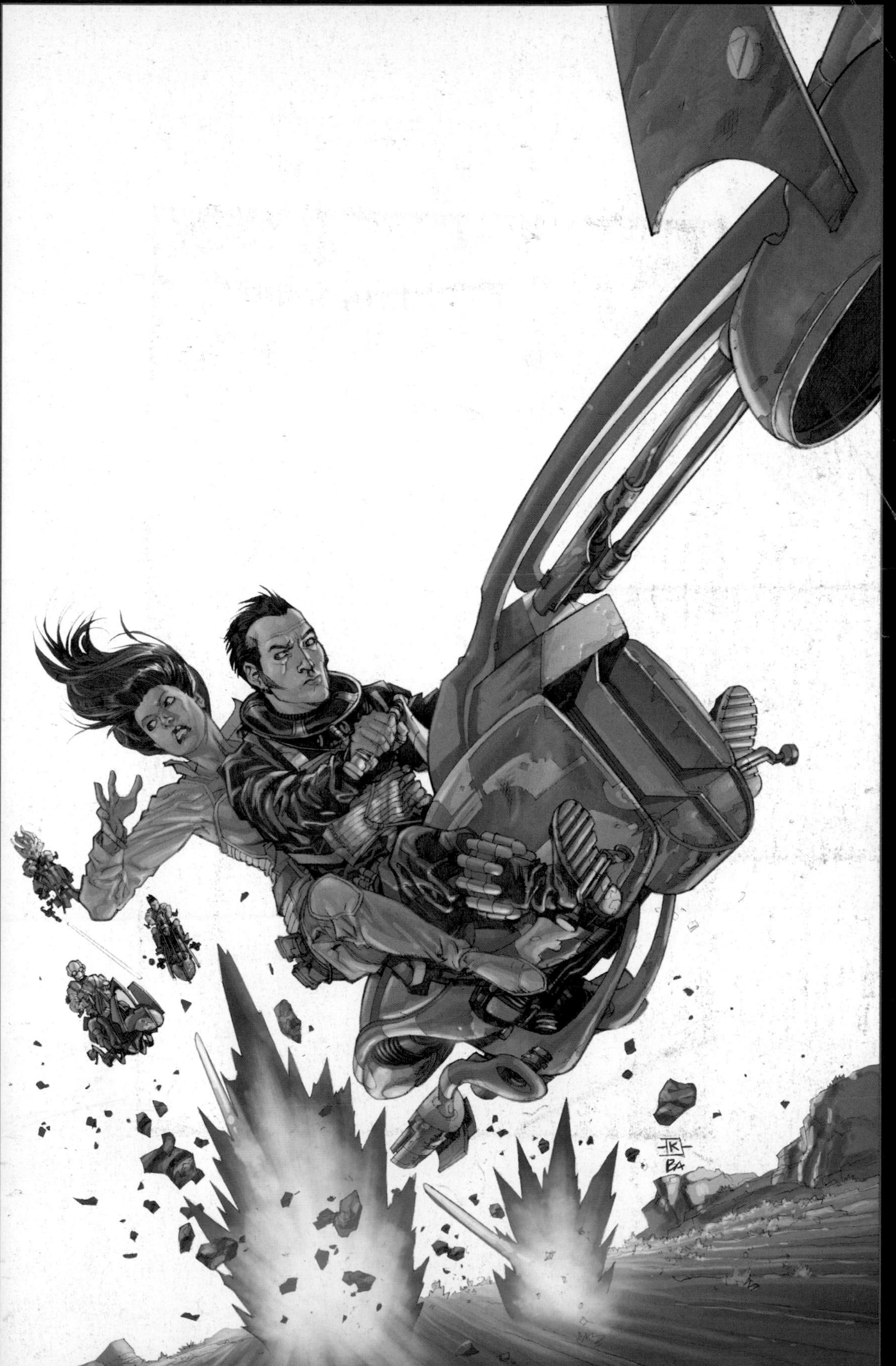

KILIAN PLUNKETT

THE BRAVERY OF
BEING OUT OF RANGE

SCRIPT JEREMY BARLOW
ART BRANDON BADEAUX
COLORS MICHAEL ATIYEH

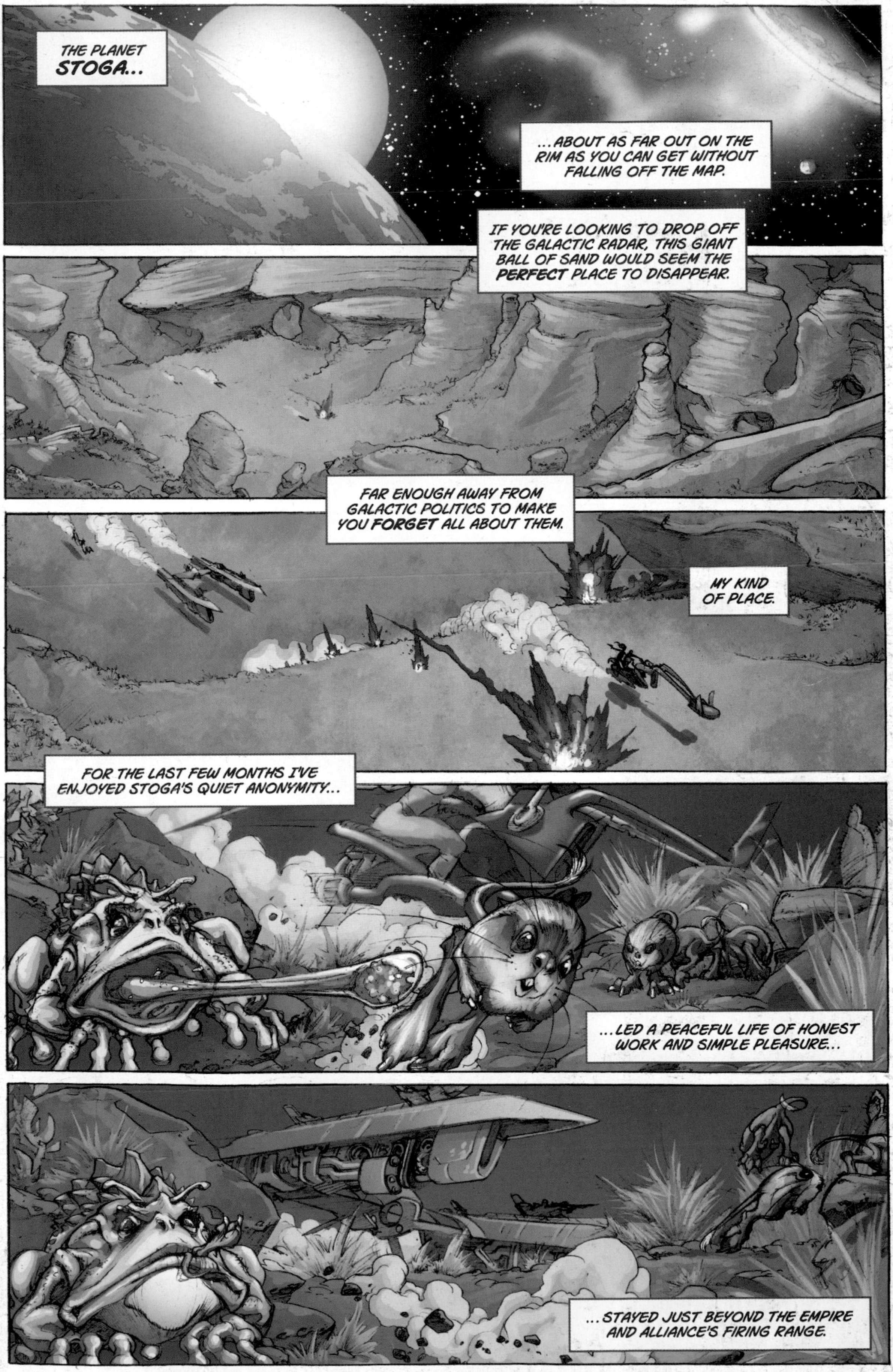

THE PLANET STOGA...
...ABOUT AS FAR OUT ON THE RIM AS YOU CAN GET WITHOUT FALLING OFF THE MAP.
IF YOU'RE LOOKING TO DROP OFF THE GALACTIC RADAR, THIS GIANT BALL OF SAND WOULD SEEM THE PERFECT PLACE TO DISAPPEAR.
FAR ENOUGH AWAY FROM GALACTIC POLITICS TO MAKE YOU FORGET ALL ABOUT THEM.
MY KIND OF PLACE.
FOR THE LAST FEW MONTHS I'VE ENJOYED STOGA'S QUIET ANONYMITY...
...LED A PEACEFUL LIFE OF HONEST WORK AND SIMPLE PLEASURE...
...STAYED JUST BEYOND THE EMPIRE AND ALLIANCE'S FIRING RANGE.

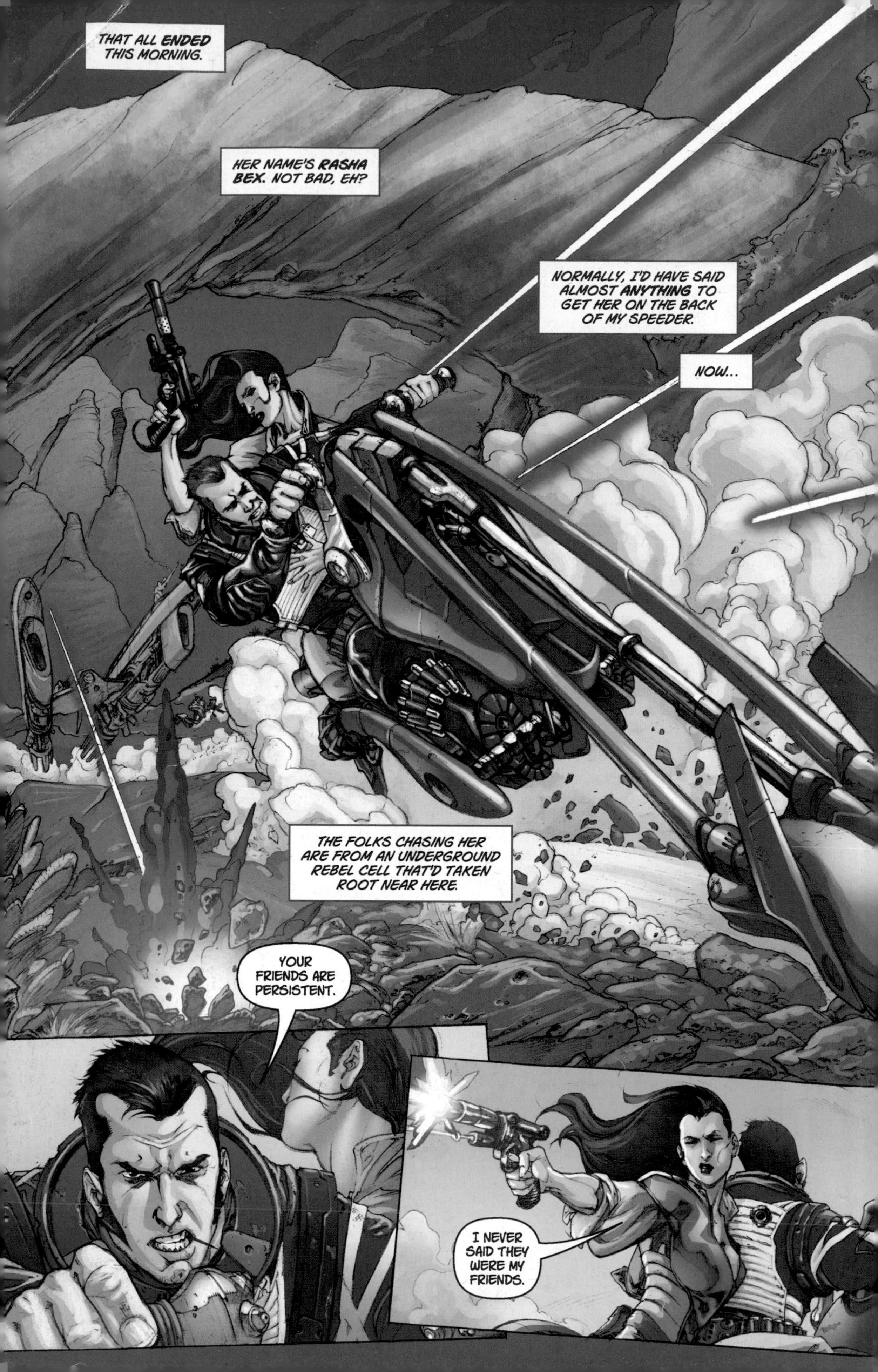
THAT ALL ENDED THIS MORNING.
HER NAME'S RASHA BEX. NOT BAD, EH?
NORMALLY, I'D HAVE SAID ALMOST ANYTHING TO GET HER ON THE BACK OF MY SPEEDER.
NOW...
THE FOLKS CHASING HER ARE FROM AN UNDERGROUND REBEL CELL THAT'D TAKEN ROOT NEAR HERE.
YOUR FRIENDS ARE PERSISTENT.
I NEVER SAID THEY WERE MY FRIENDS.

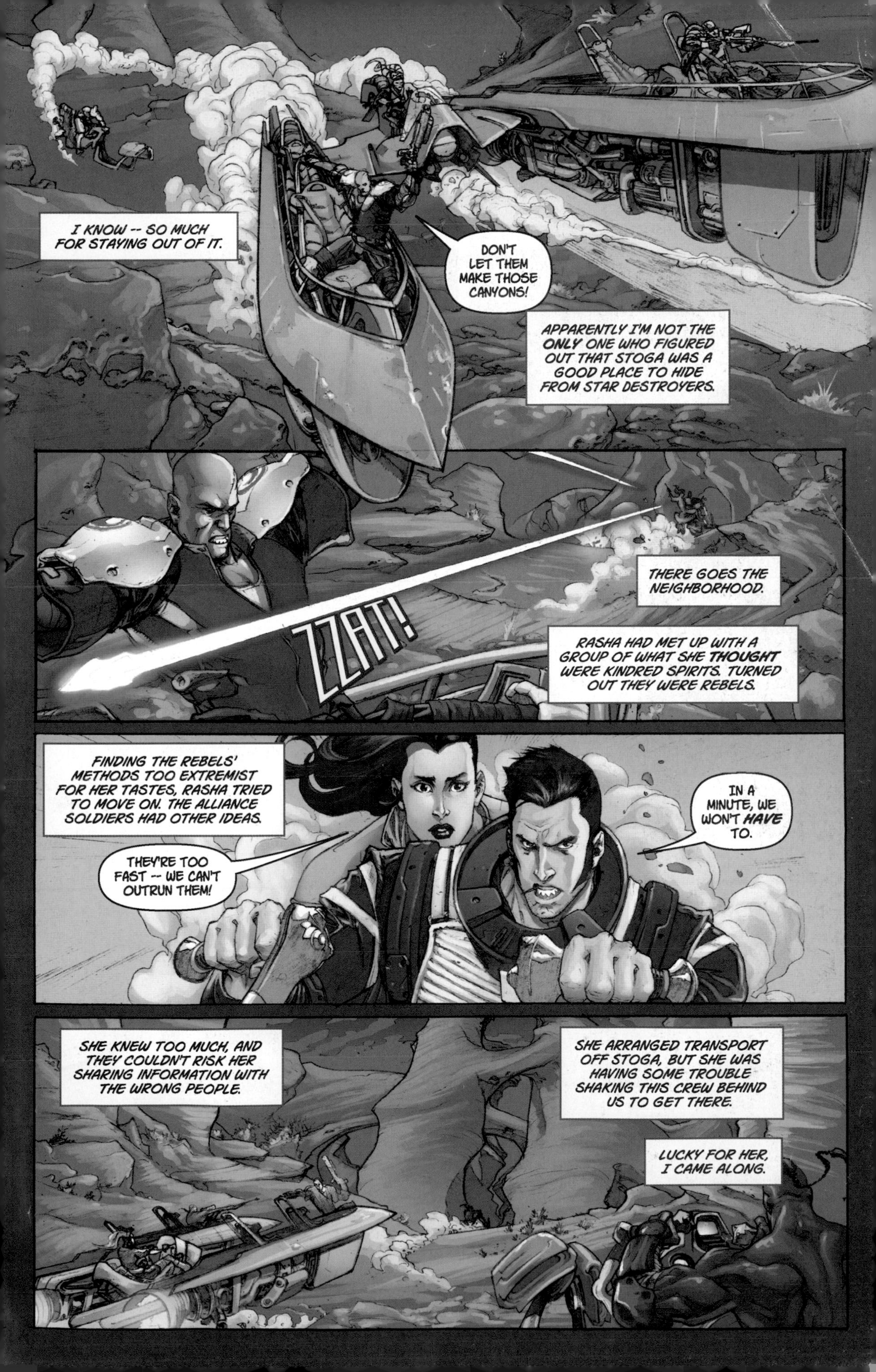

I KNOW -- SO MUCH FOR STAYING OUT OF IT.
DON'T LET THEM MAKE THOSE CANYONS!
APPARENTLY I'M NOT THE ONLY ONE WHO FIGURED OUT THAT STOGA WAS A GOOD PLACE TO HIDE FROM STAR DESTROYERS.
THERE GOES THE NEIGHBORHOOD.
ZZAT!
RASHA HAD MET UP WITH A GROUP OF WHAT SHE THOUGHT WERE KINDRED SPIRITS. TURNED OUT THEY WERE REBELS.
FINDING THE REBELS' METHODS TOO EXTREMIST FOR HER TASTES, RASHA TRIED TO MOVE ON. THE ALLIANCE SOLDIERS HAD OTHER IDEAS.
THEY'RE TOO FAST -- WE CAN'T OUTRUN THEM!
IN A MINUTE, WE WON'T HAVE TO.
SHE KNEW TOO MUCH, AND THEY COULDN'T RISK HER SHARING INFORMATION WITH THE WRONG PEOPLE.
SHE ARRANGED TRANSPORT OFF STOGA, BUT SHE WAS HAVING SOME TROUBLE SHAKING THIS CREW BEHIND US TO GET THERE.
LUCKY FOR HER, I CAME ALONG.

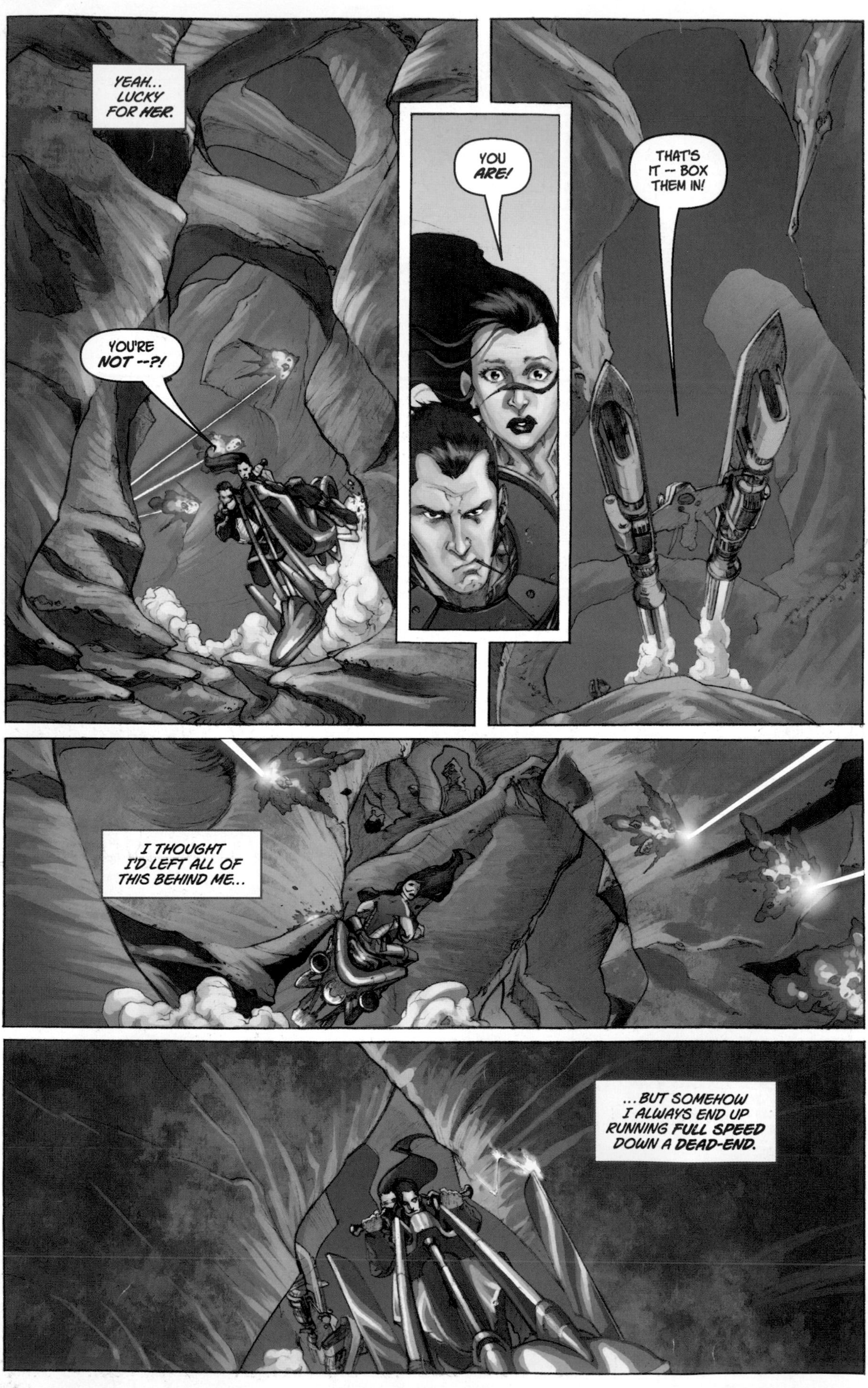
YEAH... LUCKY FOR HER.
YOU'RE NOT --?!
YOU ARE!
THAT'S IT -- BOX THEM IN!
I THOUGHT I'D LEFT ALL OF THIS BEHIND ME...
...BUT SOMEHOW I ALWAYS END UP RUNNING FULL SPEED DOWN A DEAD-END.

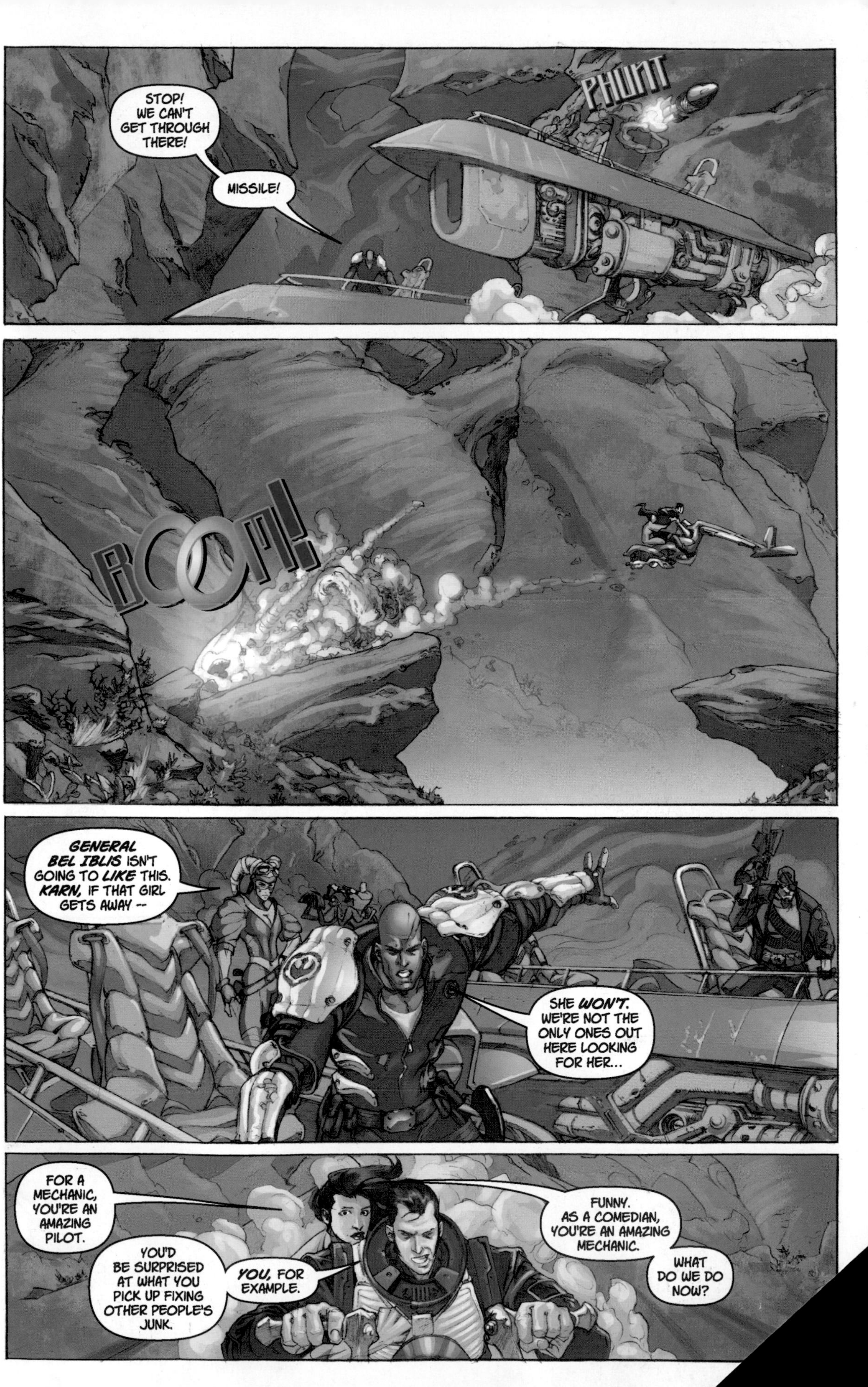
PHUNT
STOP! WE CAN'T GET THROUGH THERE!
MISSILE!
BOOM!
GENERAL BEL IBLIS ISN'T GOING TO LIKE THIS. KARN, IF THAT GIRL GETS AWAY --
SHE WON'T. WE'RE NOT THE ONLY ONES OUT HERE LOOKING FOR HER...
FOR A MECHANIC, YOU'RE AN AMAZING PILOT.
YOU'D BE SURPRISED AT WHAT YOU PICK UP FIXING OTHER PEOPLE'S JUNK.
YOU, FOR EXAMPLE.
FUNNY. AS A COMEDIAN, YOU'RE AN AMAZING MECHANIC.
WHAT DO WE DO NOW?

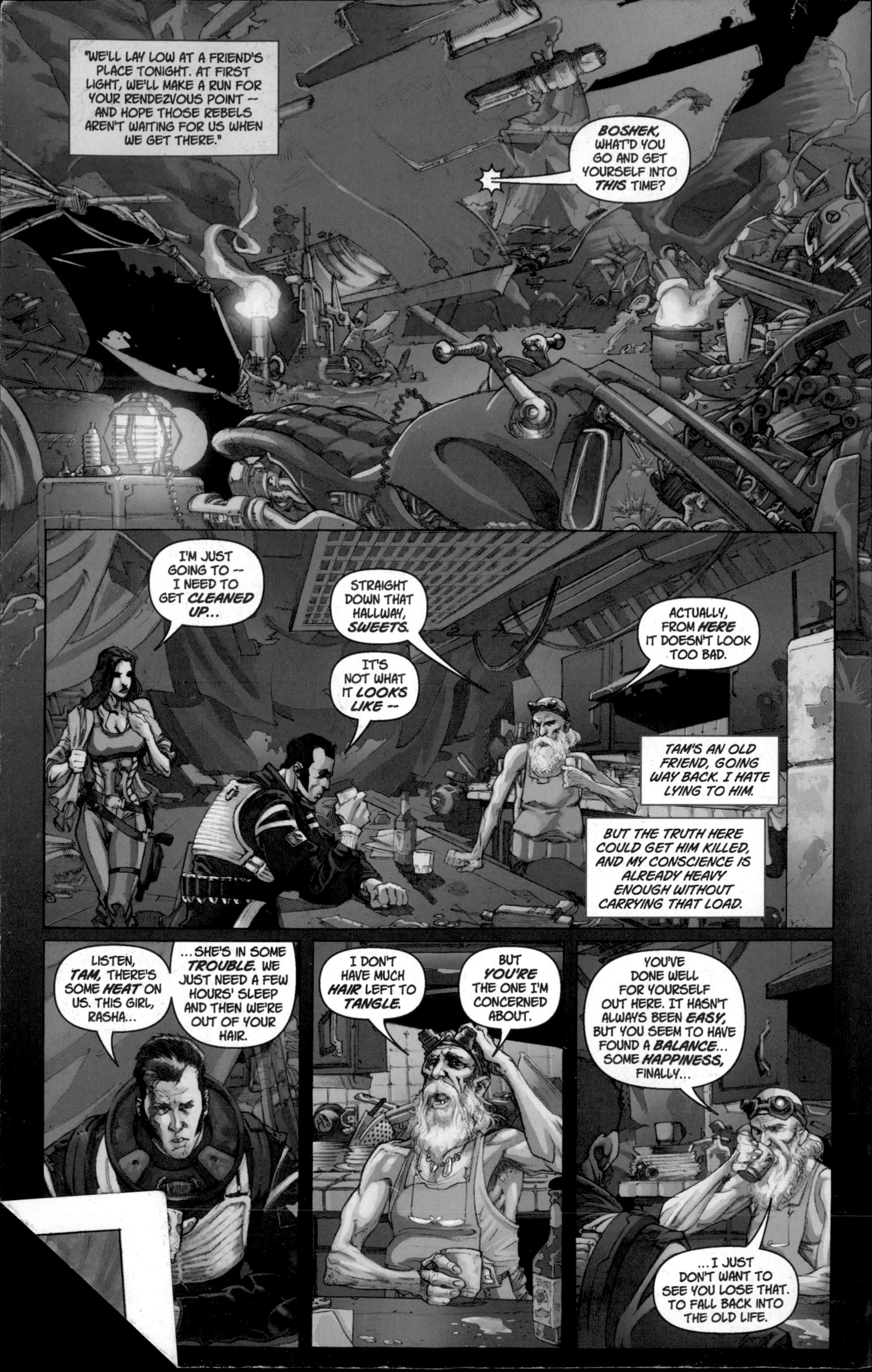
"WE'LL LAY LOW AT A FRIEND'S PLACE TONIGHT. AT FIRST LIGHT, WE'LL MAKE A RUN FOR YOUR RENDEZVOUS POINT -- AND HOPE THOSE REBELS AREN'T WAITING FOR US WHEN WE GET THERE."
BOSHEK, WHAT'D YOU GO AND GET YOURSELF INTO THIS TIME?
I'M JUST GOING TO -- I NEED TO GET CLEANED UP...
STRAIGHT DOWN THAT HALLWAY, SWEETS.
IT'S NOT WHAT IT LOOKS LIKE --
ACTUALLY, FROM HERE IT DOESN'T LOOK TOO BAD.
TAM'S AN OLD FRIEND, GOING WAY BACK. I HATE LYING TO HIM.
BUT THE TRUTH HERE COULD GET HIM KILLED, AND MY CONSCIENCE IS ALREADY HEAVY ENOUGH WITHOUT CARRYING THAT LOAD.
LISTEN, TAM, THERE'S SOME HEAT ON US. THIS GIRL, RASHA...
...SHE'S IN SOME TROUBLE. WE JUST NEED A FEW HOURS' SLEEP AND THEN WE'RE OUT OF YOUR HAIR.
I DON'T HAVE MUCH HAIR LEFT TO TANGLE.
BUT YOU'RE THE ONE I'M CONCERNED ABOUT.
YOU'VE DONE WELL FOR YOURSELF OUT HERE. IT HASN'T ALWAYS BEEN EASY, BUT YOU SEEM TO HAVE FOUND A BALANCE... SOME HAPPINESS, FINALLY...
...I JUST DON'T WANT TO SEE YOU LOSE THAT. TO FALL BACK INTO THE OLD LIFE.

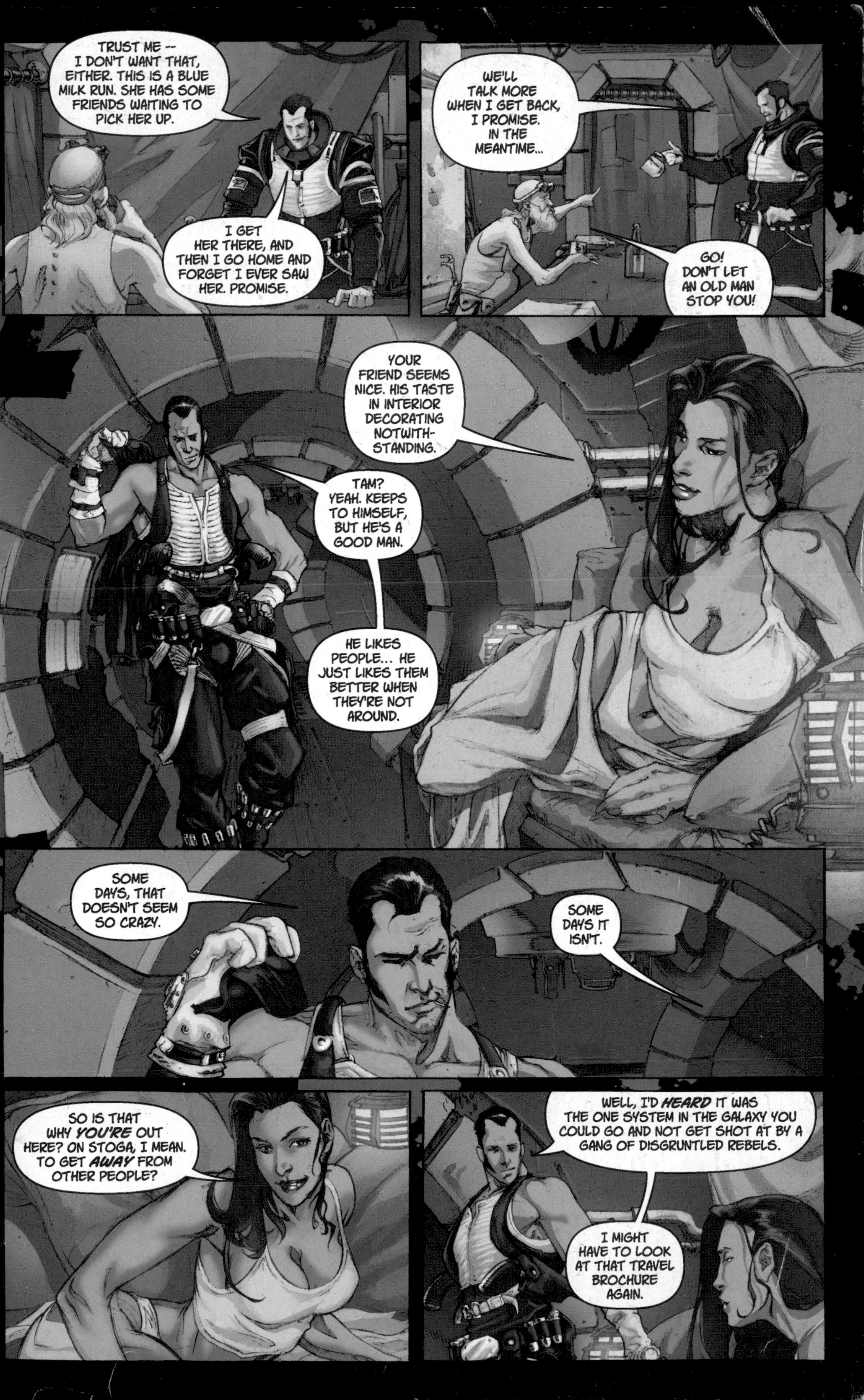
TRUST ME -- I DON'T WANT THAT, EITHER. THIS IS A BLUE MILK RUN. SHE HAS SOME FRIENDS WAITING TO PICK HER UP.
I GET HER THERE, AND THEN I GO HOME AND FORGET I EVER SAW HER. PROMISE.
WE'LL TALK MORE WHEN I GET BACK, I PROMISE. IN THE MEANTIME...
GO! DON'T LET AN OLD MAN STOP YOU!
YOUR FRIEND SEEMS NICE. HIS TASTE IN INTERIOR DECORATING NOTWITH-STANDING.
TAM? YEAH. KEEPS TO HIMSELF, BUT HE'S A GOOD MAN.
HE LIKES PEOPLE... HE JUST LIKES THEM BETTER WHEN THEY'RE NOT AROUND.
SOME DAYS, THAT DOESN'T SEEM SO CRAZY.
SOME DAYS IT ISN'T.
SO IS THAT WHY *YOU'RE* OUT HERE? ON STOGA, I MEAN. TO GET *AWAY* FROM OTHER PEOPLE?
WELL, I'D *HEARD* IT WAS THE ONE SYSTEM IN THE GALAXY YOU COULD GO AND NOT GET SHOT AT BY A GANG OF DISGRUNTLED REBELS.
I MIGHT HAVE TO LOOK AT THAT TRAVEL BROCHURE AGAIN.

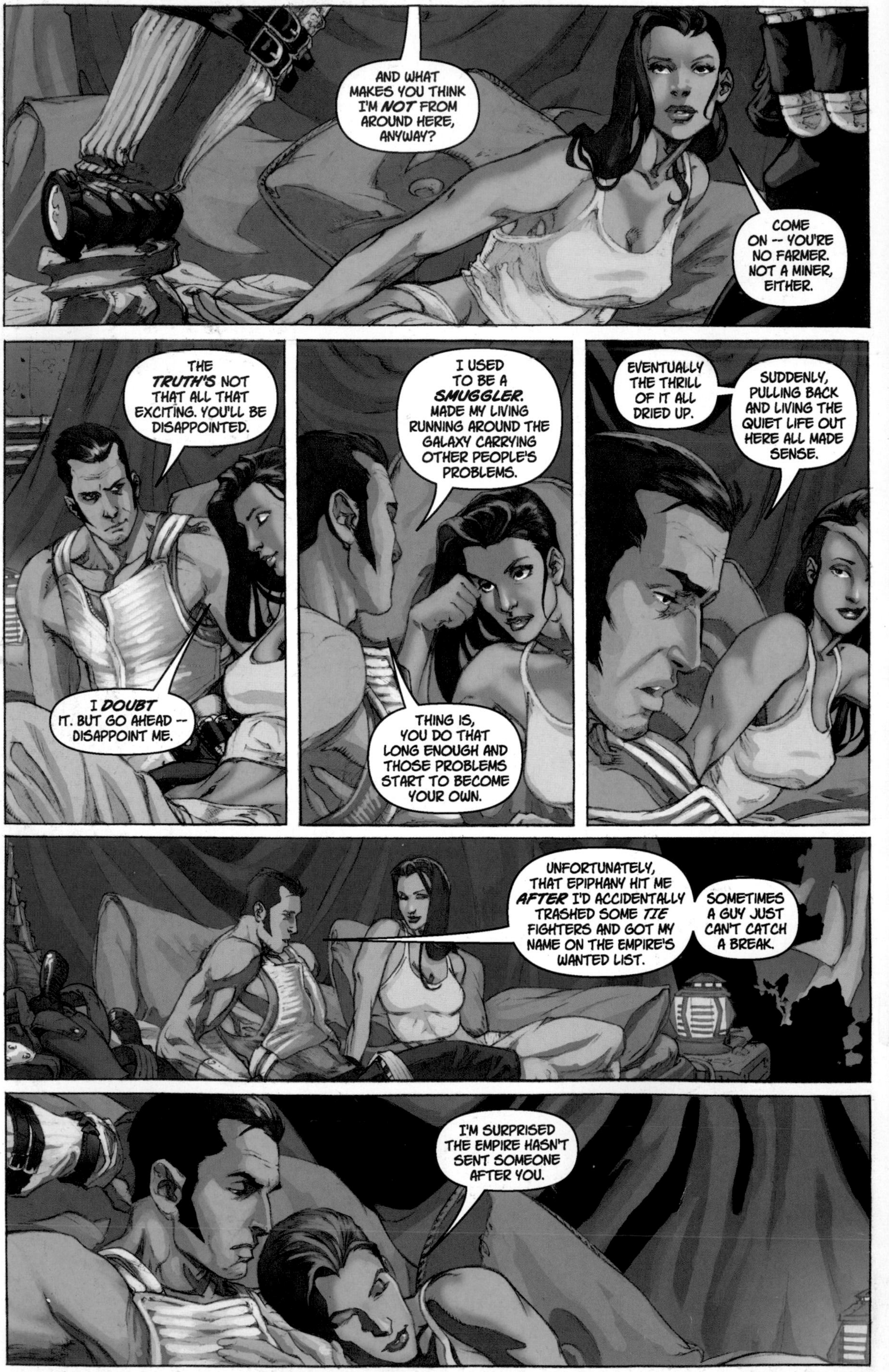

AND WHAT MAKES YOU THINK I'M *NOT* FROM AROUND HERE, ANYWAY?
COME ON -- YOU'RE NO FARMER. NOT A MINER, EITHER.
THE *TRUTH'S* NOT THAT ALL THAT EXCITING. YOU'LL BE DISAPPOINTED.
I *DOUBT* IT. BUT GO AHEAD -- DISAPPOINT ME.
I USED TO BE A *SMUGGLER*. MADE MY LIVING RUNNING AROUND THE GALAXY CARRYING OTHER PEOPLE'S PROBLEMS.
THING IS, YOU DO THAT LONG ENOUGH AND THOSE PROBLEMS START TO BECOME YOUR OWN.
EVENTUALLY THE THRILL OF IT ALL DRIED UP.
SUDDENLY, PULLING BACK AND LIVING THE QUIET LIFE OUT HERE ALL MADE SENSE.
UNFORTUNATELY, THAT EPIPHANY HIT ME *AFTER* I'D ACCIDENTALLY TRASHED SOME *TIE* FIGHTERS AND GOT MY NAME ON THE EMPIRE'S WANTED LIST.
SOMETIMES A GUY JUST CAN'T CATCH A BREAK.
I'M SURPRISED THE EMPIRE HASN'T SENT SOMEONE AFTER YOU.

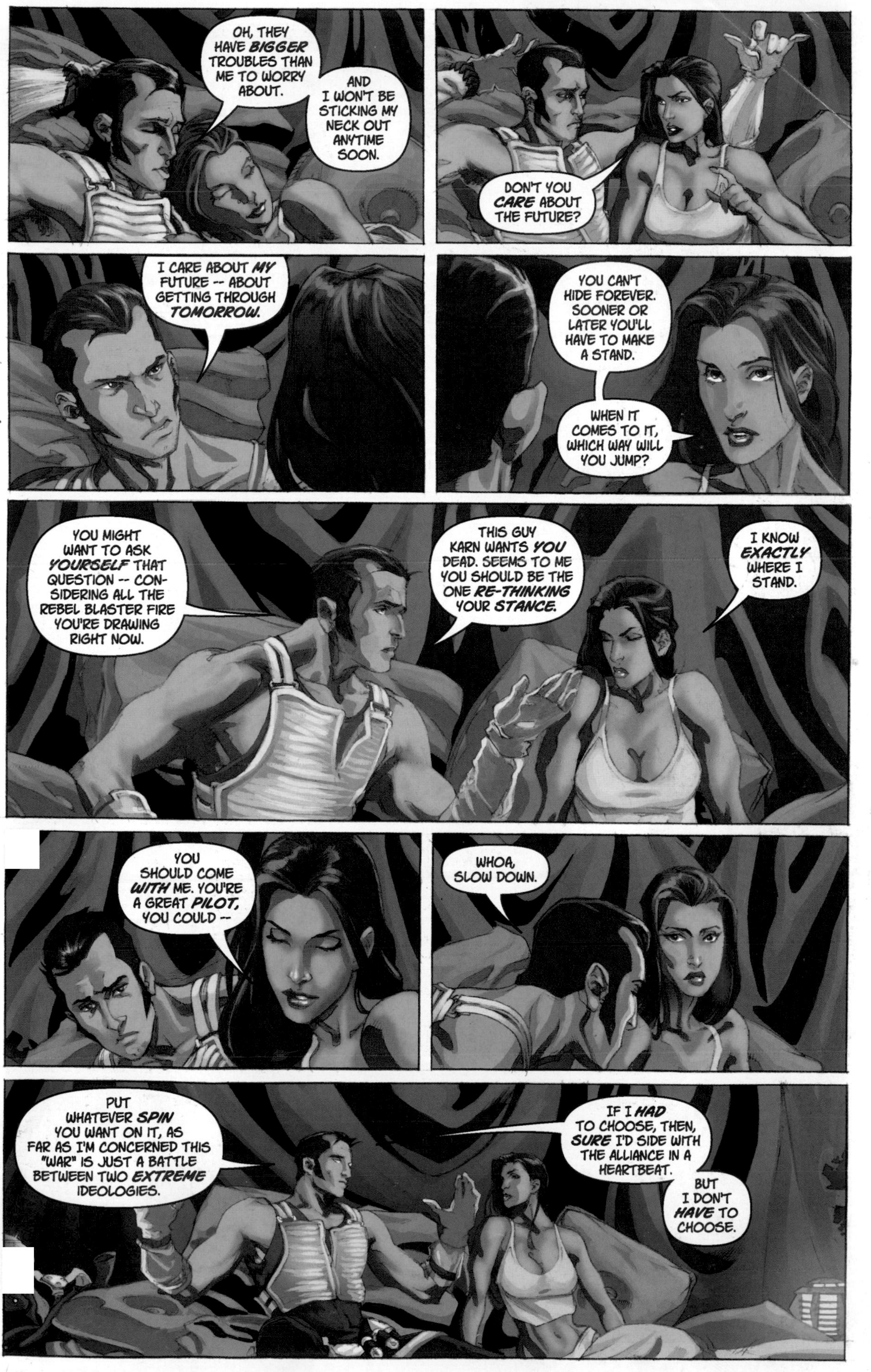
OH, THEY HAVE BIGGER TROUBLES THAN ME TO WORRY ABOUT.
AND I WON'T BE STICKING MY NECK OUT ANYTIME SOON.
DON'T YOU CARE ABOUT THE FUTURE?
I CARE ABOUT MY FUTURE -- ABOUT GETTING THROUGH TOMORROW.
YOU CAN'T HIDE FOREVER. SOONER OR LATER YOU'LL HAVE TO MAKE A STAND.
WHEN IT COMES TO IT, WHICH WAY WILL YOU JUMP?
YOU MIGHT WANT TO ASK YOURSELF THAT QUESTION -- CONSIDERING ALL THE REBEL BLASTER FIRE YOU'RE DRAWING RIGHT NOW.
THIS GUY KARN WANTS YOU DEAD. SEEMS TO ME YOU SHOULD BE THE ONE RE-THINKING YOUR STANCE.
I KNOW EXACTLY WHERE I STAND.
YOU SHOULD COME WITH ME. YOU'RE A GREAT PILOT, YOU COULD --
WHOA, SLOW DOWN.
PUT WHATEVER SPIN YOU WANT ON IT, AS FAR AS I'M CONCERNED THIS "WAR" IS JUST A BATTLE BETWEEN TWO EXTREME IDEOLOGIES.
IF I HAD TO CHOOSE, THEN, SURE I'D SIDE WITH THE ALLIANCE IN A HEARTBEAT.
BUT I DON'T HAVE TO CHOOSE.

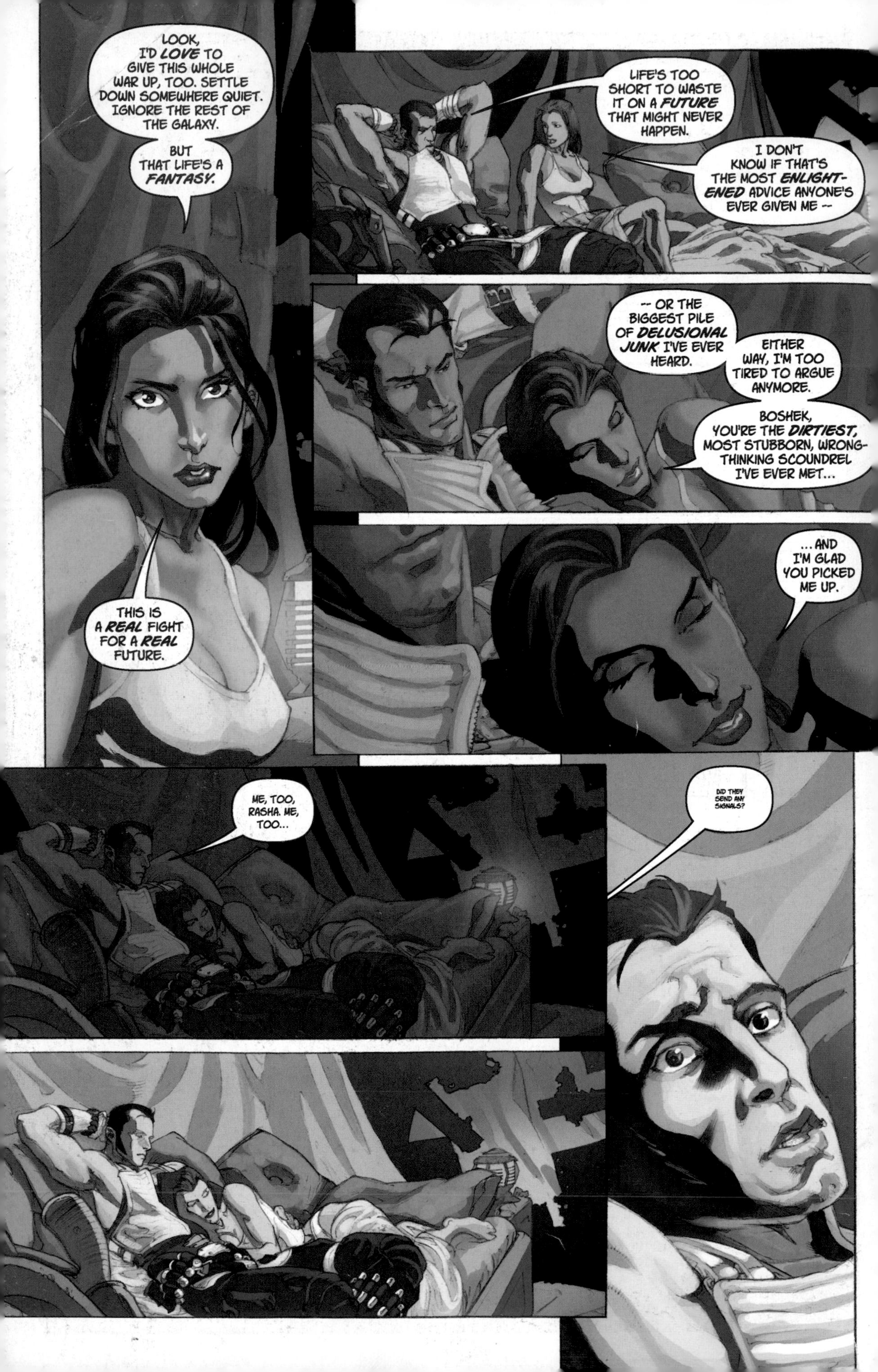
LOOK, I'D *LOVE* TO GIVE THIS WHOLE WAR UP, TOO. SETTLE DOWN SOMEWHERE QUIET. IGNORE THE REST OF THE GALAXY.
BUT THAT LIFE'S A *FANTASY.*
THIS IS A *REAL* FIGHT FOR A *REAL* FUTURE.
LIFE'S TOO SHORT TO WASTE IT ON A *FUTURE* THAT MIGHT NEVER HAPPEN.
I DON'T KNOW IF THAT'S THE MOST *ENLIGHT-ENED* ADVICE ANYONE'S EVER GIVEN ME --
-- OR THE BIGGEST PILE OF *DELUSIONAL JUNK* I'VE EVER HEARD.
EITHER WAY, I'M TOO TIRED TO ARGUE ANYMORE.
BOSHEK, YOU'RE THE *DIRTIEST,* MOST STUBBORN, WRONG-THINKING SCOUNDREL I'VE EVER MET...
...AND I'M GLAD YOU PICKED ME UP.
ME, TOO, RASHA. ME, TOO...
DID THEY SEND ANY SIGNALS?

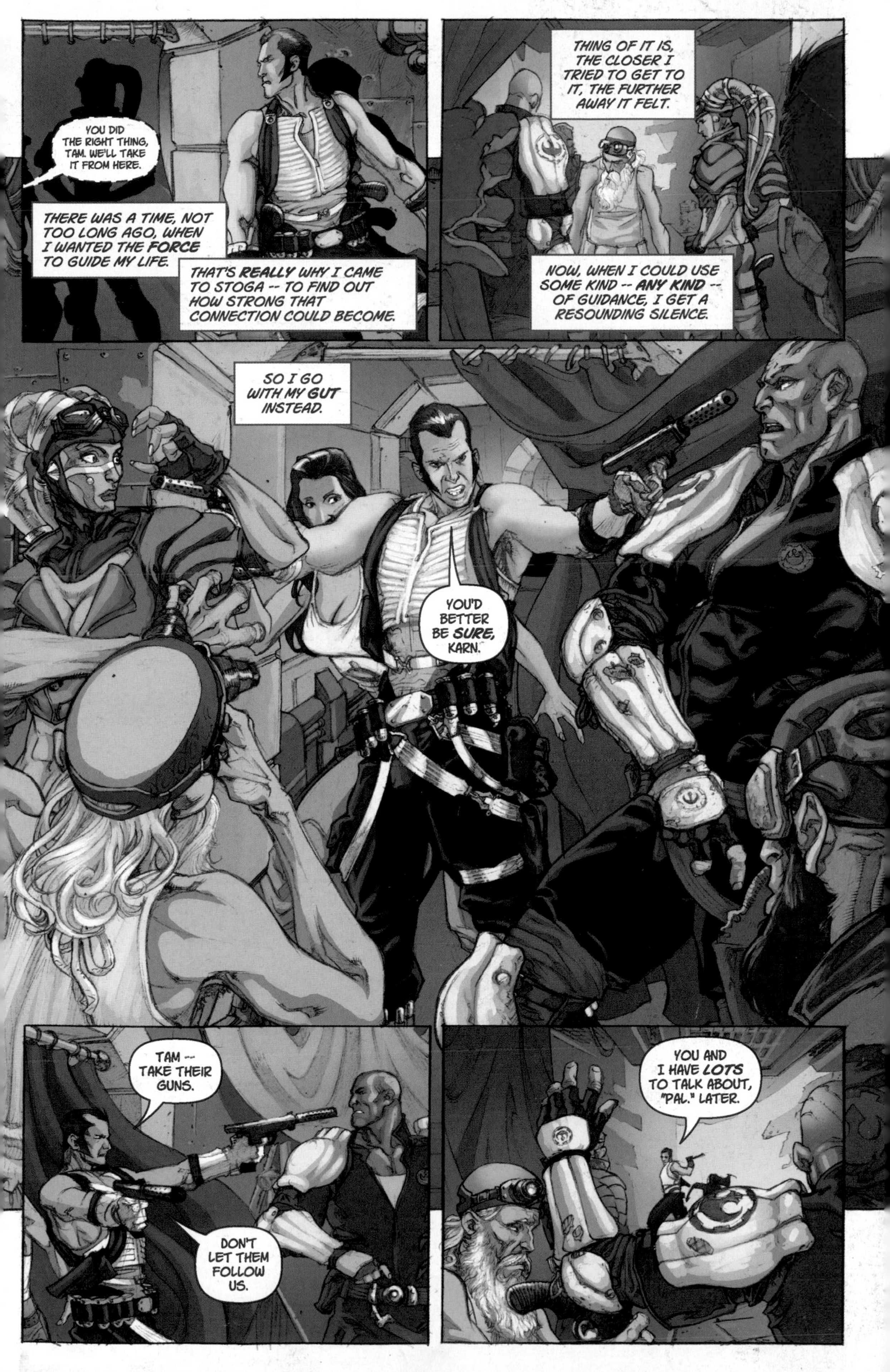
YOU DID THE RIGHT THING, TAM. WE'LL TAKE IT FROM HERE.
THERE WAS A TIME, NOT TOO LONG AGO, WHEN I WANTED THE FORCE TO GUIDE MY LIFE.
THAT'S REALLY WHY I CAME TO STOGA -- TO FIND OUT HOW STRONG THAT CONNECTION COULD BECOME.
THING OF IT IS, THE CLOSER I TRIED TO GET TO IT, THE FURTHER AWAY IT FELT.
NOW, WHEN I COULD USE SOME KIND -- ANY KIND -- OF GUIDANCE, I GET A RESOUNDING SILENCE.
SO I GO WITH MY GUT INSTEAD.
YOU'D BETTER BE SURE, KARN.
TAM -- TAKE THEIR GUNS.
DON'T LET THEM FOLLOW US.
YOU AND I HAVE LOTS TO TALK ABOUT, "PAL." LATER.

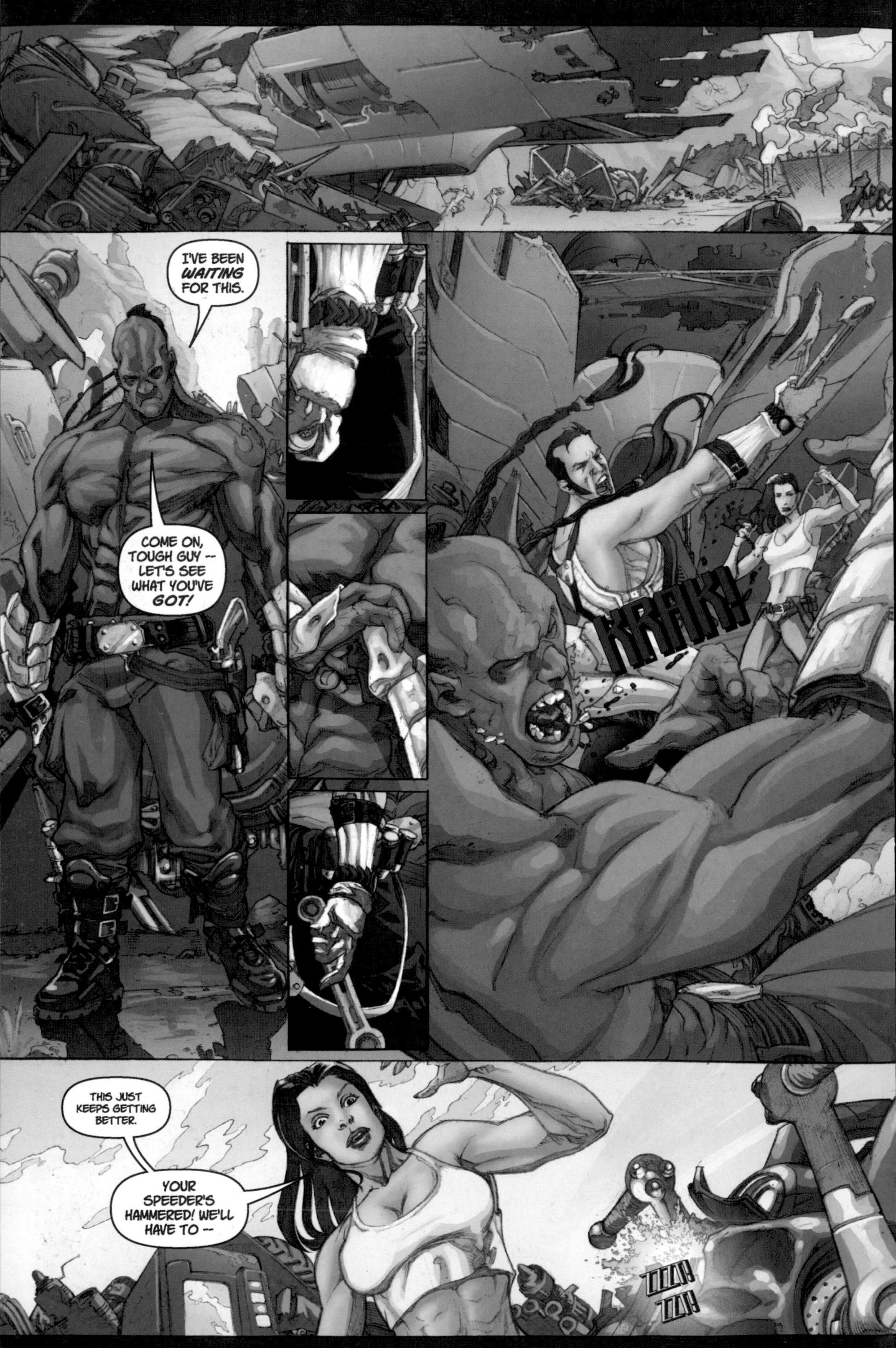
I'VE BEEN WAITING FOR THIS.
COME ON, TOUGH GUY -- LET'S SEE WHAT YOU'VE GOT!
KRAK!
THIS JUST KEEPS GETTING BETTER.
YOUR SPEEDER'S HAMMERED! WE'LL HAVE TO --

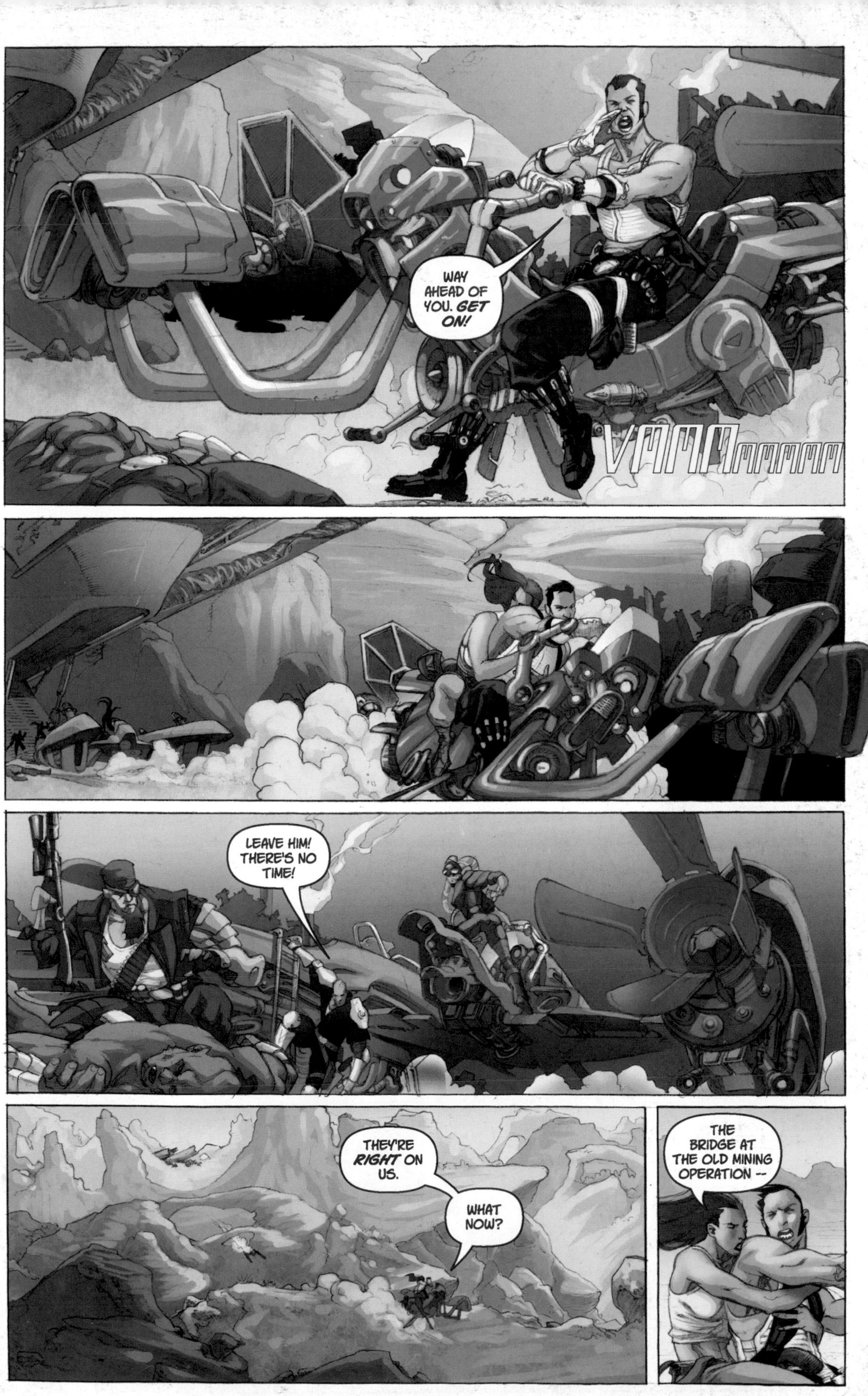
WAY AHEAD OF YOU. GET ON!
VMMMmmmmmm
LEAVE HIM! THERE'S NO TIME!
THEY'RE RIGHT ON US.
WHAT NOW?
THE BRIDGE AT THE OLD MINING OPERATION --

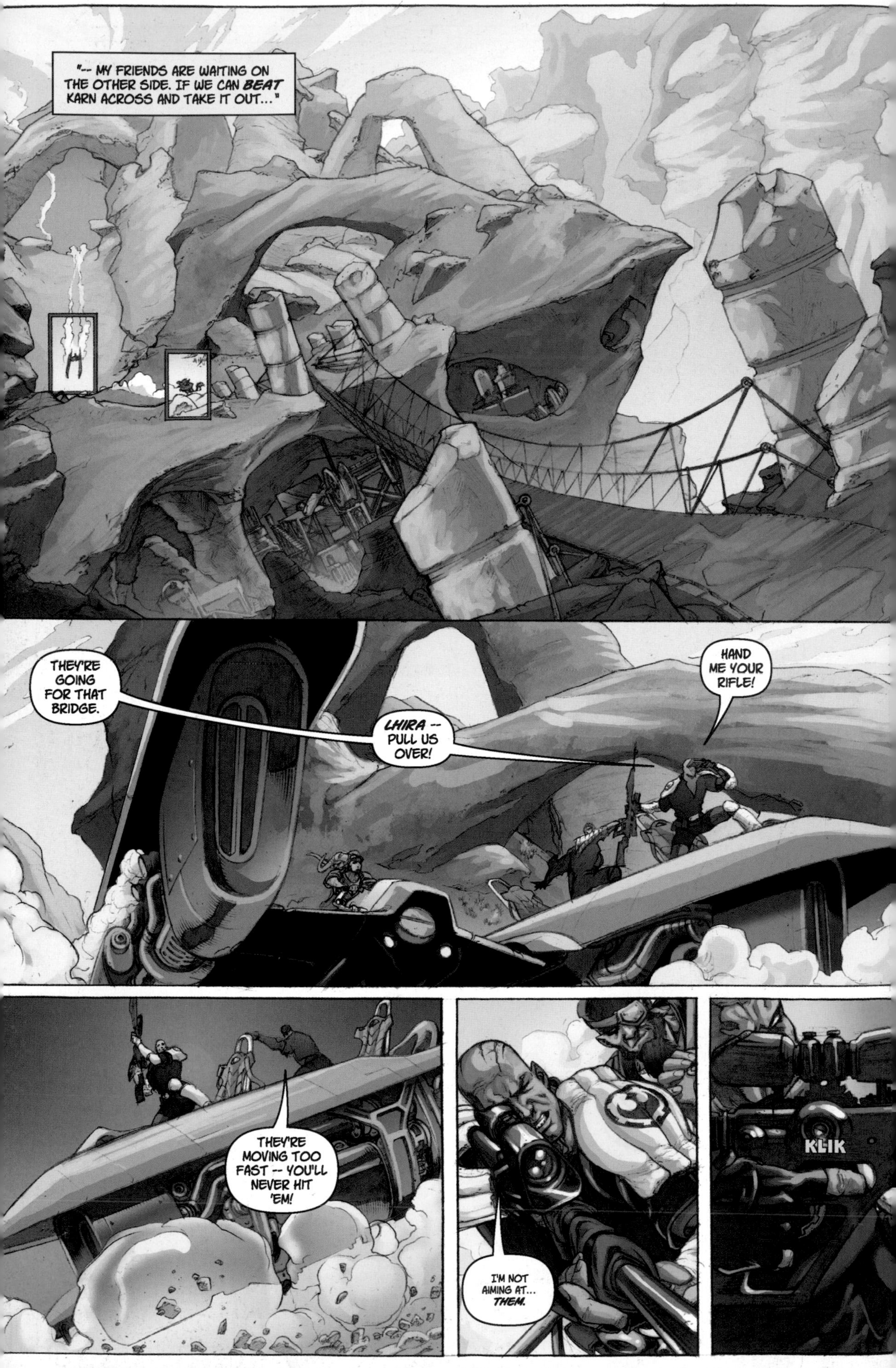
"-- MY FRIENDS ARE WAITING ON THE OTHER SIDE. IF WE CAN *BEAT* KARN ACROSS AND TAKE IT OUT..."
THEY'RE GOING FOR THAT BRIDGE.
LHIRA -- PULL US OVER!
HAND ME YOUR RIFLE!
THEY'RE MOVING TOO FAST -- YOU'LL NEVER HIT 'EM!
I'M NOT AIMING AT... *THEM.*
KLIK

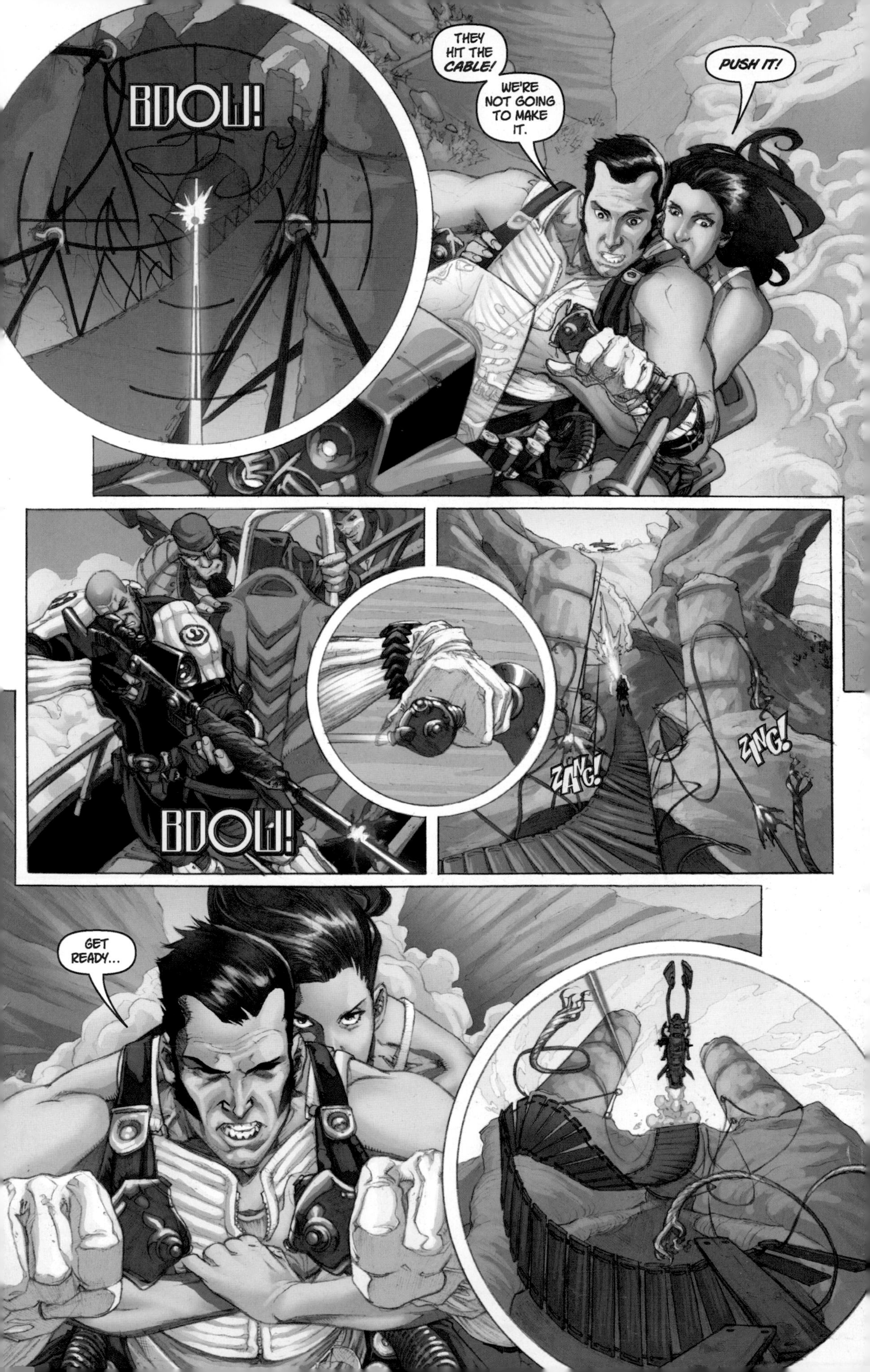
BDOW!
THEY HIT THE CABLE!
WE'RE NOT GOING TO MAKE IT.
PUSH IT!
BDOW!
ZANG!
ZING!
GET READY...

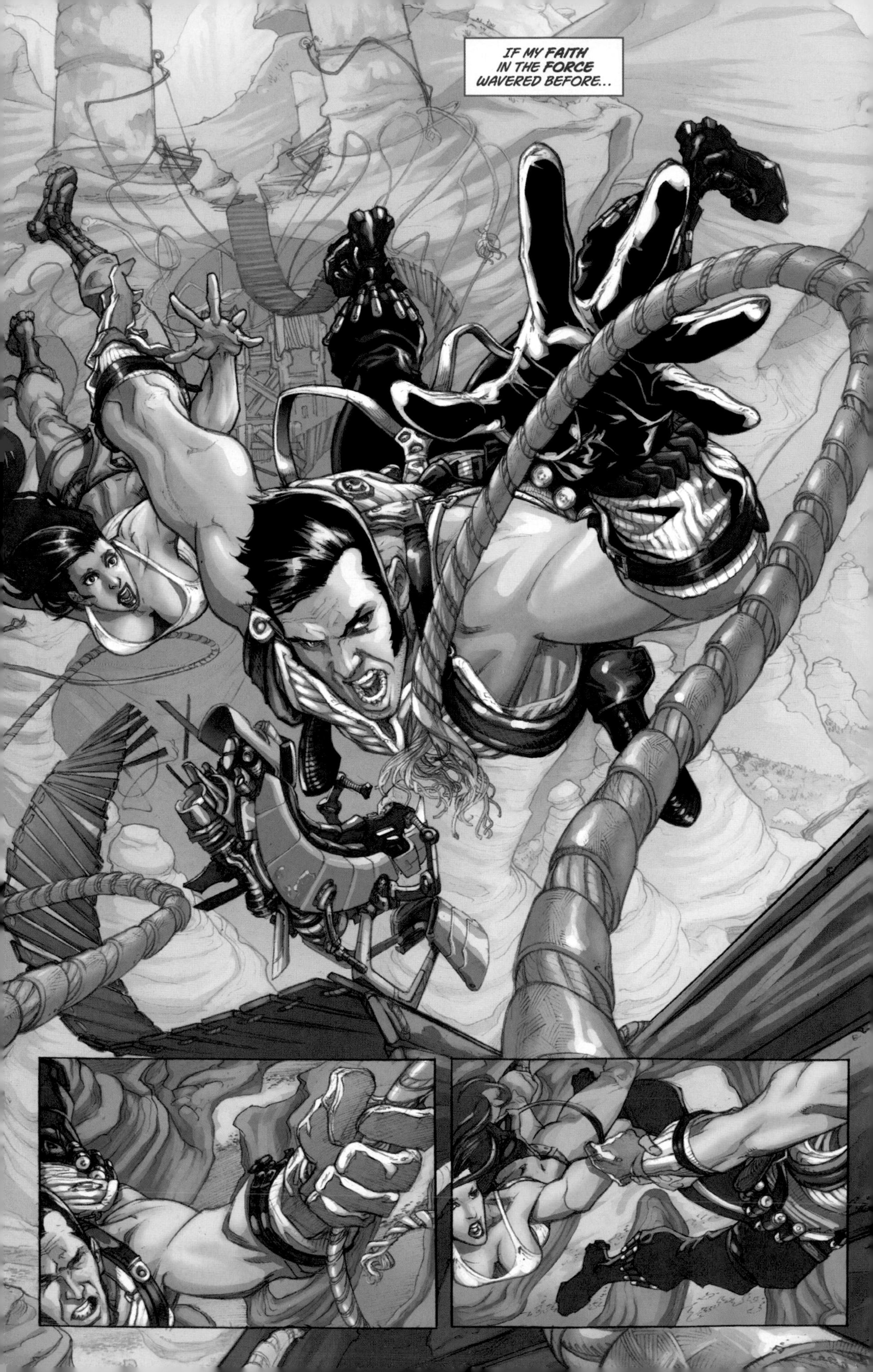
IF MY FAITH IN THE FORCE WAVERED BEFORE...

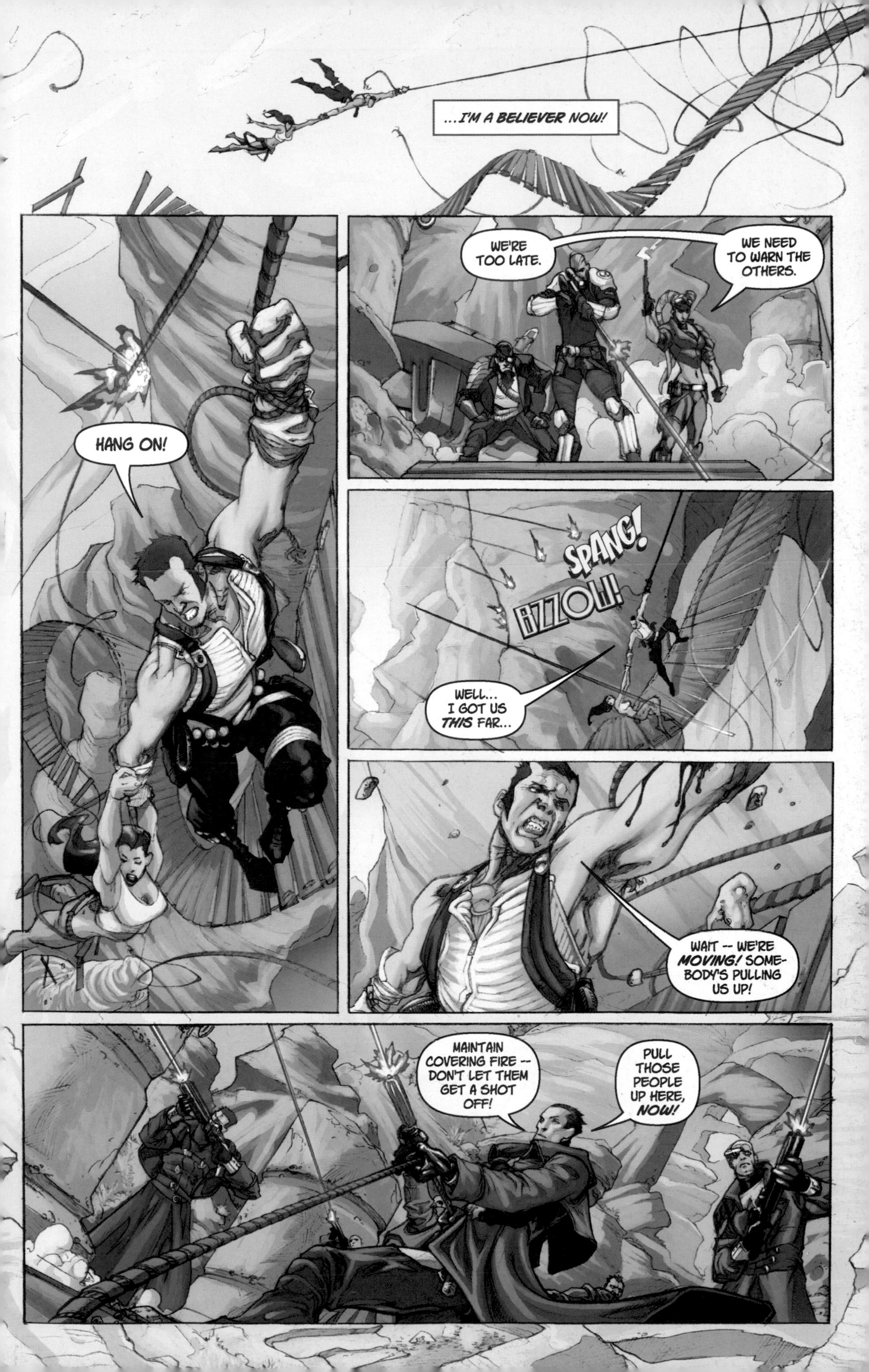

...I'M A BELIEVER NOW!
HANG ON!
WE'RE TOO LATE.
WE NEED TO WARN THE OTHERS.
SPANG!
BZZOW!
WELL... I GOT US THIS FAR...
WAIT -- WE'RE MOVING! SOMEBODY'S PULLING US UP!
MAINTAIN COVERING FIRE -- DON'T LET THEM GET A SHOT OFF!
PULL THOSE PEOPLE UP HERE, NOW!

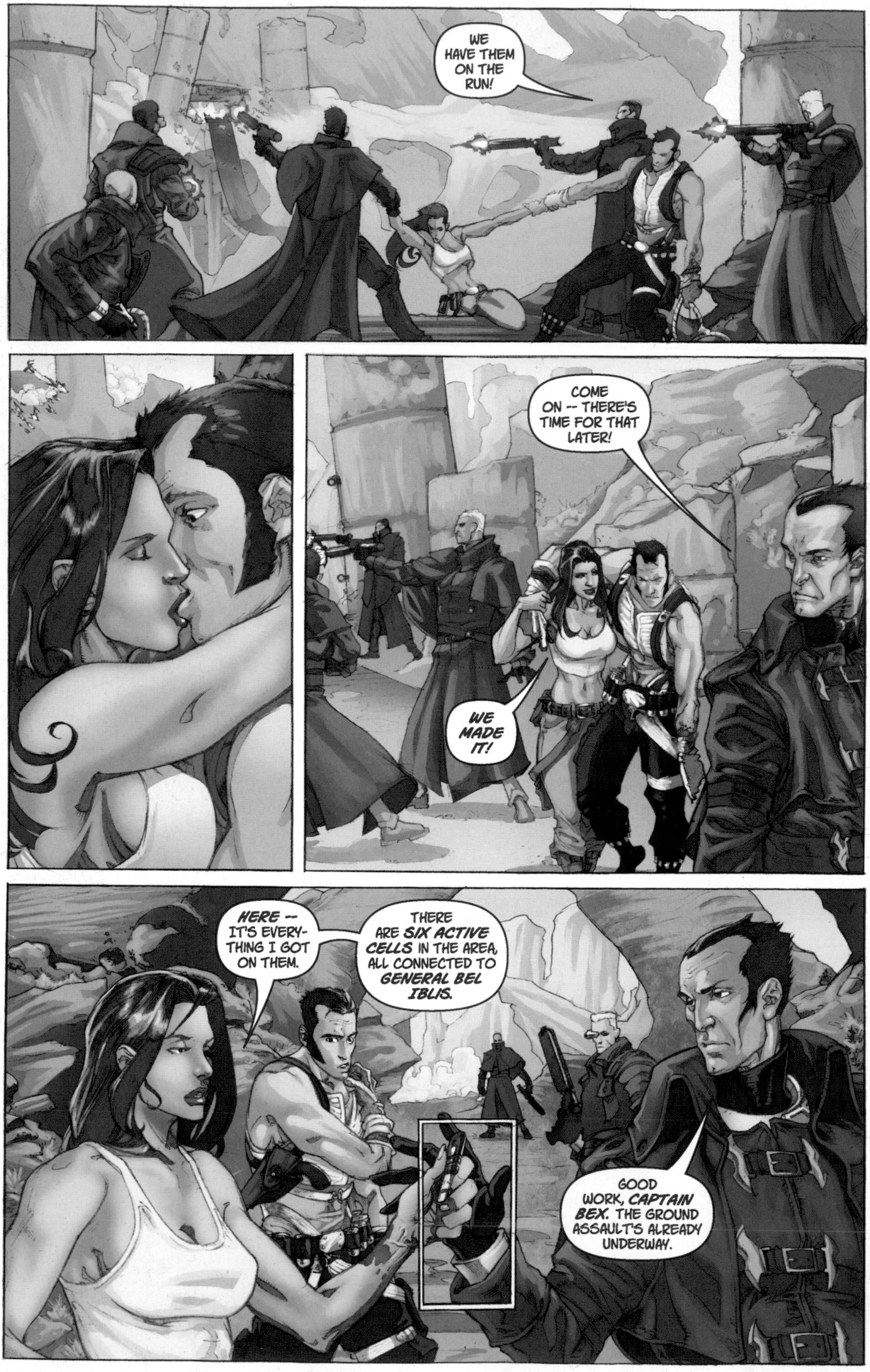
WE HAVE THEM ON THE RUN!
COME ON -- THERE'S TIME FOR THAT LATER!
WE MADE IT!
HERE -- IT'S EVERY-THING I GOT ON THEM.
THERE ARE SIX ACTIVE CELLS IN THE AREA, ALL CONNECTED TO GENERAL BEL IBLIS.
GOOD WORK, CAPTAIN BEX. THE GROUND ASSAULT'S ALREADY UNDERWAY.

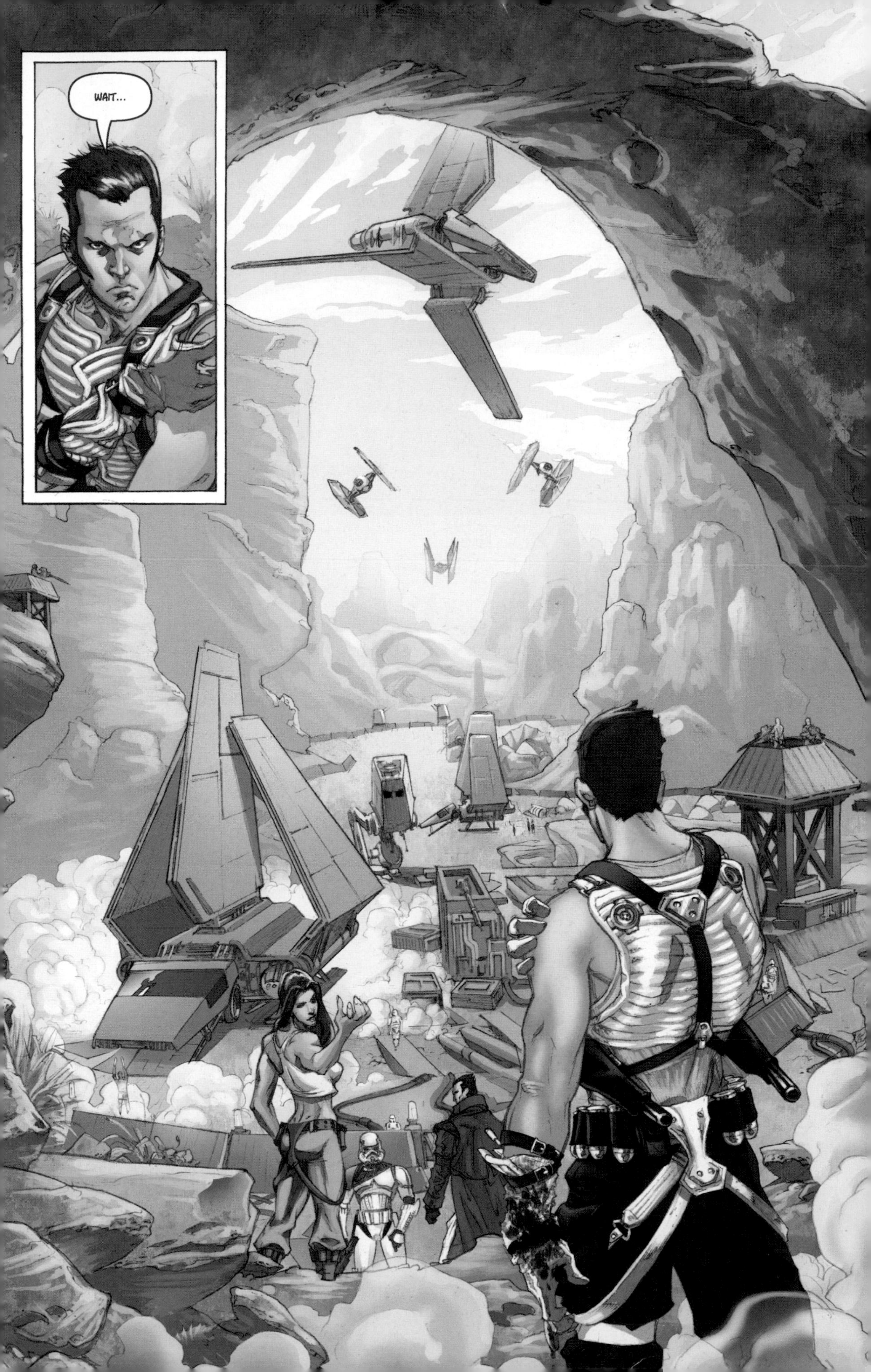
WAIT...

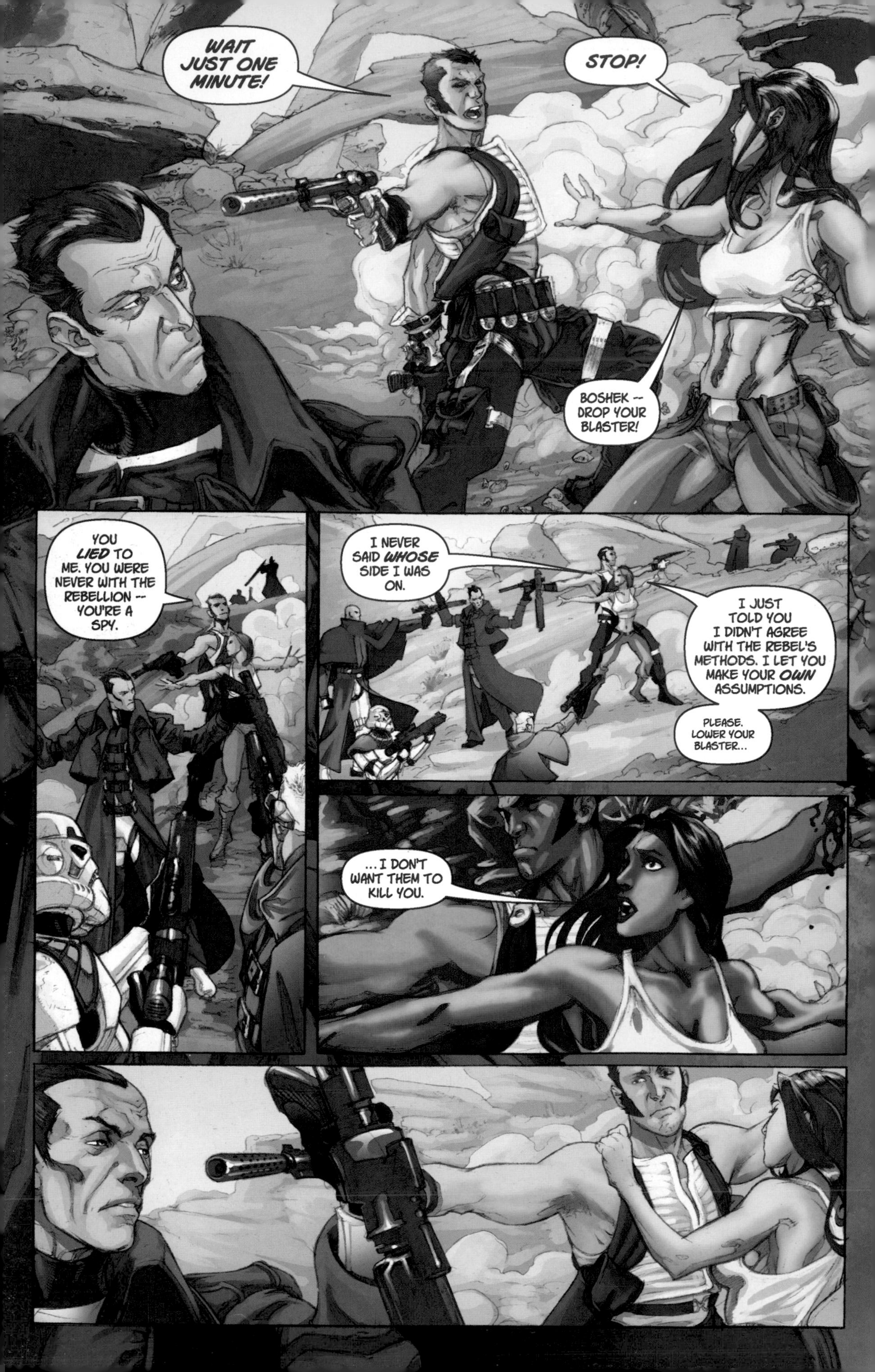
WAIT JUST ONE MINUTE!
STOP!
BOSHEK -- DROP YOUR BLASTER!
YOU LIED TO ME. YOU WERE NEVER WITH THE REBELLION -- YOU'RE A SPY.
I NEVER SAID WHOSE SIDE I WAS ON.
I JUST TOLD YOU I DIDN'T AGREE WITH THE REBEL'S METHODS. I LET YOU MAKE YOUR OWN ASSUMPTIONS.
PLEASE. LOWER YOUR BLASTER...
...I DON'T WANT THEM TO KILL YOU.

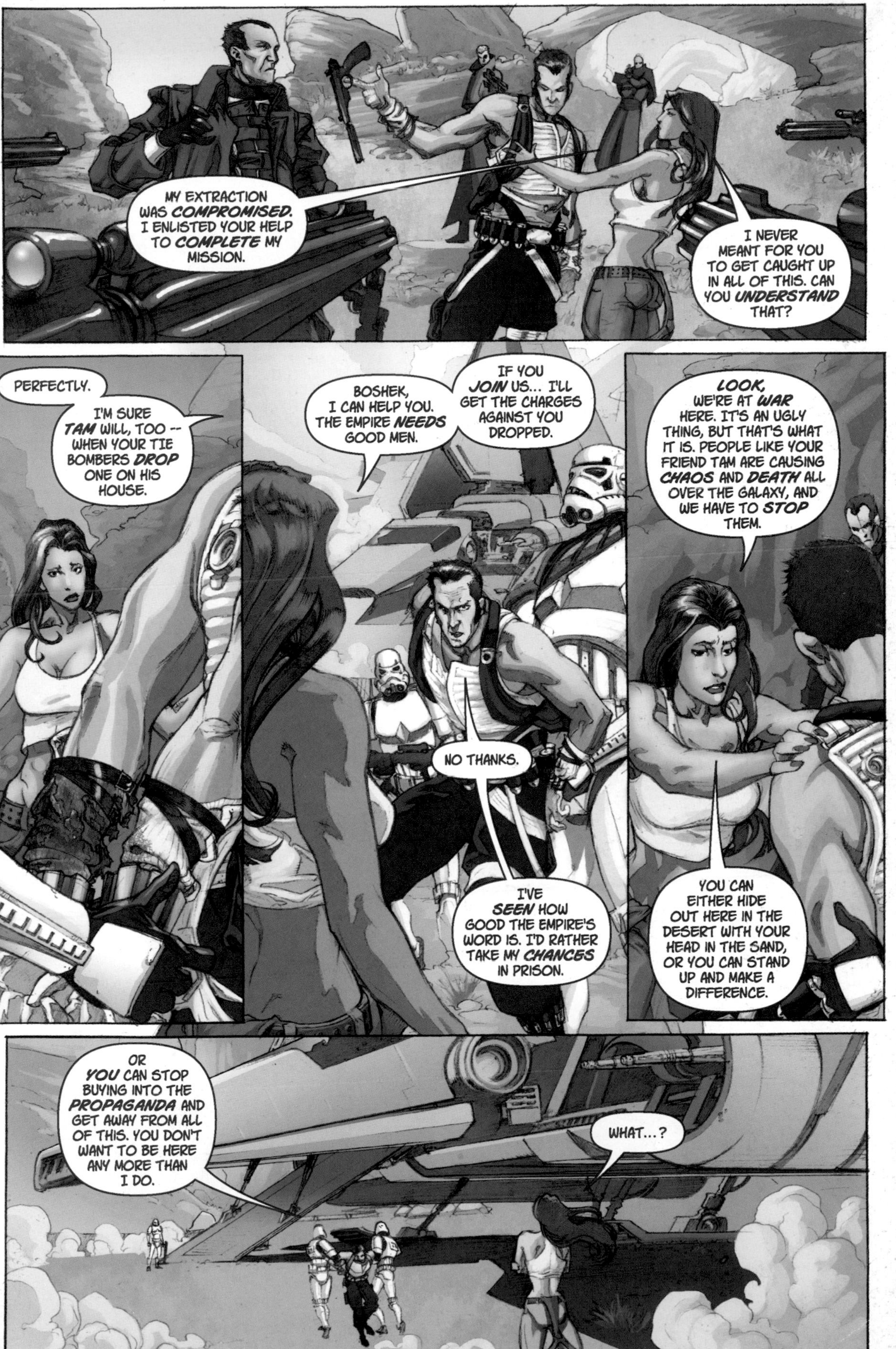

MY EXTRACTION WAS COMPROMISED. I ENLISTED YOUR HELP TO COMPLETE MY MISSION.
I NEVER MEANT FOR YOU TO GET CAUGHT UP IN ALL OF THIS. CAN YOU UNDERSTAND THAT?
PERFECTLY.
I'M SURE TAM WILL, TOO -- WHEN YOUR TIE BOMBERS DROP ONE ON HIS HOUSE.
BOSHEK, I CAN HELP YOU. THE EMPIRE NEEDS GOOD MEN.
IF YOU JOIN US... I'LL GET THE CHARGES AGAINST YOU DROPPED.
NO THANKS.
I'VE SEEN HOW GOOD THE EMPIRE'S WORD IS. I'D RATHER TAKE MY CHANCES IN PRISON.
LOOK, WE'RE AT WAR HERE. IT'S AN UGLY THING, BUT THAT'S WHAT IT IS. PEOPLE LIKE YOUR FRIEND TAM ARE CAUSING CHAOS AND DEATH ALL OVER THE GALAXY, AND WE HAVE TO STOP THEM.
YOU CAN EITHER HIDE OUT HERE IN THE DESERT WITH YOUR HEAD IN THE SAND, OR YOU CAN STAND UP AND MAKE A DIFFERENCE.
OR YOU CAN STOP BUYING INTO THE PROPAGANDA AND GET AWAY FROM ALL OF THIS. YOU DON'T WANT TO BE HERE ANY MORE THAN I DO.
WHAT...?

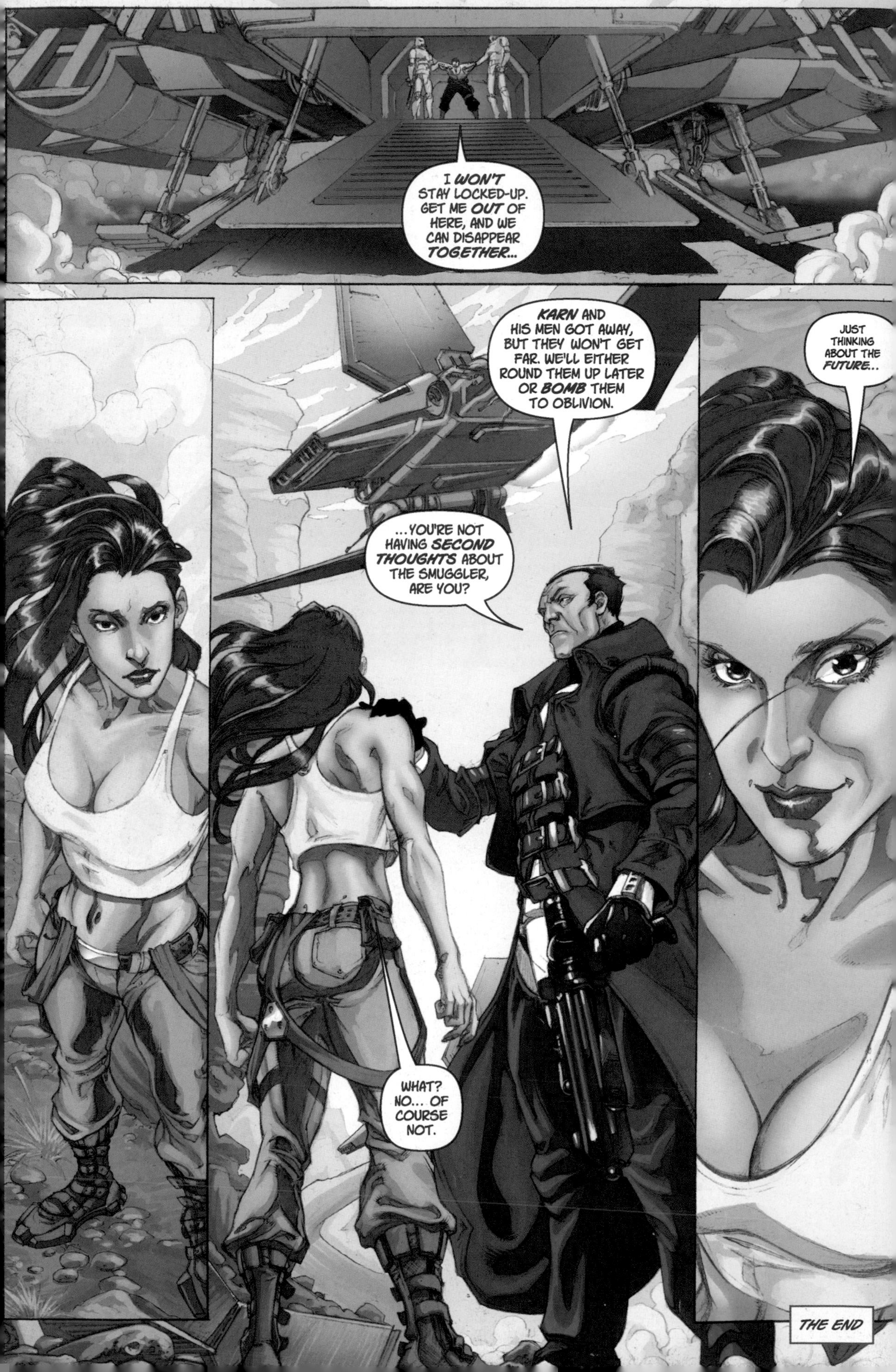

I WON'T STAY LOCKED-UP. GET ME OUT OF HERE, AND WE CAN DISAPPEAR TOGETHER...
KARN AND HIS MEN GOT AWAY, BUT THEY WON'T GET FAR. WE'LL EITHER ROUND THEM UP LATER OR BOMB THEM TO OBLIVION.
...YOU'RE NOT HAVING SECOND THOUGHTS ABOUT THE SMUGGLER, ARE YOU?
WHAT? NO... OF COURSE NOT.
JUST THINKING ABOUT THE FUTURE...
THE END

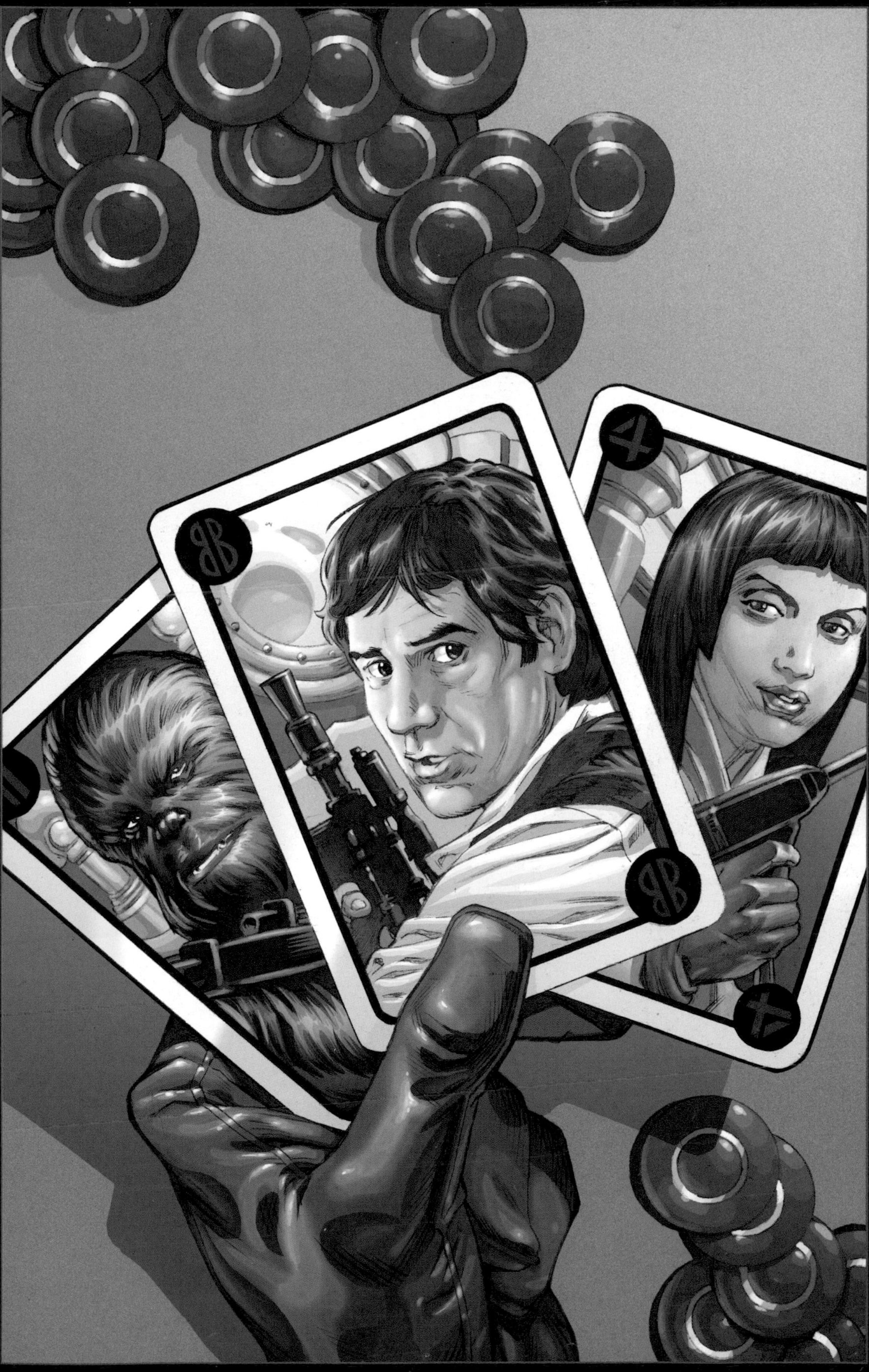

Jeff Johnson
Colors Brad Anderson

IDIOT'S ARRAY

Script RON MARZ
Art JEFF JOHNSON and JOE CORRONEY
Colors MICHAEL ATIYEH

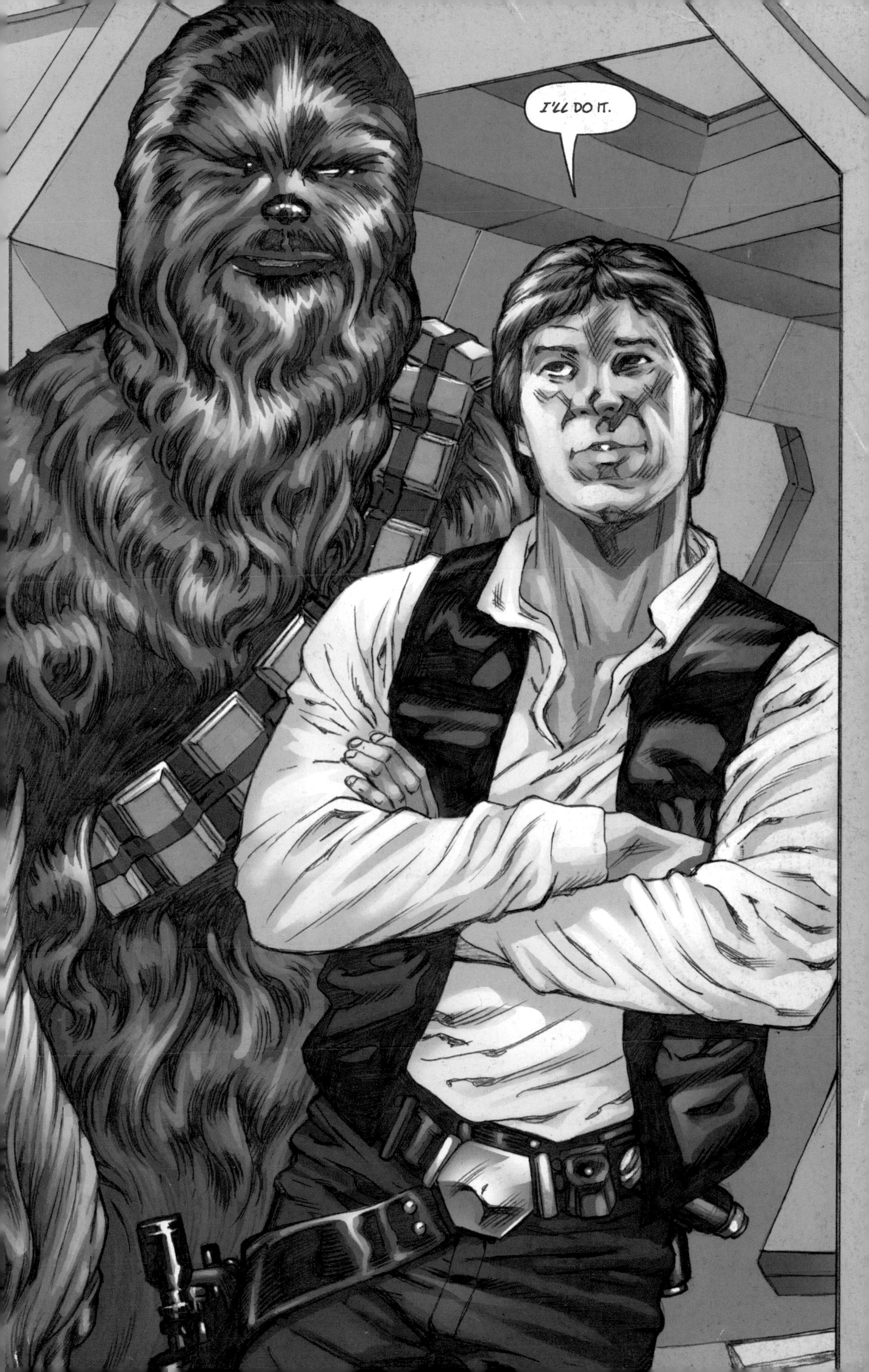
I'LL DO IT.

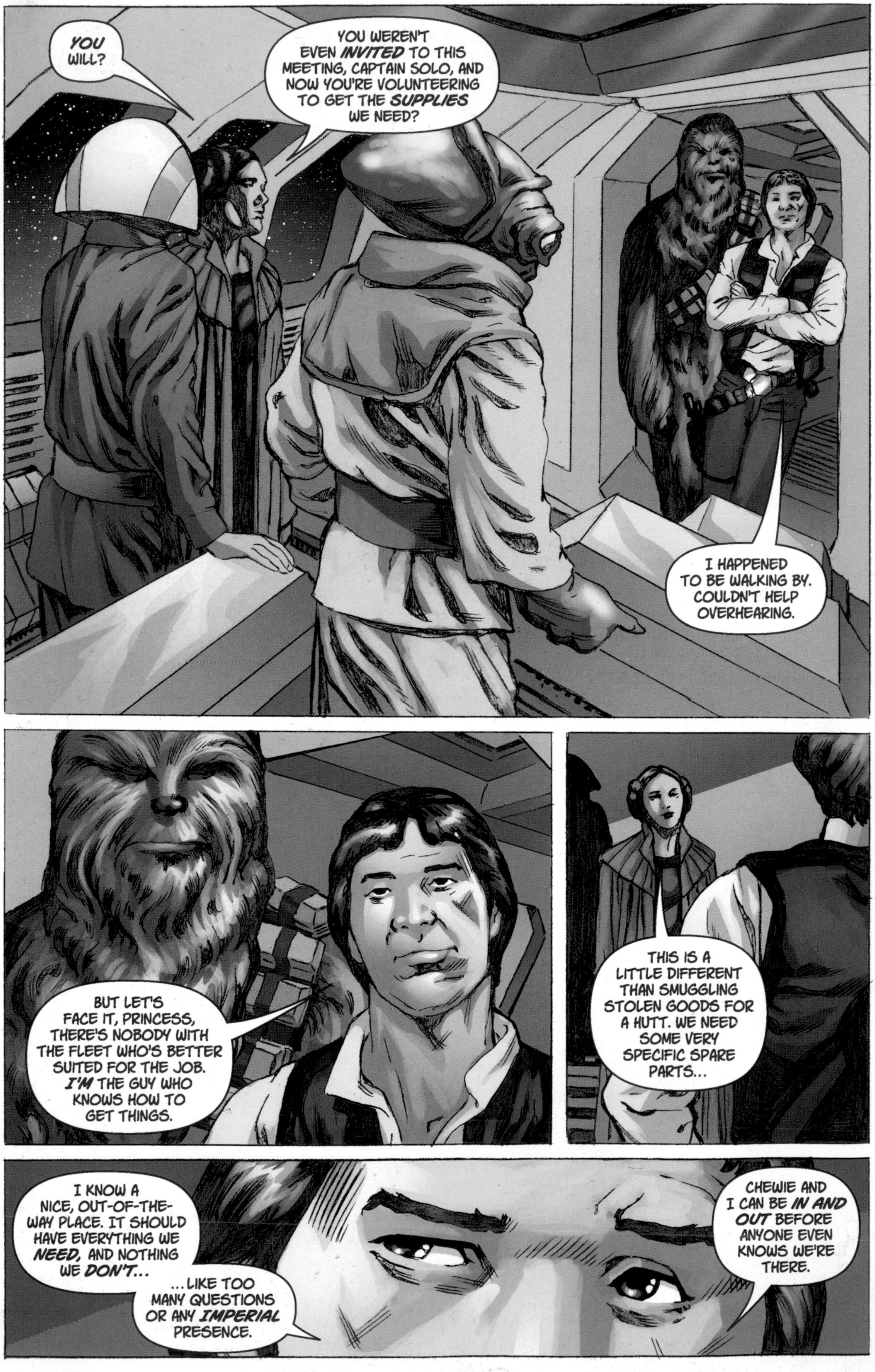
YOU WILL?
YOU WEREN'T EVEN INVITED TO THIS MEETING, CAPTAIN SOLO, AND NOW YOU'RE VOLUNTEERING TO GET THE SUPPLIES WE NEED?
I HAPPENED TO BE WALKING BY. COULDN'T HELP OVERHEARING.
BUT LET'S FACE IT, PRINCESS, THERE'S NOBODY WITH THE FLEET WHO'S BETTER SUITED FOR THE JOB. I'M THE GUY WHO KNOWS HOW TO GET THINGS.
THIS IS A LITTLE DIFFERENT THAN SMUGGLING STOLEN GOODS FOR A HUTT. WE NEED SOME VERY SPECIFIC SPARE PARTS...
I KNOW A NICE, OUT-OF-THE-WAY PLACE. IT SHOULD HAVE EVERYTHING WE NEED, AND NOTHING WE DON'T...
...LIKE TOO MANY QUESTIONS OR ANY IMPERIAL PRESENCE.
CHEWIE AND I CAN BE IN AND OUT BEFORE ANYONE EVEN KNOWS WE'RE THERE.

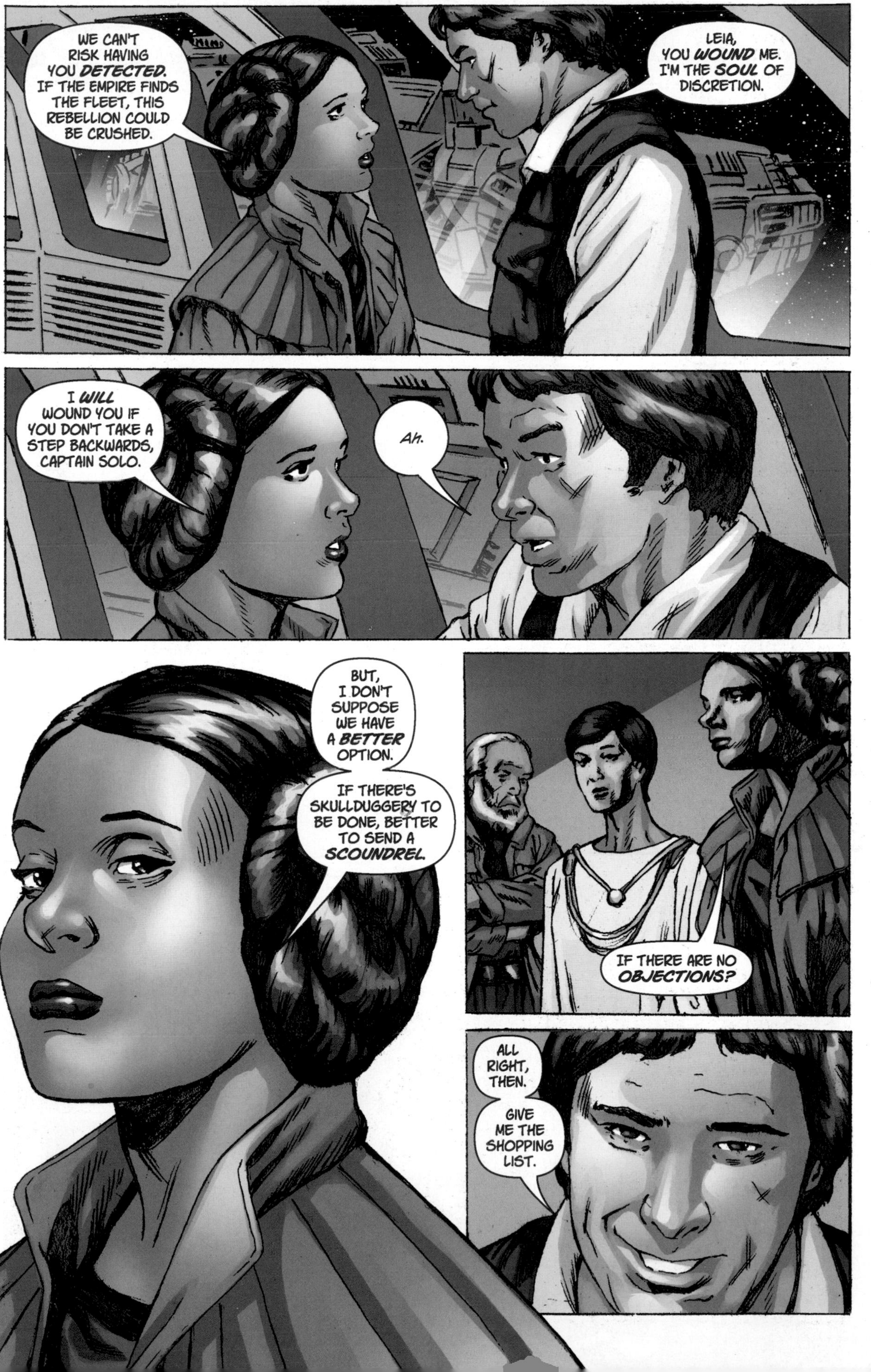
WE CAN'T RISK HAVING YOU DETECTED. IF THE EMPIRE FINDS THE FLEET, THIS REBELLION COULD BE CRUSHED.
LEIA, YOU WOUND ME. I'M THE SOUL OF DISCRETION.
I WILL WOUND YOU IF YOU DON'T TAKE A STEP BACKWARDS, CAPTAIN SOLO.
Ah.
BUT, I DON'T SUPPOSE WE HAVE A BETTER OPTION.
IF THERE'S SKULLDUGGERY TO BE DONE, BETTER TO SEND A SCOUNDREL.
IF THERE ARE NO OBJECTIONS?
ALL RIGHT, THEN.
GIVE ME THE SHOPPING LIST.

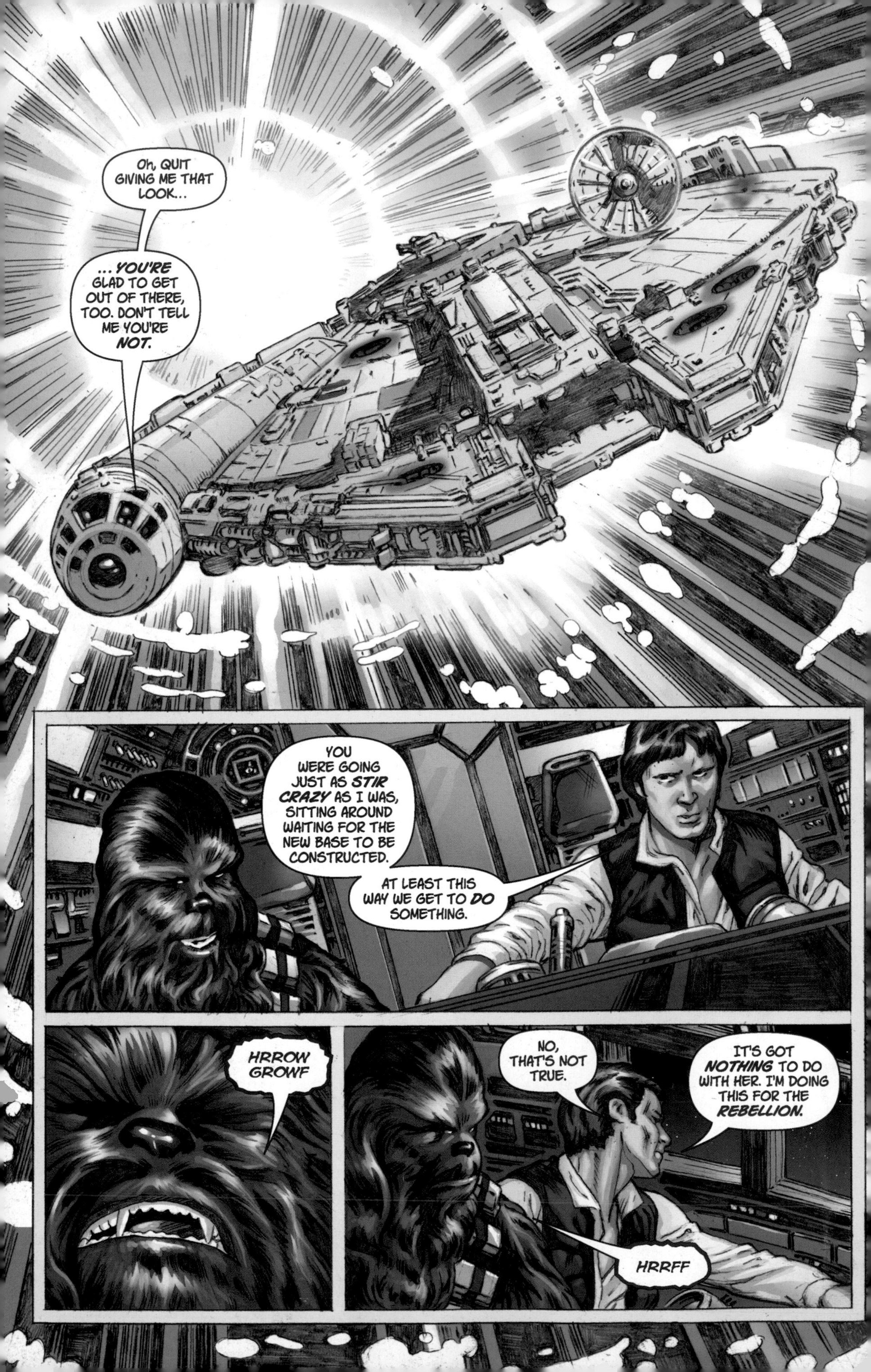
Oh, QUIT GIVING ME THAT LOOK...
...YOU'RE GLAD TO GET OUT OF THERE, TOO. DON'T TELL ME YOU'RE NOT.
YOU WERE GOING JUST AS STIR CRAZY AS I WAS, SITTING AROUND WAITING FOR THE NEW BASE TO BE CONSTRUCTED.
AT LEAST THIS WAY WE GET TO DO SOMETHING.
HRROW GROWF
NO, THAT'S NOT TRUE.
IT'S GOT NOTHING TO DO WITH HER. I'M DOING THIS FOR THE REBELLION.
HRRFF

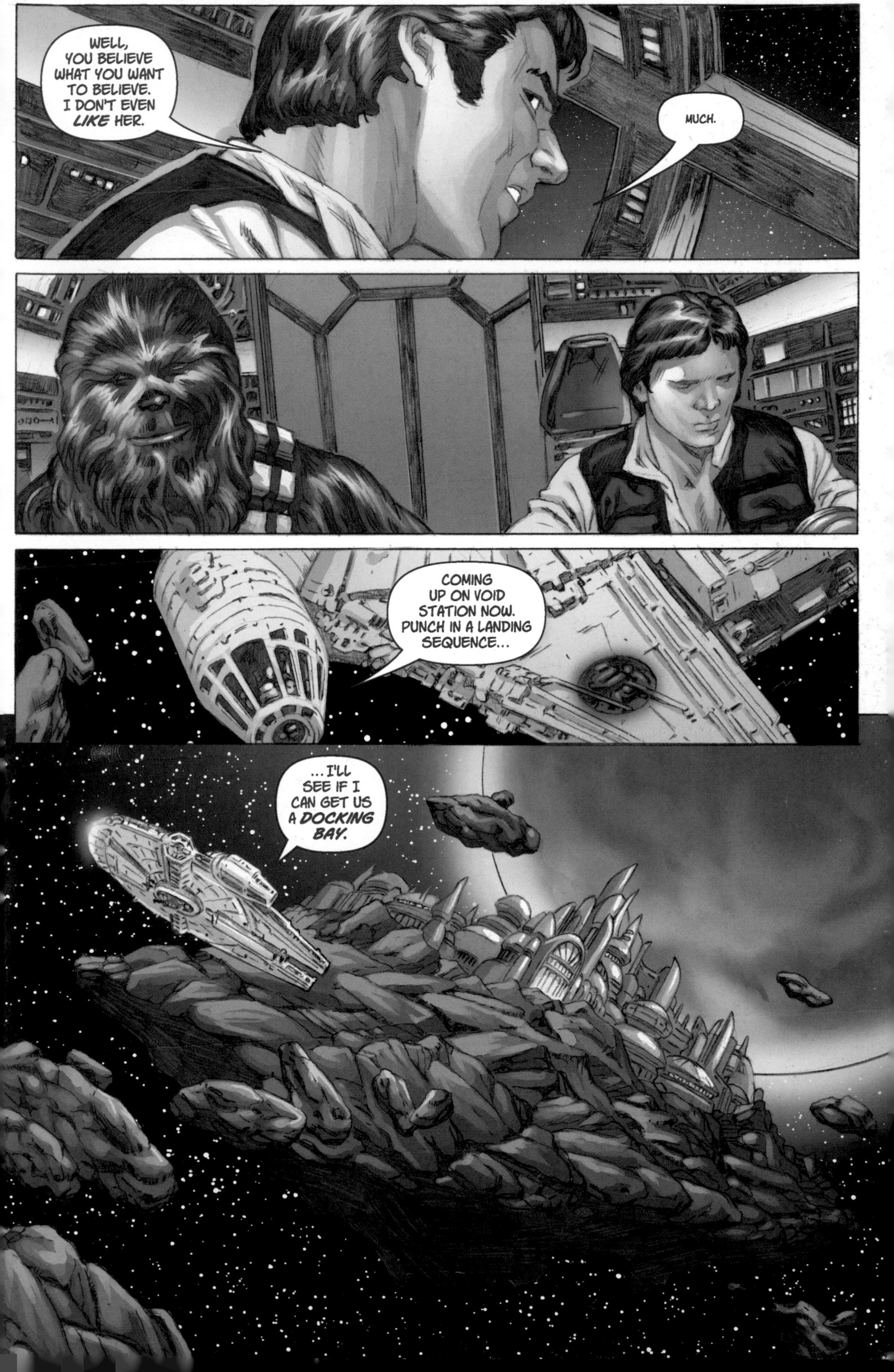
WELL, YOU BELIEVE WHAT YOU WANT TO BELIEVE. I DON'T EVEN *LIKE* HER.
MUCH.
COMING UP ON VOID STATION NOW. PUNCH IN A LANDING SEQUENCE...
...I'LL SEE IF I CAN GET US A *DOCKING BAY.*

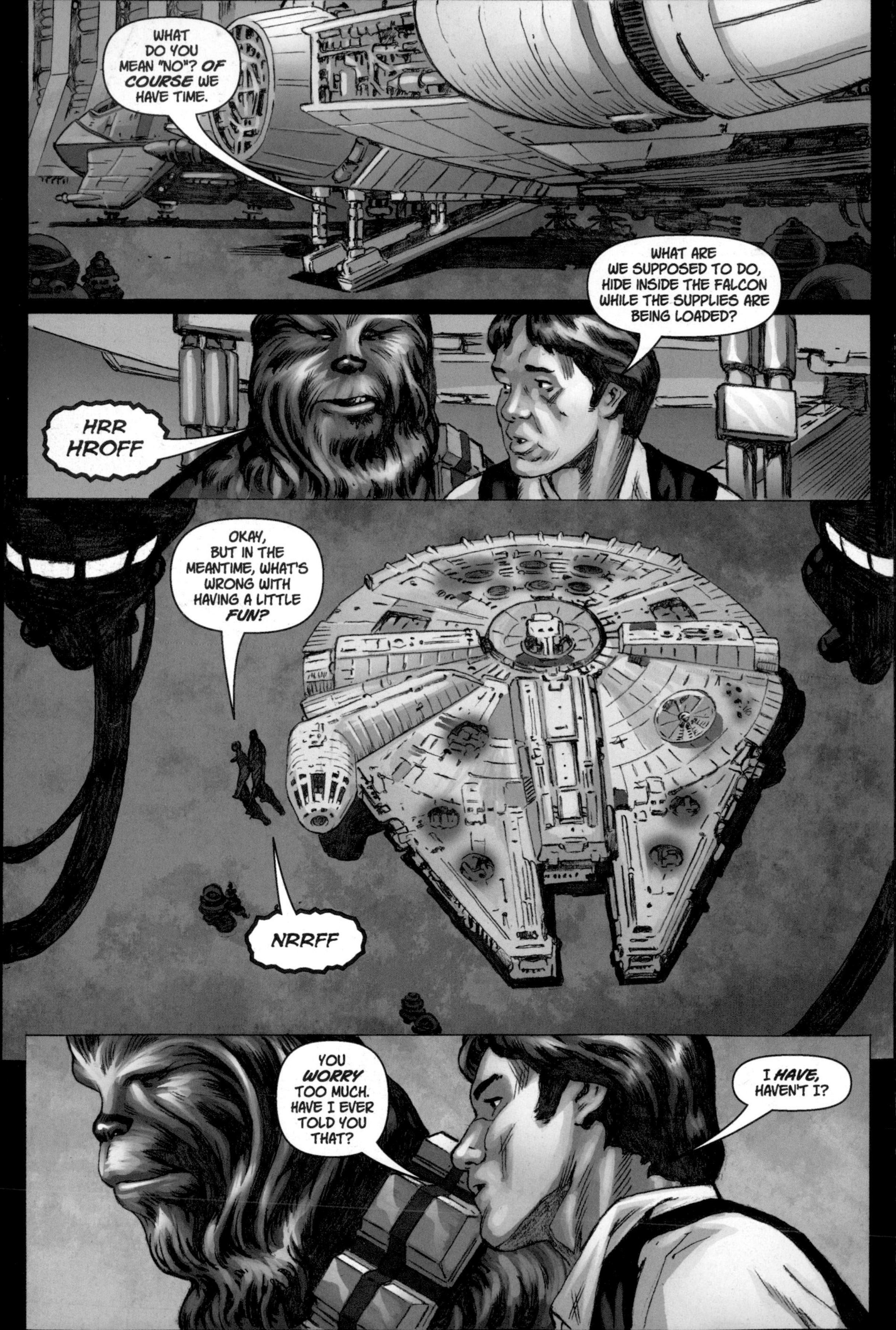
WHAT DO YOU MEAN "NO"? *OF COURSE* WE HAVE TIME.
WHAT ARE WE SUPPOSED TO DO, HIDE INSIDE THE FALCON WHILE THE SUPPLIES ARE BEING LOADED?
HRR HROFF
OKAY, BUT IN THE MEANTIME, WHAT'S WRONG WITH HAVING A LITTLE *FUN?*
NRRFF
YOU *WORRY* TOO MUCH. HAVE I EVER TOLD YOU THAT?
I *HAVE,* HAVEN'T I?

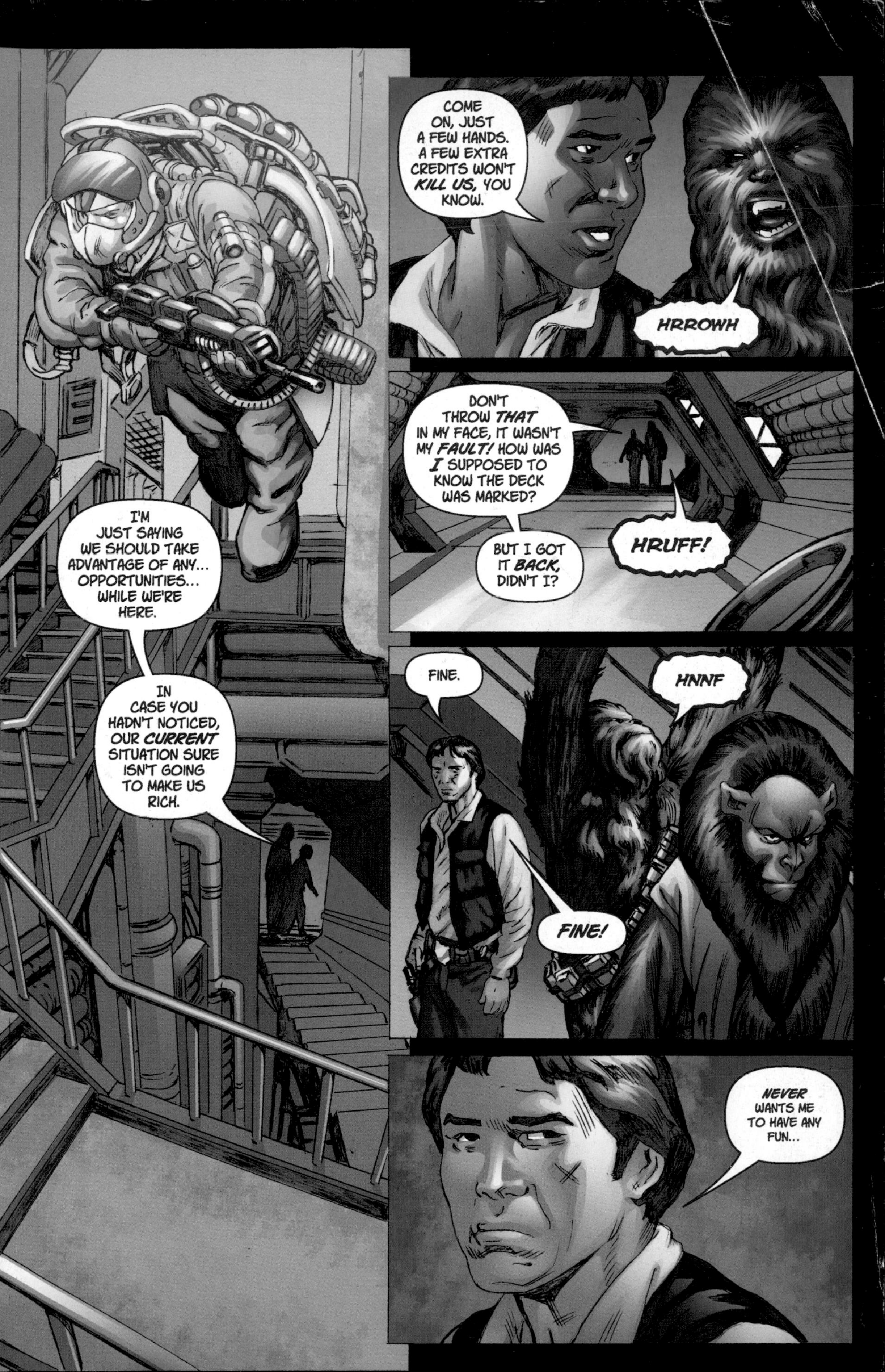
COME ON, JUST A FEW HANDS. A FEW EXTRA CREDITS WON'T KILL US, YOU KNOW.
HRROWH
DON'T THROW THAT IN MY FACE, IT WASN'T MY FAULT! HOW WAS I SUPPOSED TO KNOW THE DECK WAS MARKED?
BUT I GOT IT BACK, DIDN'T I?
HRUFF!
I'M JUST SAYING WE SHOULD TAKE ADVANTAGE OF ANY... OPPORTUNITIES... WHILE WE'RE HERE.
IN CASE YOU HADN'T NOTICED, OUR CURRENT SITUATION SURE ISN'T GOING TO MAKE US RICH.
FINE.
HNNF
FINE!
NEVER WANTS ME TO HAVE ANY FUN...

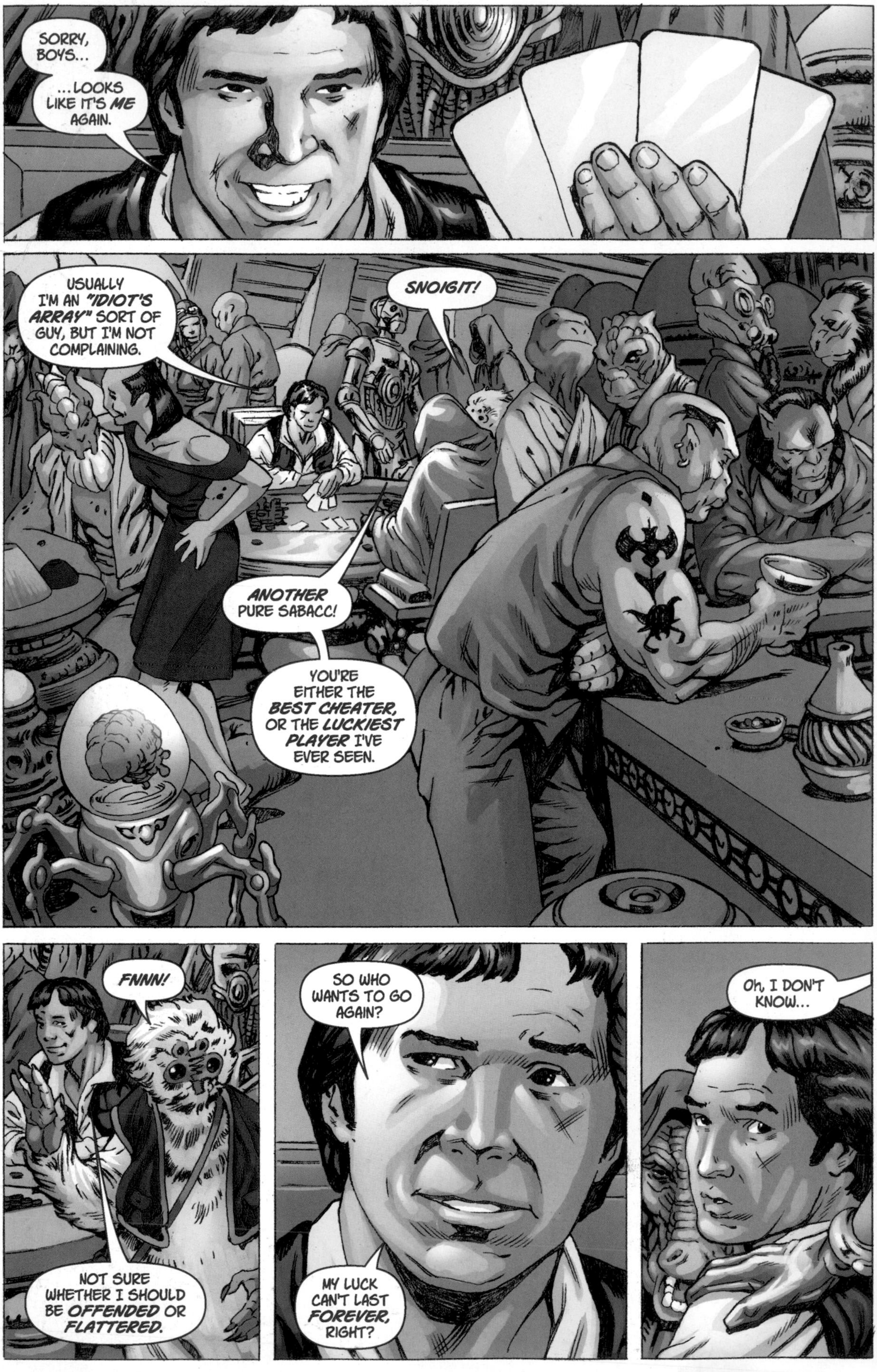
SORRY, BOYS...
...LOOKS LIKE IT'S ME AGAIN.
USUALLY I'M AN "IDIOT'S ARRAY" SORT OF GUY, BUT I'M NOT COMPLAINING.
SNOIGIT!
ANOTHER PURE SABACC!
YOU'RE EITHER THE BEST CHEATER, OR THE LUCKIEST PLAYER I'VE EVER SEEN.
FNNN!
NOT SURE WHETHER I SHOULD BE OFFENDED OR FLATTERED.
SO WHO WANTS TO GO AGAIN?
MY LUCK CAN'T LAST FOREVER, RIGHT?
Oh, I DON'T KNOW...

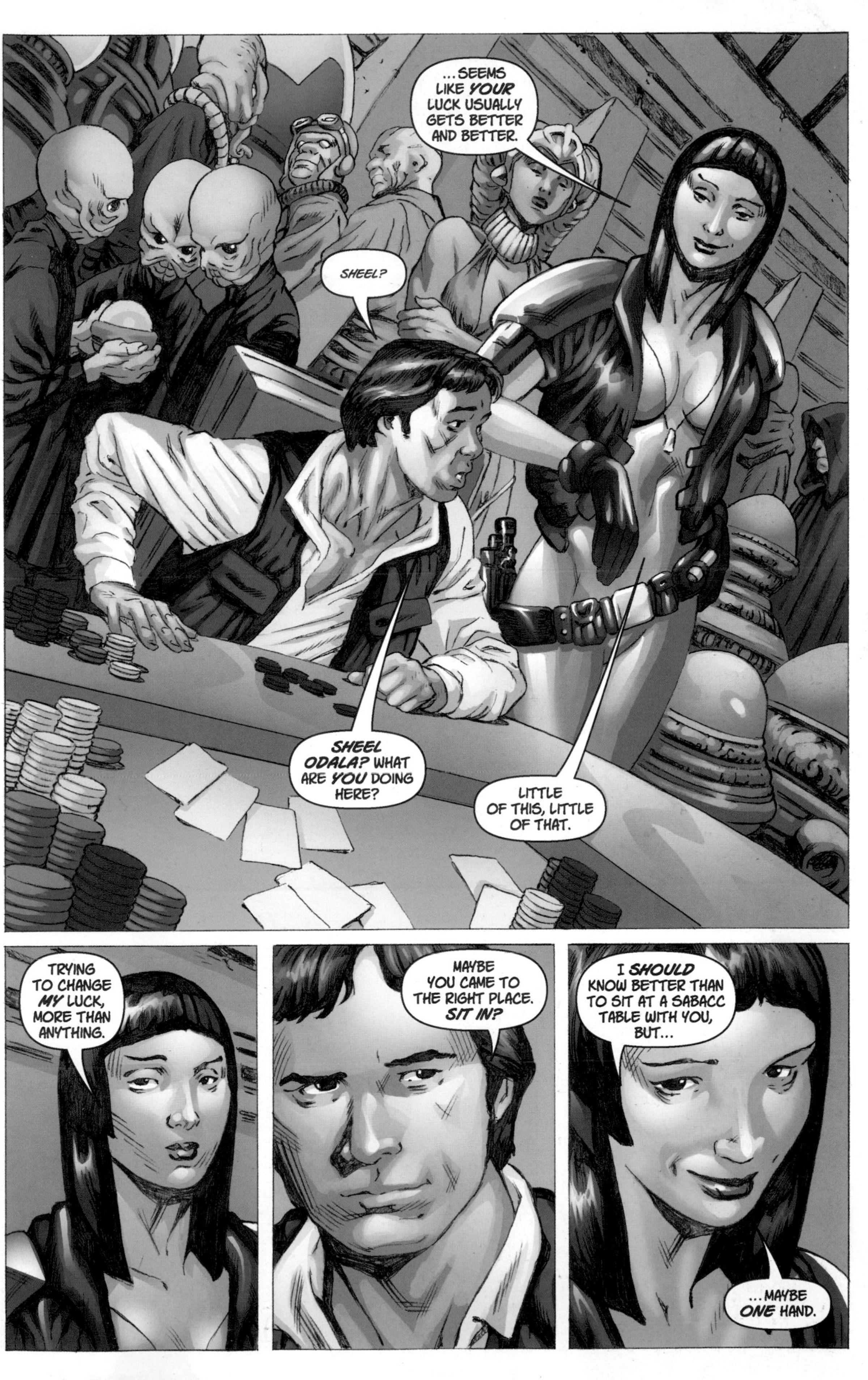
...SEEMS LIKE YOUR LUCK USUALLY GETS BETTER AND BETTER.
SHEEL?
SHEEL ODALA? WHAT ARE YOU DOING HERE?
LITTLE OF THIS, LITTLE OF THAT.
TRYING TO CHANGE MY LUCK, MORE THAN ANYTHING.
MAYBE YOU CAME TO THE RIGHT PLACE. SIT IN?
I SHOULD KNOW BETTER THAN TO SIT AT A SABACC TABLE WITH YOU, BUT...
...MAYBE ONE HAND.

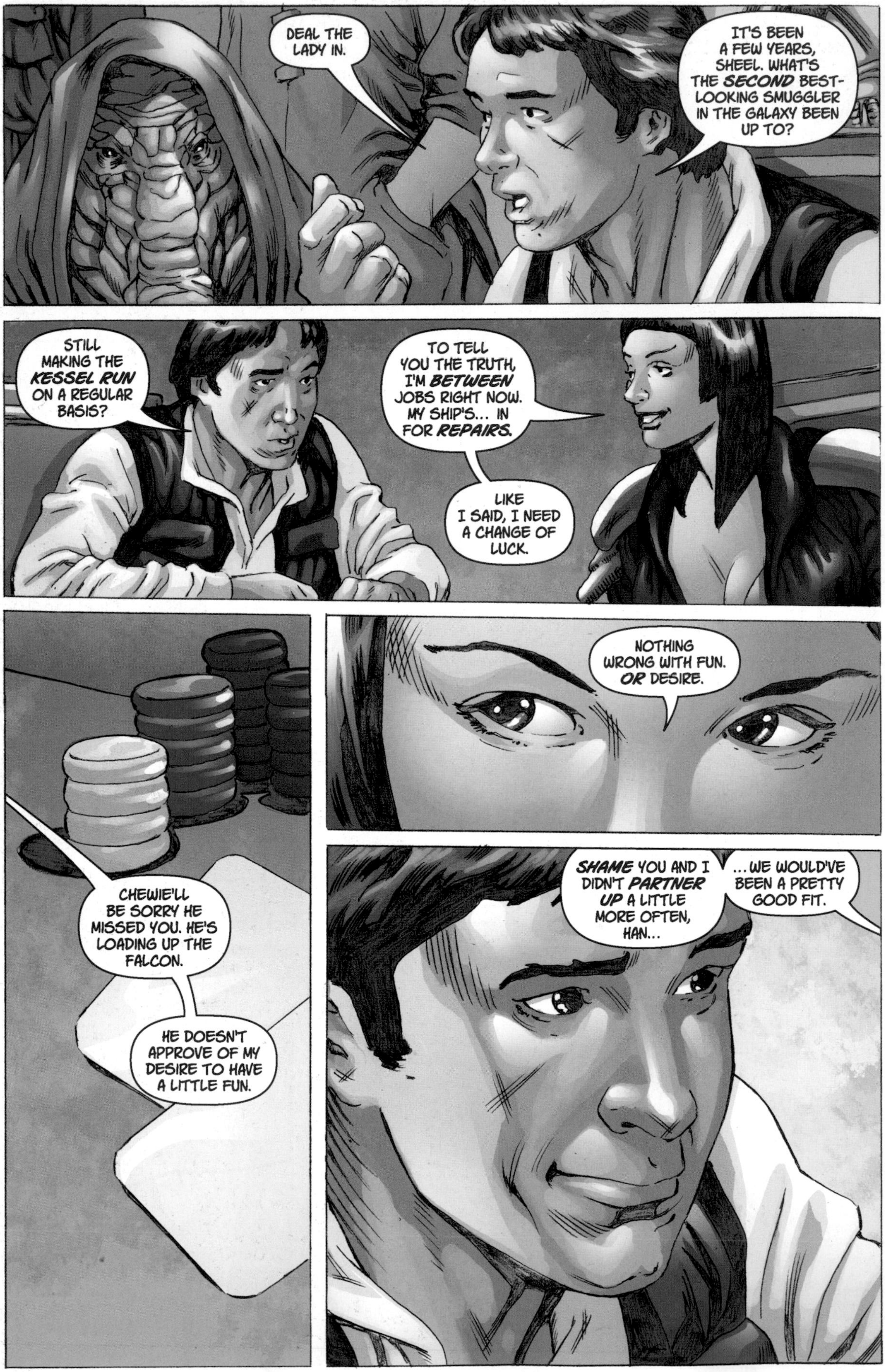
DEAL THE LADY IN.
IT'S BEEN A FEW YEARS, SHEEL. WHAT'S THE *SECOND* BEST-LOOKING SMUGGLER IN THE GALAXY BEEN UP TO?
STILL MAKING THE *KESSEL RUN* ON A REGULAR BASIS?
TO TELL YOU THE TRUTH, I'M *BETWEEN* JOBS RIGHT NOW. MY SHIP'S... IN FOR *REPAIRS*.
LIKE I SAID, I NEED A CHANGE OF LUCK.
CHEWIE'LL BE SORRY HE MISSED YOU. HE'S LOADING UP THE FALCON.
HE DOESN'T APPROVE OF MY DESIRE TO HAVE A LITTLE FUN.
NOTHING WRONG WITH FUN. *OR* DESIRE.
SHAME YOU AND I DIDN'T *PARTNER UP* A LITTLE MORE OFTEN, HAN...
...WE WOULD'VE BEEN A PRETTY GOOD FIT.

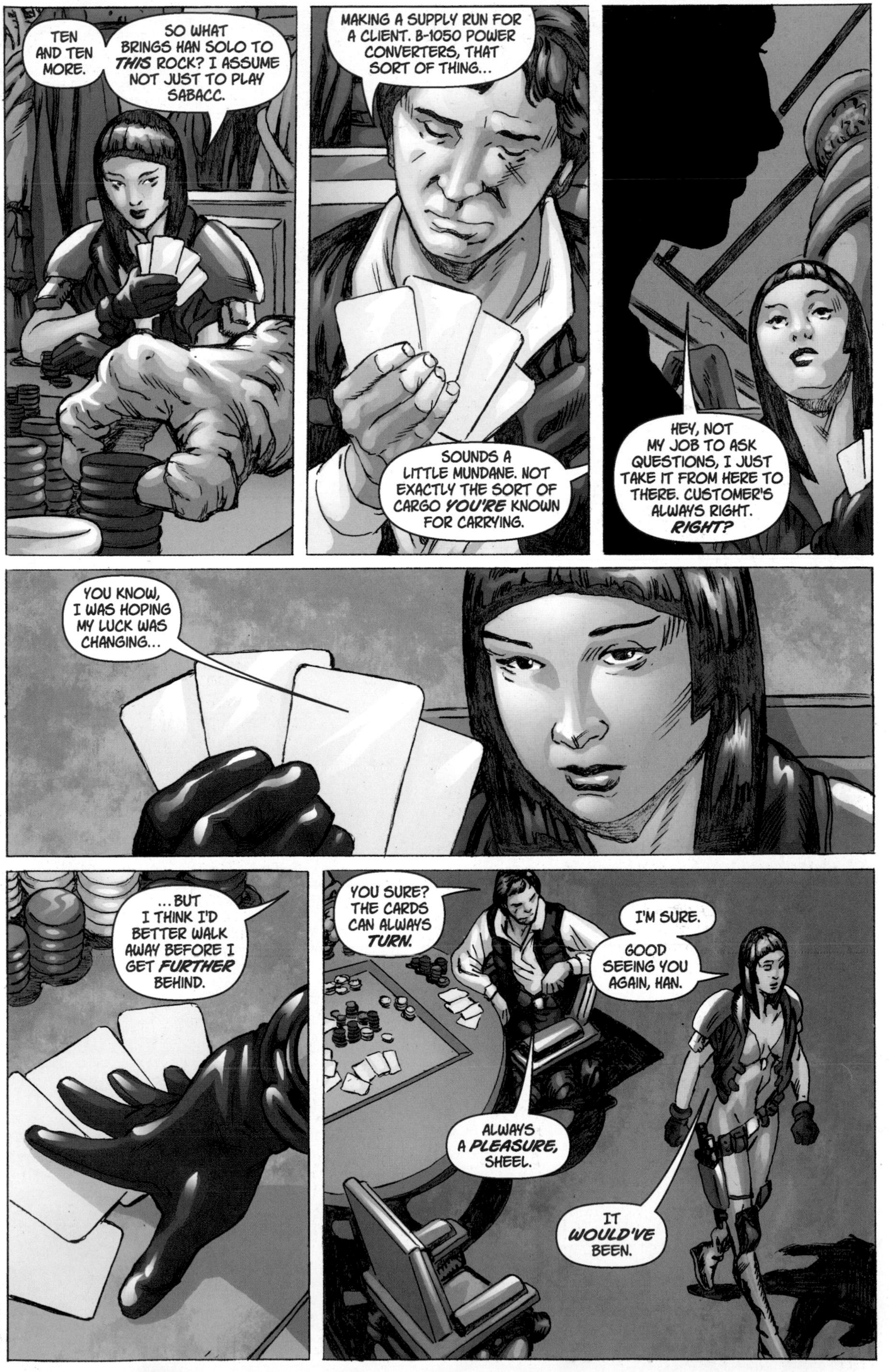
TEN AND TEN MORE.
SO WHAT BRINGS HAN SOLO TO *THIS* ROCK? I ASSUME NOT JUST TO PLAY SABACC.
MAKING A SUPPLY RUN FOR A CLIENT. B-1050 POWER CONVERTERS, THAT SORT OF THING...
SOUNDS A LITTLE MUNDANE. NOT EXACTLY THE SORT OF CARGO *YOU'RE* KNOWN FOR CARRYING.
HEY, NOT MY JOB TO ASK QUESTIONS, I JUST TAKE IT FROM HERE TO THERE. CUSTOMER'S ALWAYS RIGHT. ***RIGHT?***
YOU KNOW, I WAS HOPING MY LUCK WAS CHANGING...
...BUT I THINK I'D BETTER WALK AWAY BEFORE I GET ***FURTHER*** BEHIND.
YOU SURE? THE CARDS CAN ALWAYS ***TURN.***
I'M SURE.
GOOD SEEING YOU AGAIN, HAN.
ALWAYS A ***PLEASURE,*** SHEEL.
IT ***WOULD'VE*** BEEN.

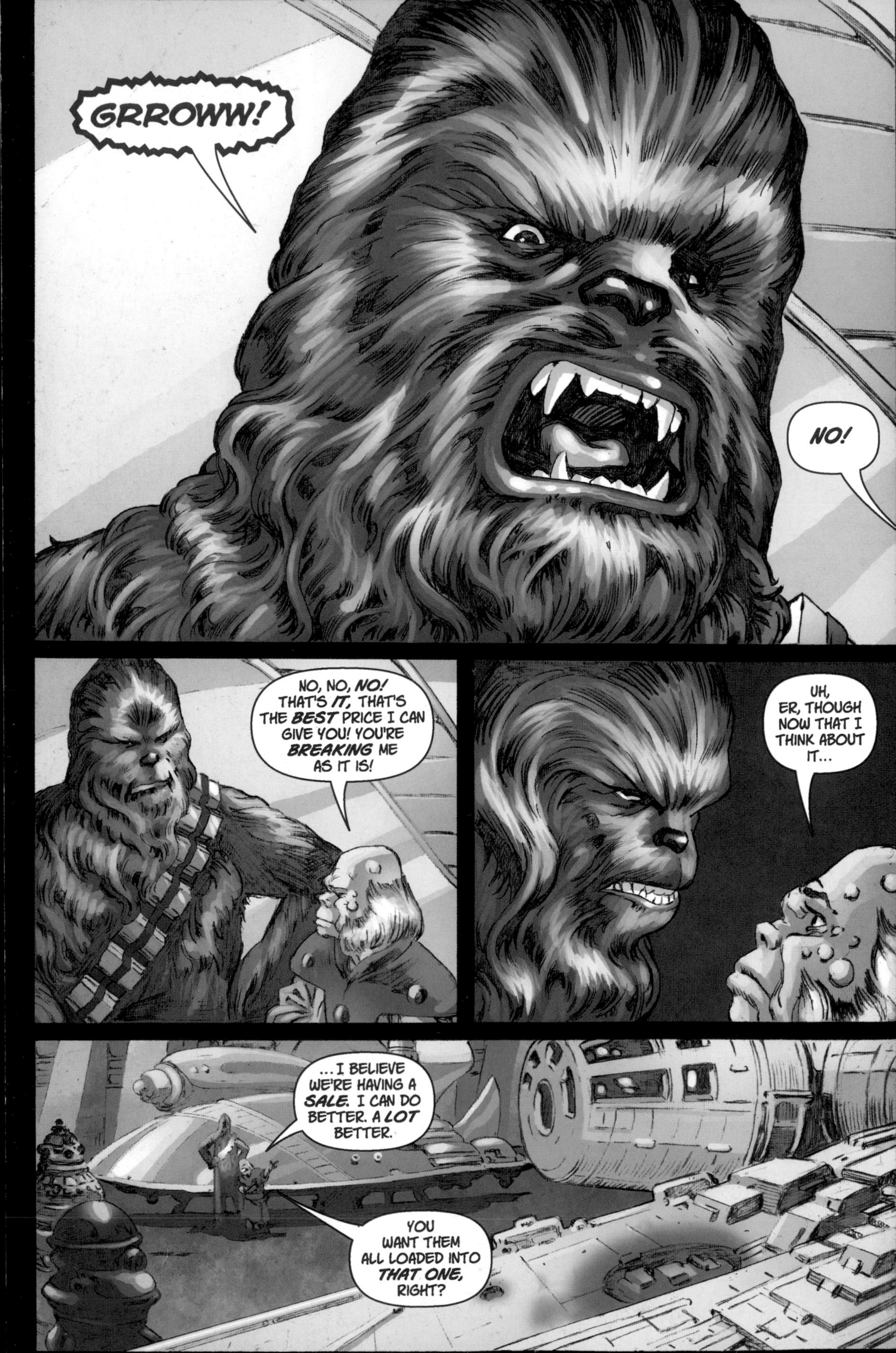
GRROWW!
NO!
NO, NO, NO! THAT'S IT, THAT'S THE BEST PRICE I CAN GIVE YOU! YOU'RE BREAKING ME AS IT IS!
UH, ER, THOUGH NOW THAT I THINK ABOUT IT...
...I BELIEVE WE'RE HAVING A SALE. I CAN DO BETTER. A LOT BETTER.
YOU WANT THEM ALL LOADED INTO THAT ONE, RIGHT?

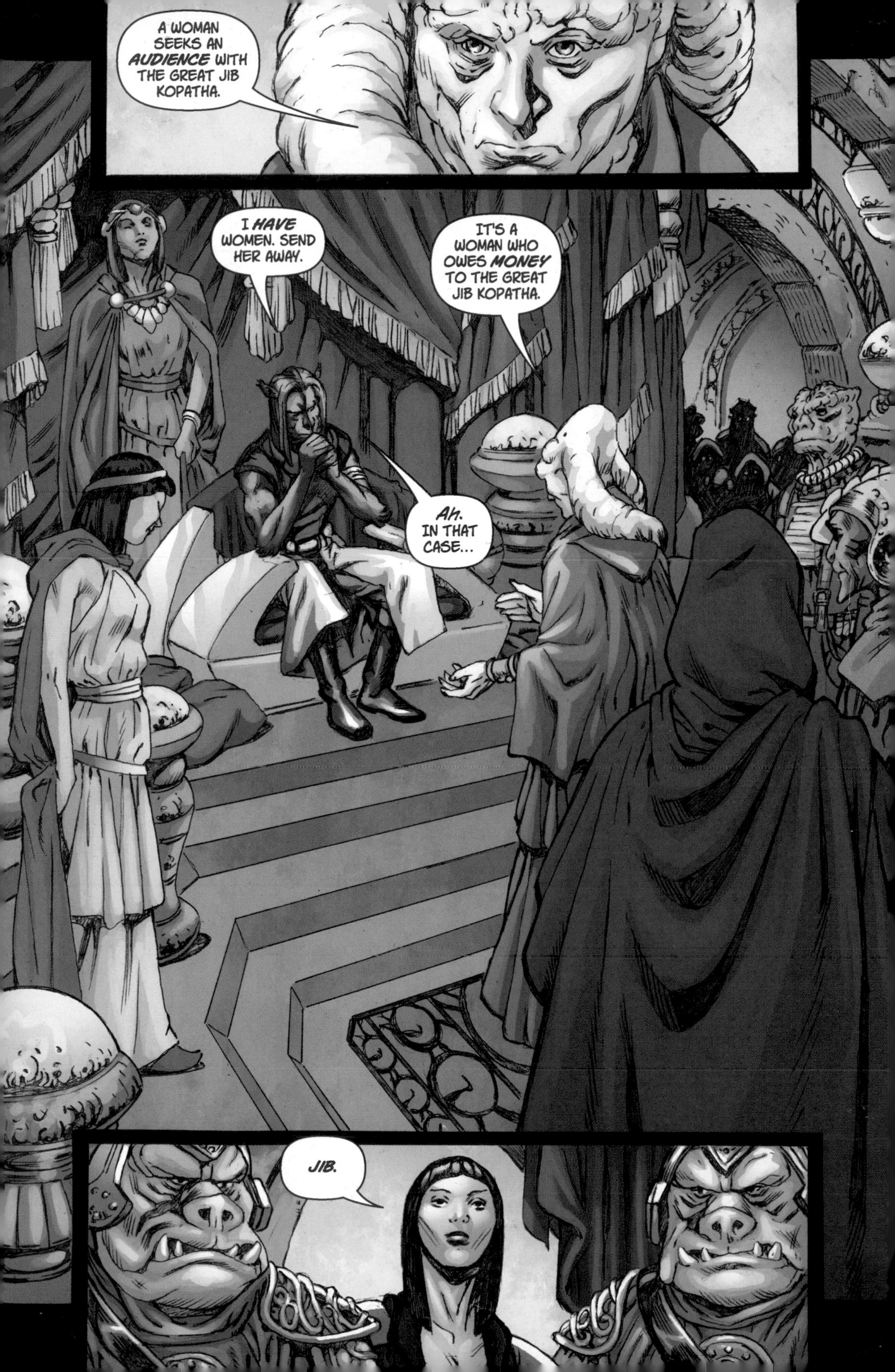
A WOMAN SEEKS AN AUDIENCE WITH THE GREAT JIB KOPATHA.
I HAVE WOMEN. SEND HER AWAY.
IT'S A WOMAN WHO OWES MONEY TO THE GREAT JIB KOPATHA.
Ah. IN THAT CASE...
JIB.

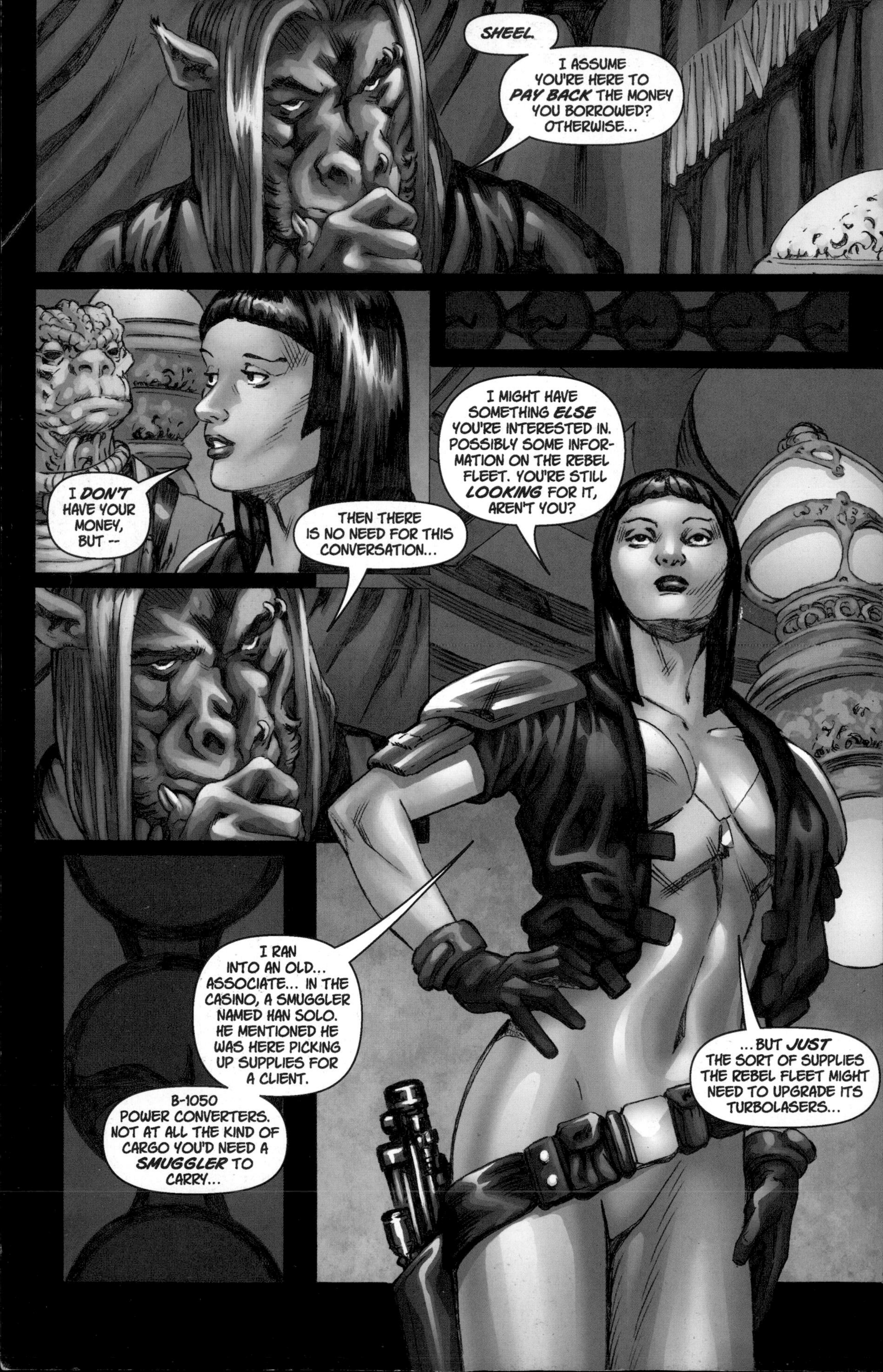
SHEEL.
I ASSUME YOU'RE HERE TO PAY BACK THE MONEY YOU BORROWED? OTHERWISE...
I DON'T HAVE YOUR MONEY, BUT --
THEN THERE IS NO NEED FOR THIS CONVERSATION...
I MIGHT HAVE SOMETHING ELSE YOU'RE INTERESTED IN. POSSIBLY SOME INFORMATION ON THE REBEL FLEET. YOU'RE STILL LOOKING FOR IT, AREN'T YOU?
I RAN INTO AN OLD... ASSOCIATE... IN THE CASINO, A SMUGGLER NAMED HAN SOLO. HE MENTIONED HE WAS HERE PICKING UP SUPPLIES FOR A CLIENT.
B-1050 POWER CONVERTERS. NOT AT ALL THE KIND OF CARGO YOU'D NEED A SMUGGLER TO CARRY...
...BUT JUST THE SORT OF SUPPLIES THE REBEL FLEET MIGHT NEED TO UPGRADE ITS TURBOLASERS...

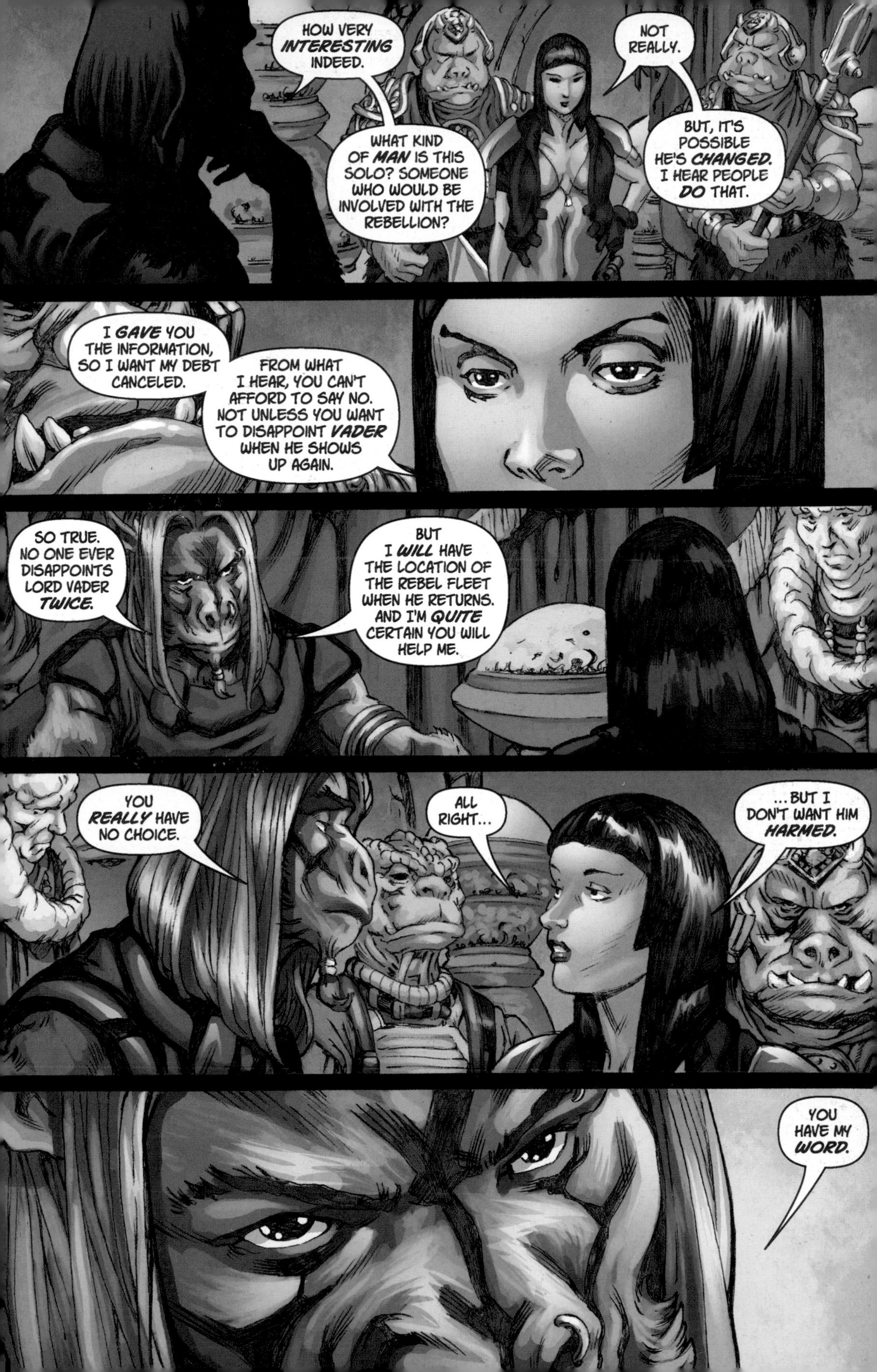
HOW VERY INTERESTING INDEED.
WHAT KIND OF MAN IS THIS SOLO? SOMEONE WHO WOULD BE INVOLVED WITH THE REBELLION?
NOT REALLY.
BUT, IT'S POSSIBLE HE'S CHANGED. I HEAR PEOPLE DO THAT.
I GAVE YOU THE INFORMATION, SO I WANT MY DEBT CANCELED.
FROM WHAT I HEAR, YOU CAN'T AFFORD TO SAY NO. NOT UNLESS YOU WANT TO DISAPPOINT VADER WHEN HE SHOWS UP AGAIN.
SO TRUE. NO ONE EVER DISAPPOINTS LORD VADER TWICE.
BUT I WILL HAVE THE LOCATION OF THE REBEL FLEET WHEN HE RETURNS. AND I'M QUITE CERTAIN YOU WILL HELP ME.
YOU REALLY HAVE NO CHOICE.
ALL RIGHT...
...BUT I DON'T WANT HIM HARMED.
YOU HAVE MY WORD.

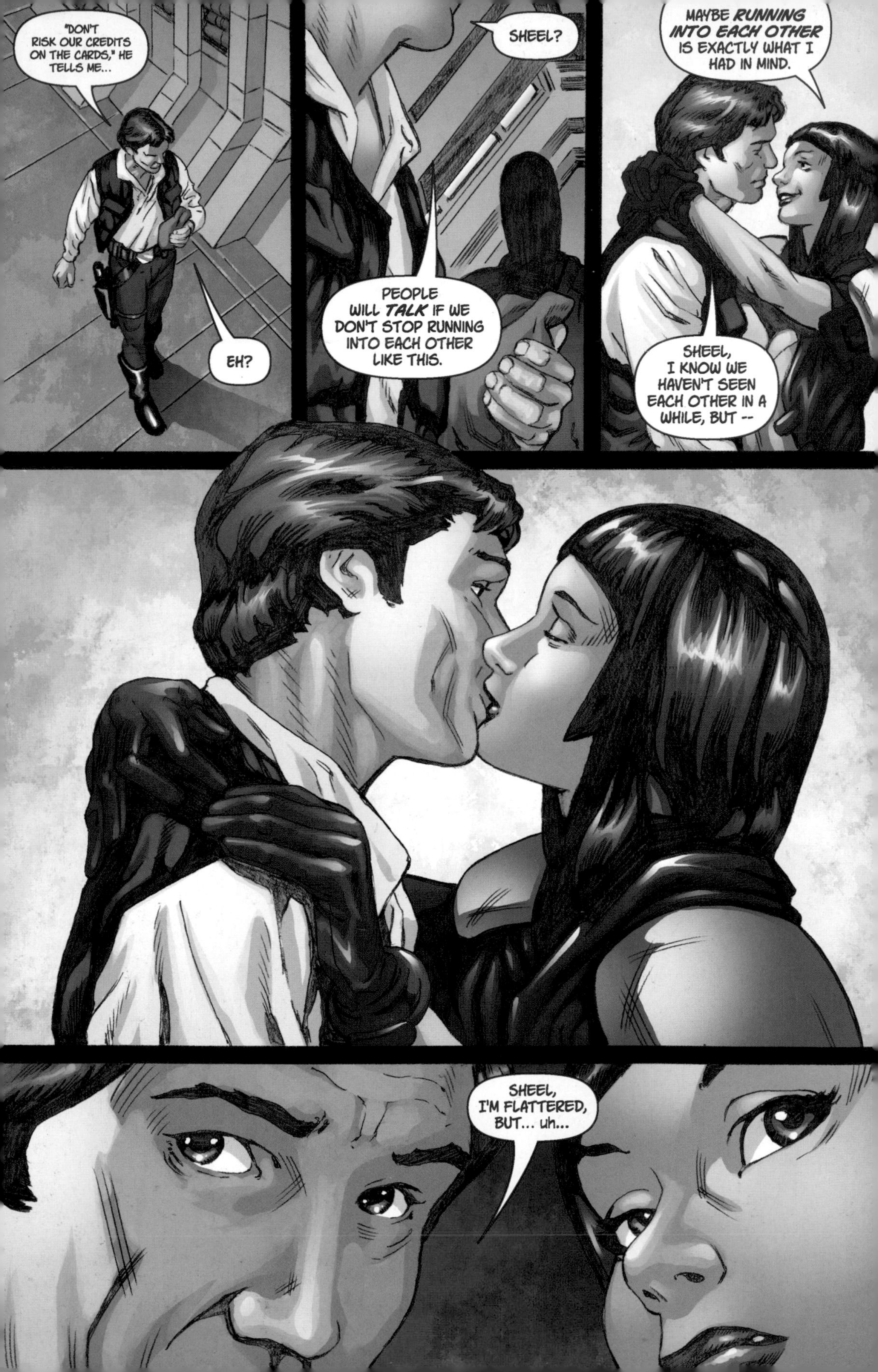
"DON'T RISK OUR CREDITS ON THE CARDS," HE TELLS ME...
EH?
SHEEL?
PEOPLE WILL TALK IF WE DON'T STOP RUNNING INTO EACH OTHER LIKE THIS.
MAYBE RUNNING INTO EACH OTHER IS EXACTLY WHAT I HAD IN MIND.
SHEEL, I KNOW WE HAVEN'T SEEN EACH OTHER IN A WHILE, BUT --
SHEEL, I'M FLATTERED, BUT... uh...

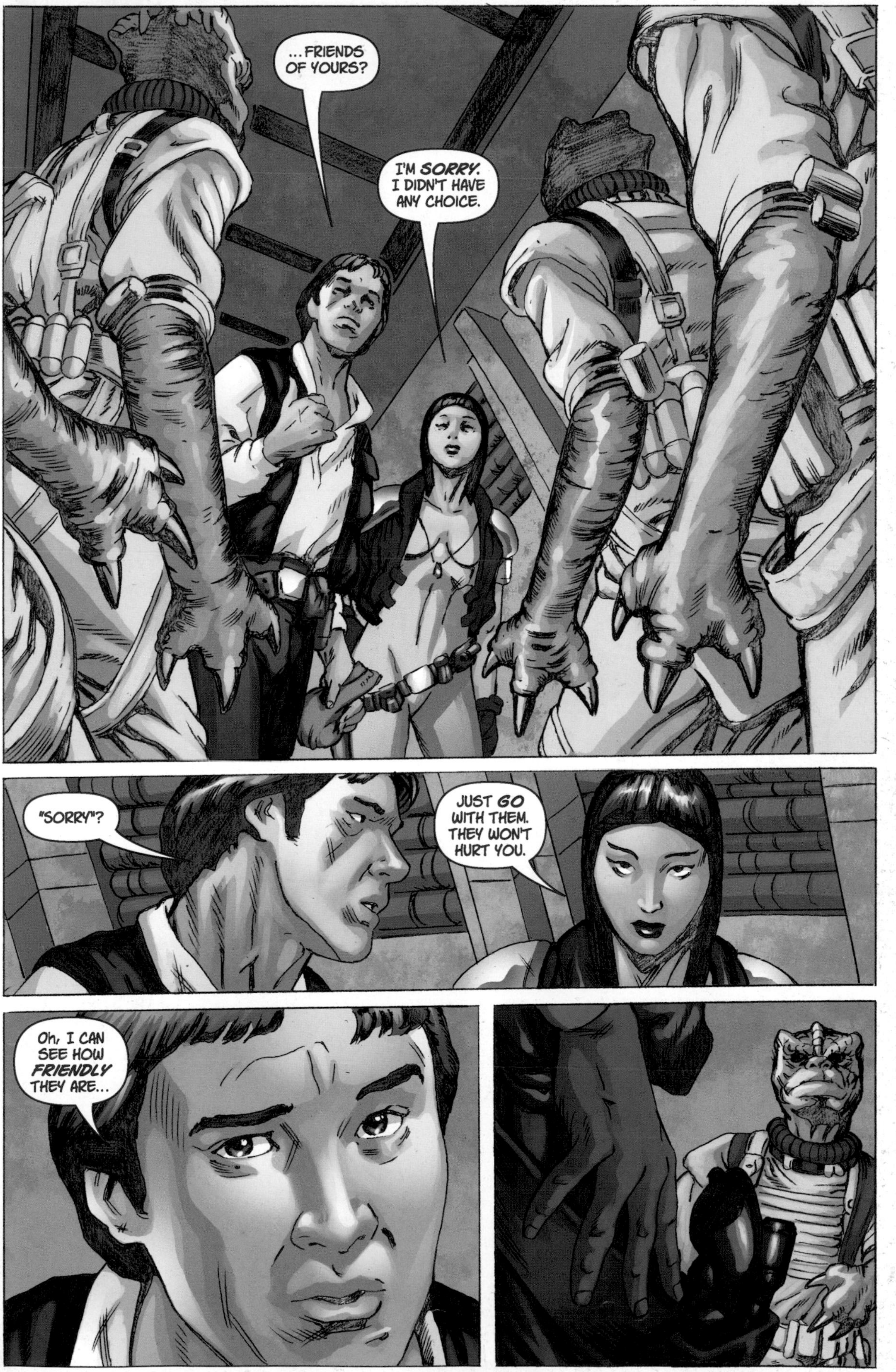

...FRIENDS OF YOURS?
I'M SORRY. I DIDN'T HAVE ANY CHOICE.
"SORRY"?
JUST GO WITH THEM. THEY WON'T HURT YOU.
Oh, I CAN SEE HOW FRIENDLY THEY ARE...

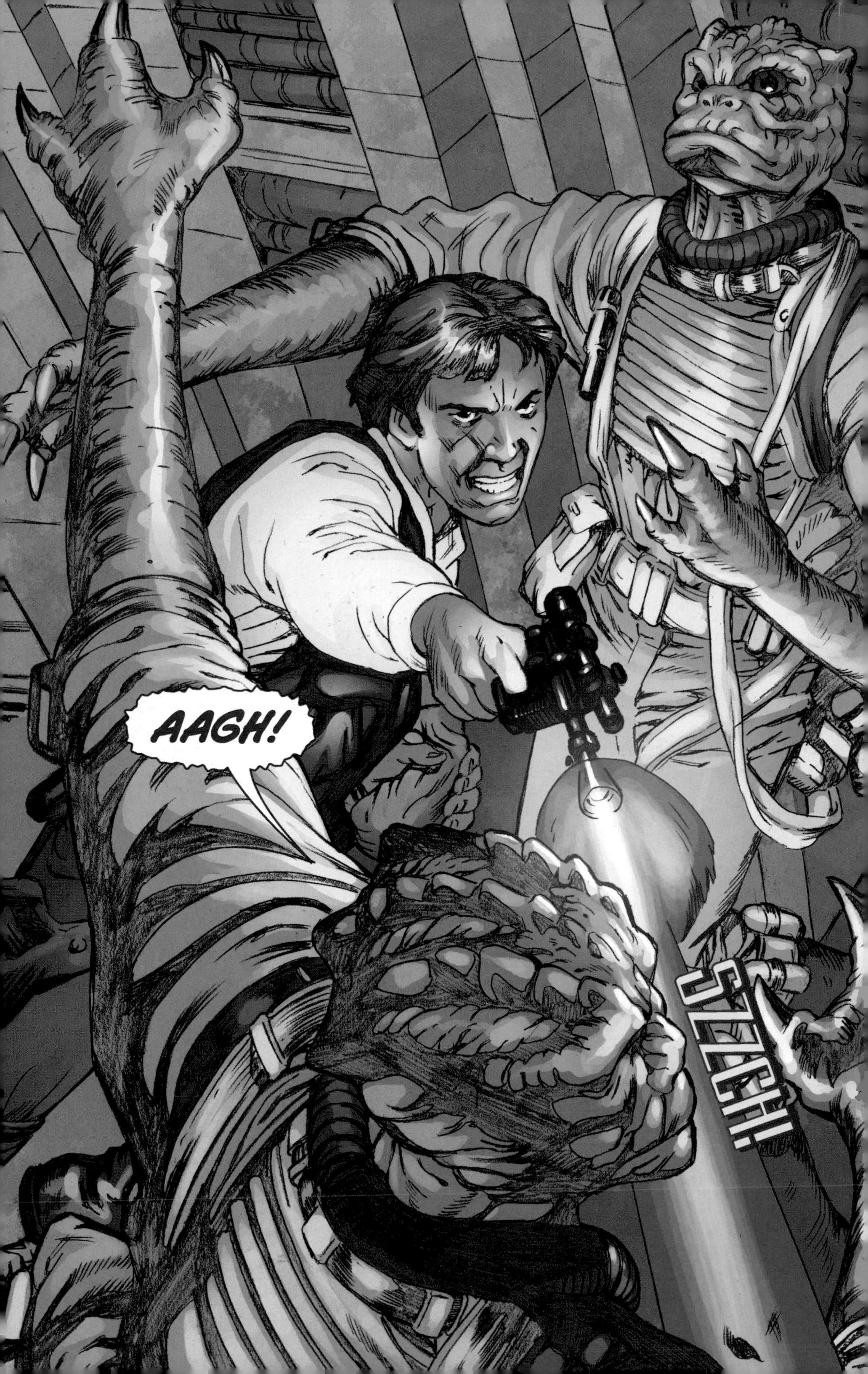
AAGH!
SZZCHH!

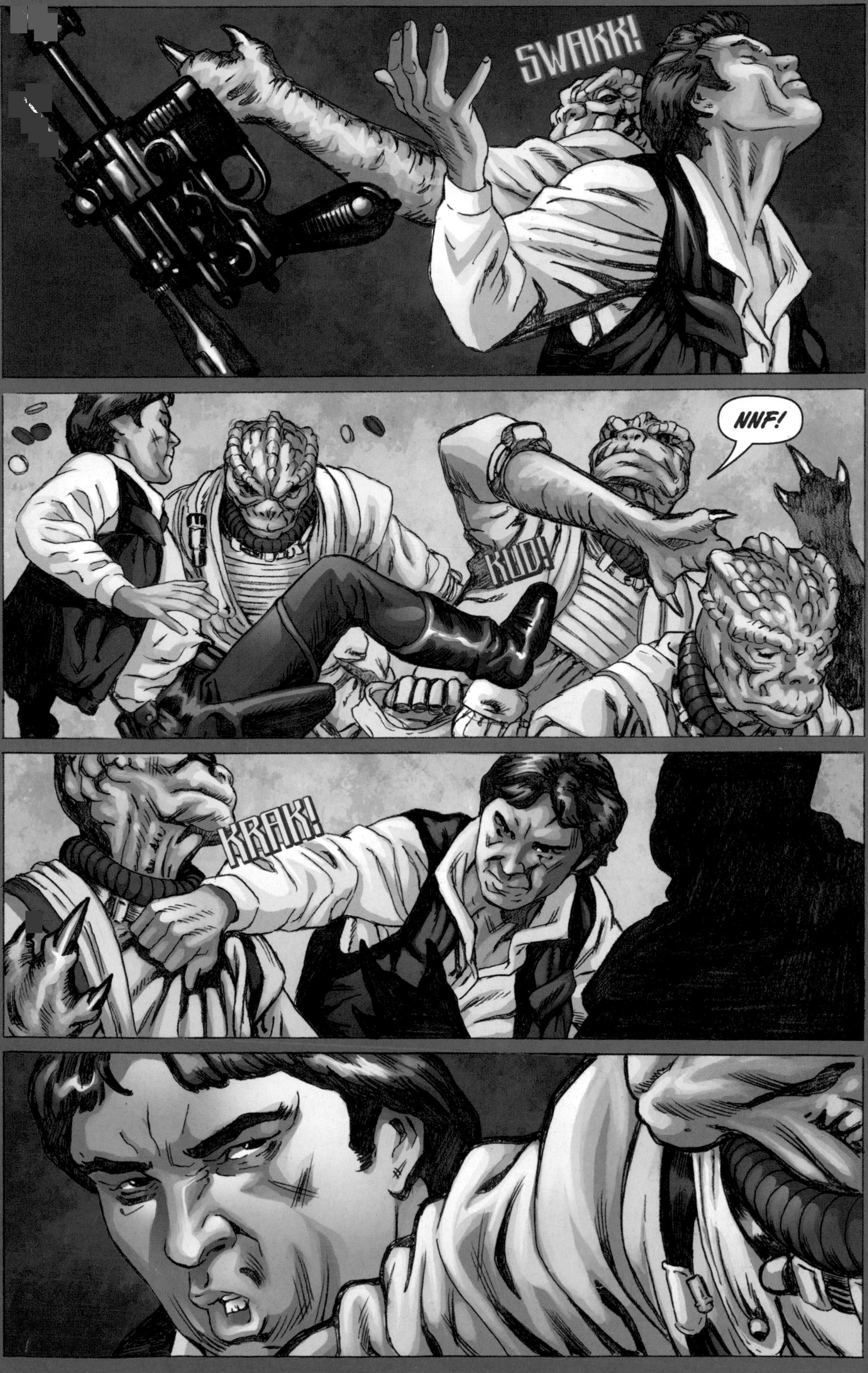
SWAKK!
KUD!
NNF!
KRAK!

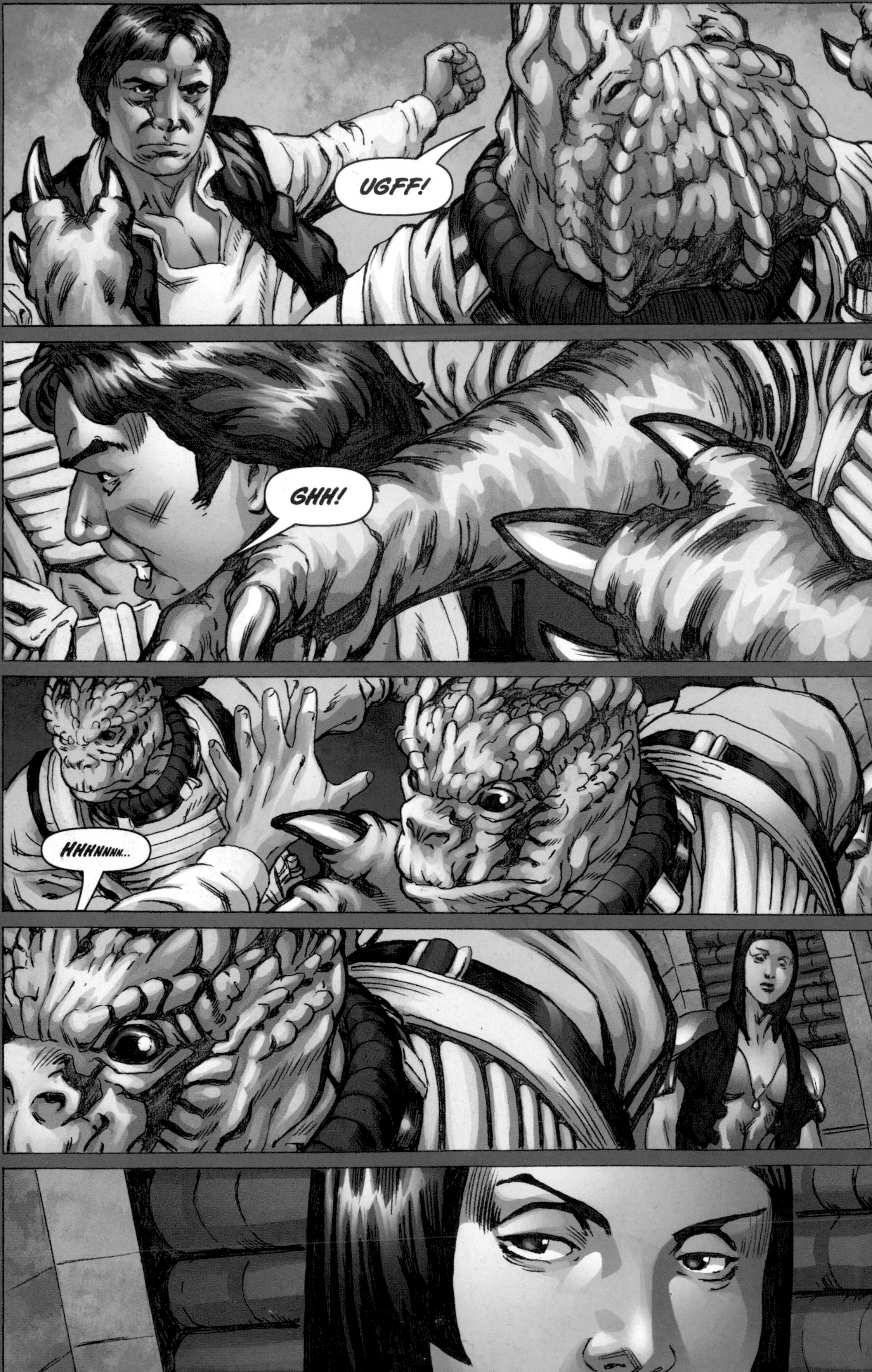
UGFF!
GHH!
HHHNNNN...

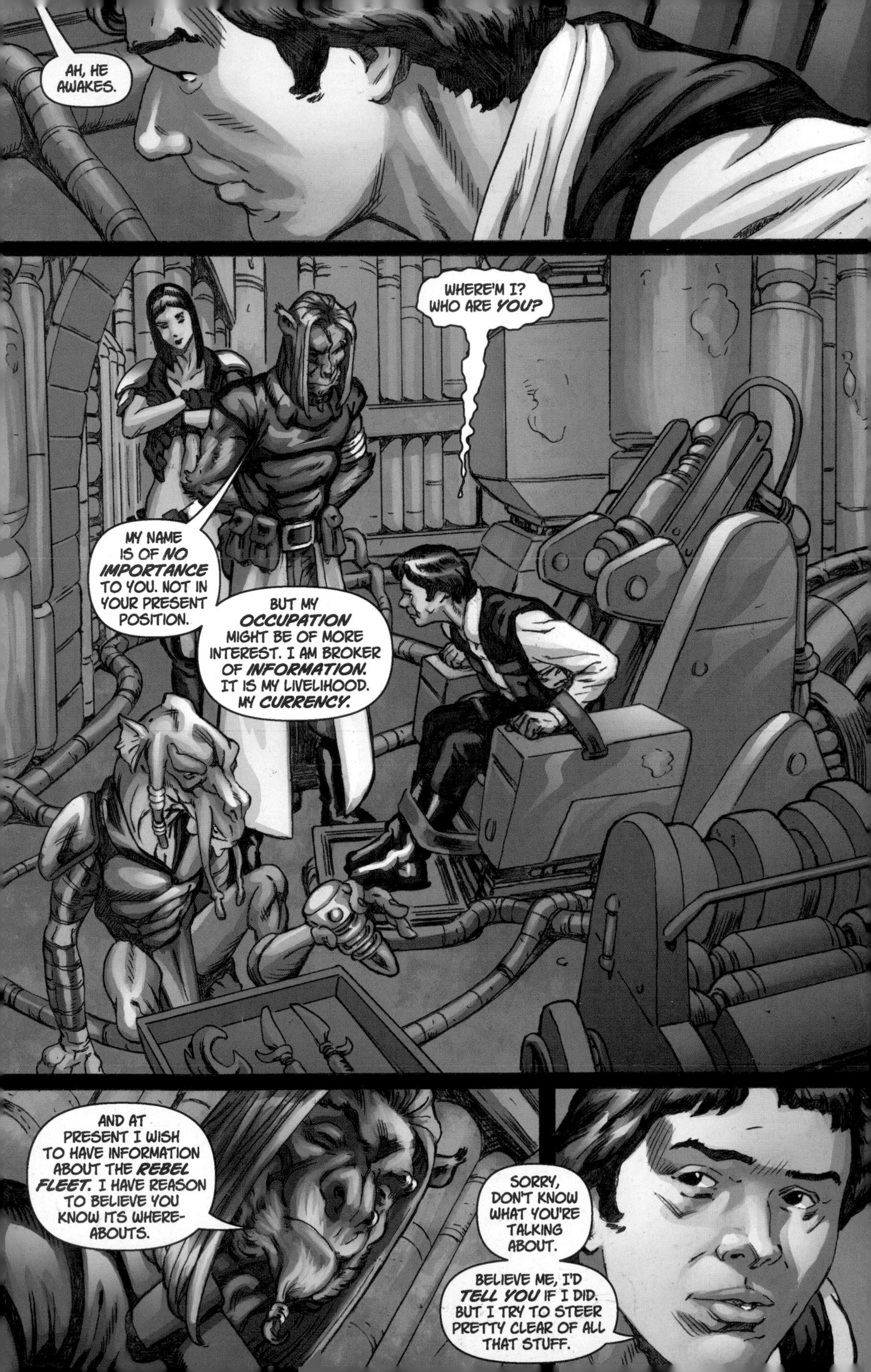
AH, HE AWAKES.
WHERE'M I? WHO ARE *YOU?*
MY NAME IS OF ***NO IMPORTANCE*** TO YOU. NOT IN YOUR PRESENT POSITION.
BUT MY ***OCCUPATION*** MIGHT BE OF MORE INTEREST. I AM BROKER OF ***INFORMATION.*** IT IS MY LIVELIHOOD. MY ***CURRENCY.***
AND AT PRESENT I WISH TO HAVE INFORMATION ABOUT THE ***REBEL FLEET.*** I HAVE REASON TO BELIEVE YOU KNOW ITS WHERE-ABOUTS.
SORRY, DON'T KNOW WHAT YOU'RE TALKING ABOUT.
BELIEVE ME, I'D ***TELL YOU*** IF I DID. BUT I TRY TO STEER PRETTY CLEAR OF ALL THAT STUFF.

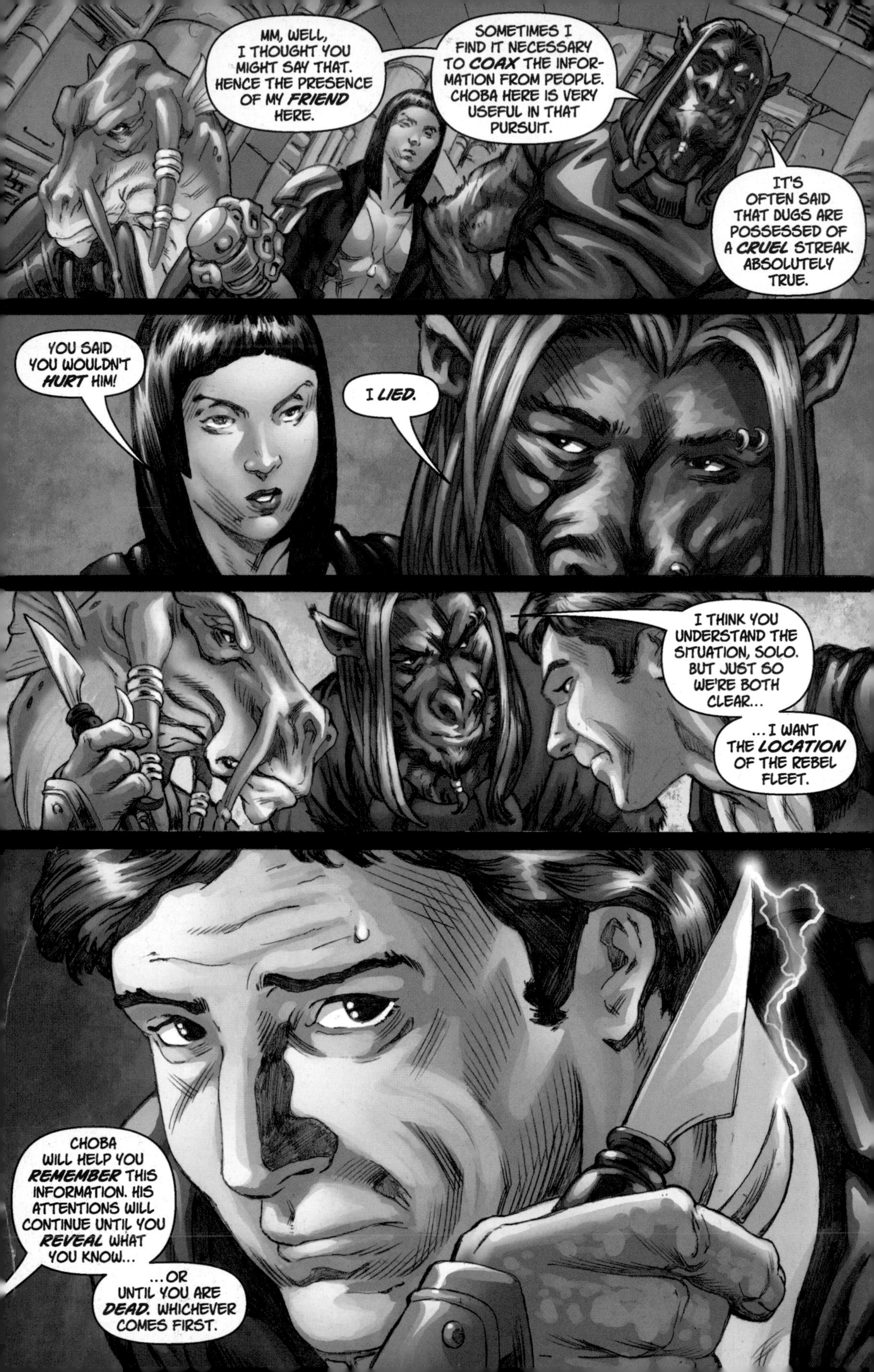
MM, WELL, I THOUGHT YOU MIGHT SAY THAT. HENCE THE PRESENCE OF MY *FRIEND* HERE.
SOMETIMES I FIND IT NECESSARY TO *COAX* THE INFORMATION FROM PEOPLE. CHOBA HERE IS VERY USEFUL IN THAT PURSUIT.
IT'S OFTEN SAID THAT DUGS ARE POSSESSED OF A *CRUEL* STREAK. ABSOLUTELY TRUE.
YOU SAID YOU WOULDN'T *HURT* HIM!
I *LIED*.
I THINK YOU UNDERSTAND THE SITUATION, SOLO. BUT JUST SO WE'RE BOTH CLEAR...
...I WANT THE *LOCATION* OF THE REBEL FLEET.
CHOBA WILL HELP YOU *REMEMBER* THIS INFORMATION. HIS ATTENTIONS WILL CONTINUE UNTIL YOU *REVEAL* WHAT YOU KNOW...
...OR UNTIL YOU ARE *DEAD*. WHICHEVER COMES FIRST.

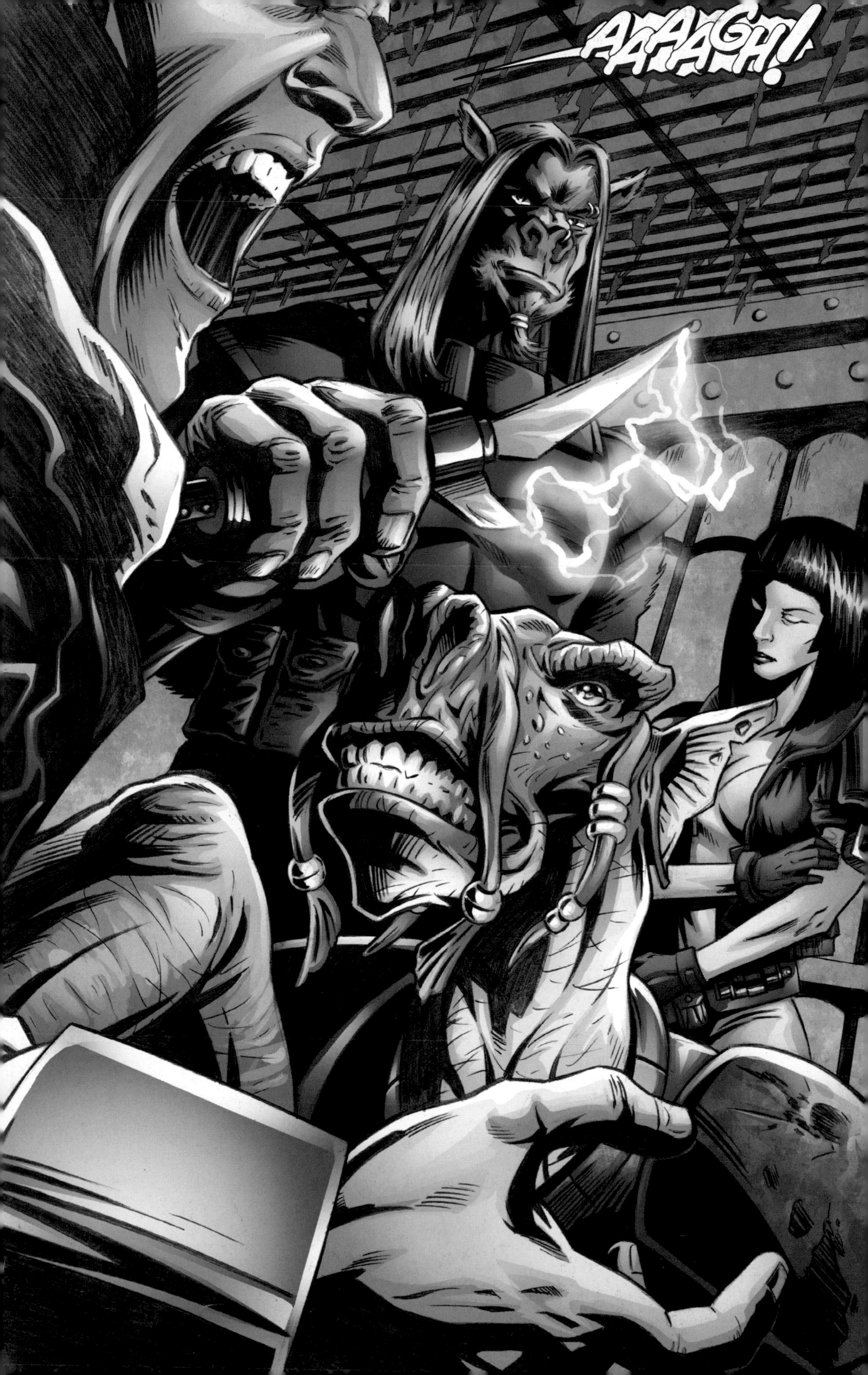
AAAAGH!

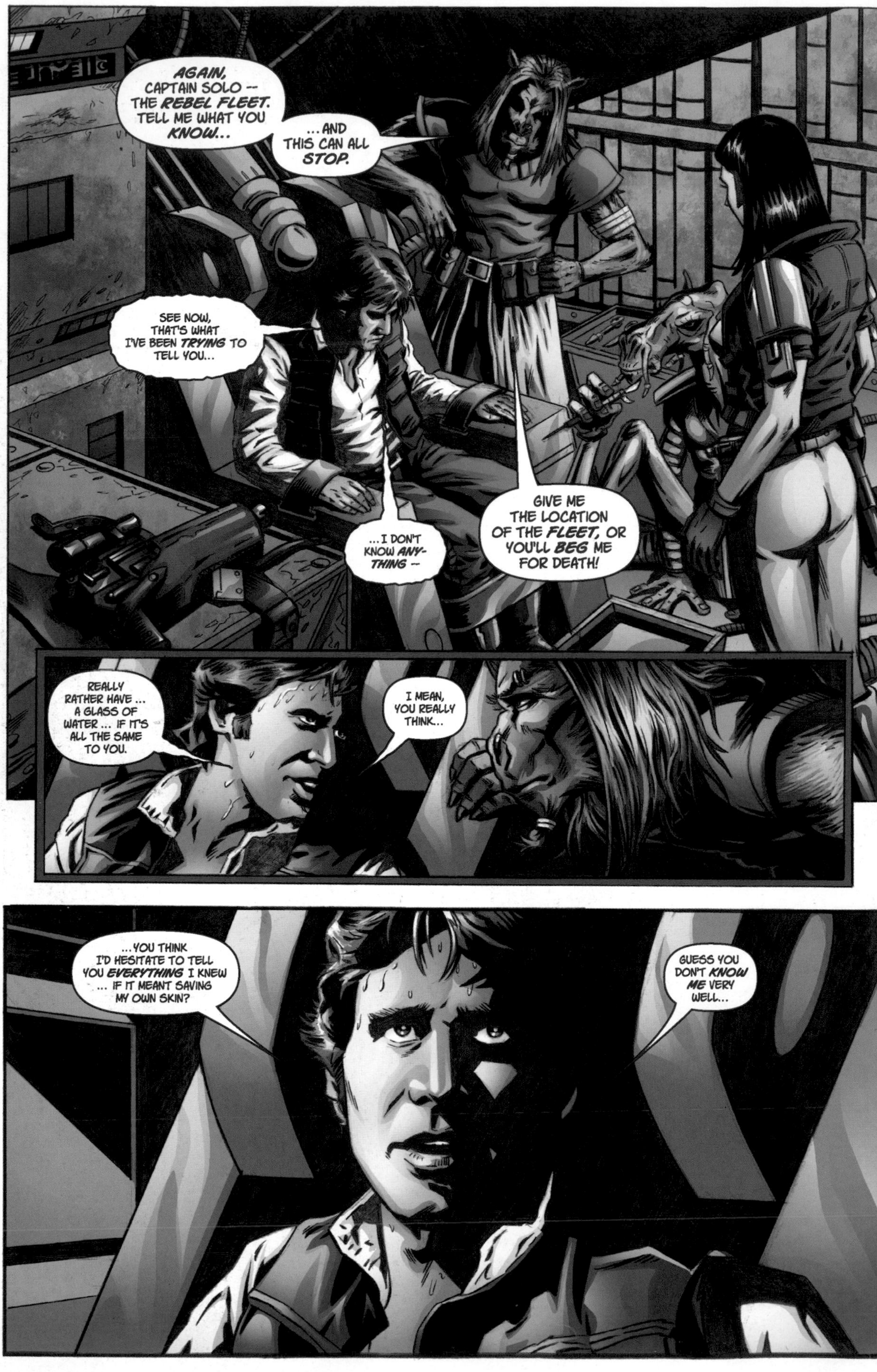
AGAIN, CAPTAIN SOLO -- THE REBEL FLEET. TELL ME WHAT YOU KNOW...
...AND THIS CAN ALL STOP.
SEE NOW, THAT'S WHAT I'VE BEEN TRYING TO TELL YOU...
...I DON'T KNOW ANY-THING --
GIVE ME THE LOCATION OF THE FLEET, OR YOU'LL BEG ME FOR DEATH!
REALLY RATHER HAVE ... A GLASS OF WATER ... IF IT'S ALL THE SAME TO YOU.
I MEAN, YOU REALLY THINK...
...YOU THINK I'D HESITATE TO TELL YOU EVERYTHING I KNEW ... IF IT MEANT SAVING MY OWN SKIN?
GUESS YOU DON'T KNOW ME VERY WELL...

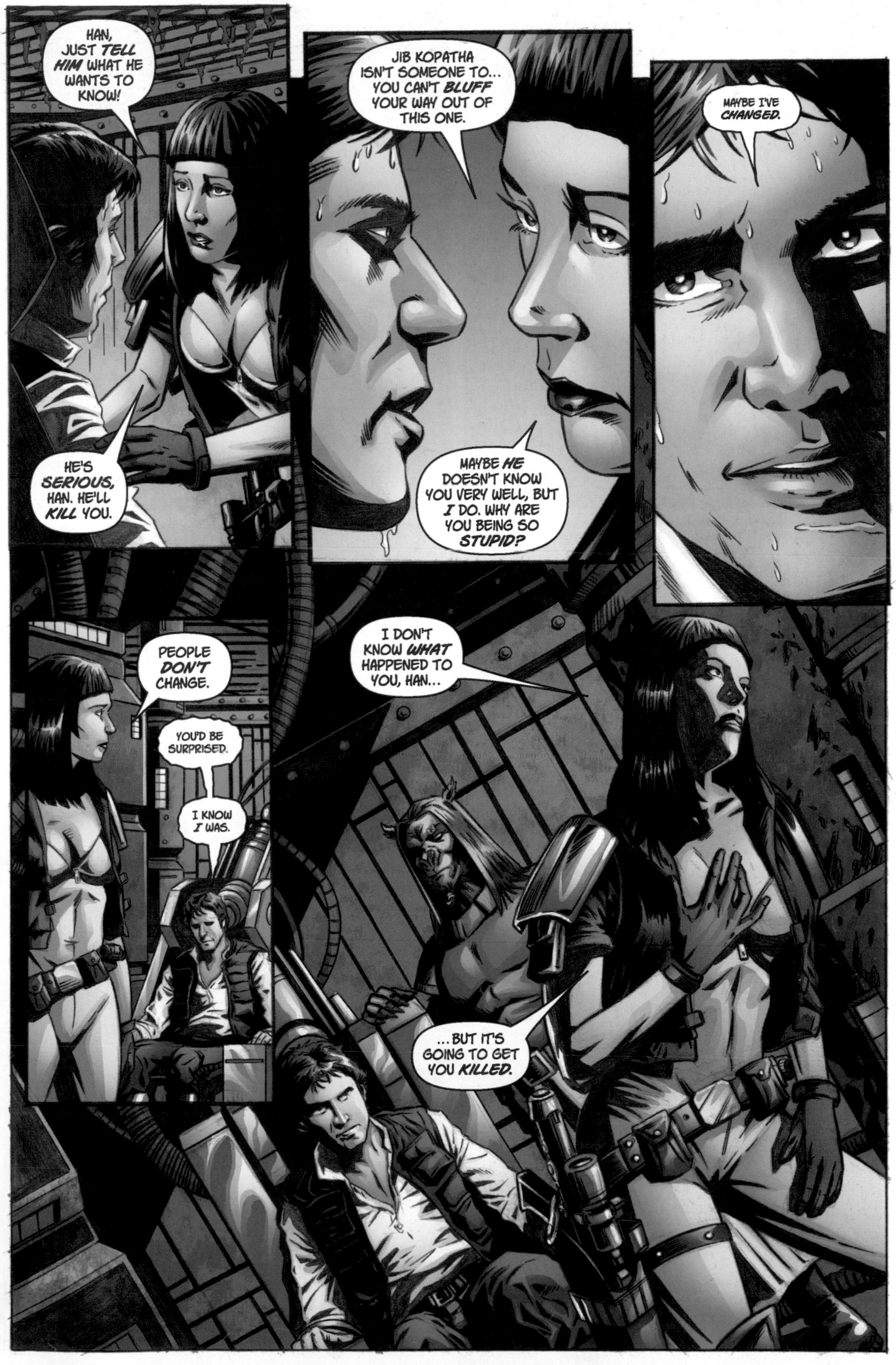
HAN, JUST TELL HIM WHAT HE WANTS TO KNOW!
HE'S SERIOUS, HAN. HE'LL KILL YOU.
JIB KOPATHA ISN'T SOMEONE TO... YOU CAN'T BLUFF YOUR WAY OUT OF THIS ONE.
MAYBE HE DOESN'T KNOW YOU VERY WELL, BUT I DO. WHY ARE YOU BEING SO STUPID?
MAYBE I'VE CHANGED.
PEOPLE DON'T CHANGE.
YOU'D BE SURPRISED.
I KNOW I WAS.
I DON'T KNOW WHAT HAPPENED TO YOU, HAN...
...BUT IT'S GOING TO GET YOU KILLED.

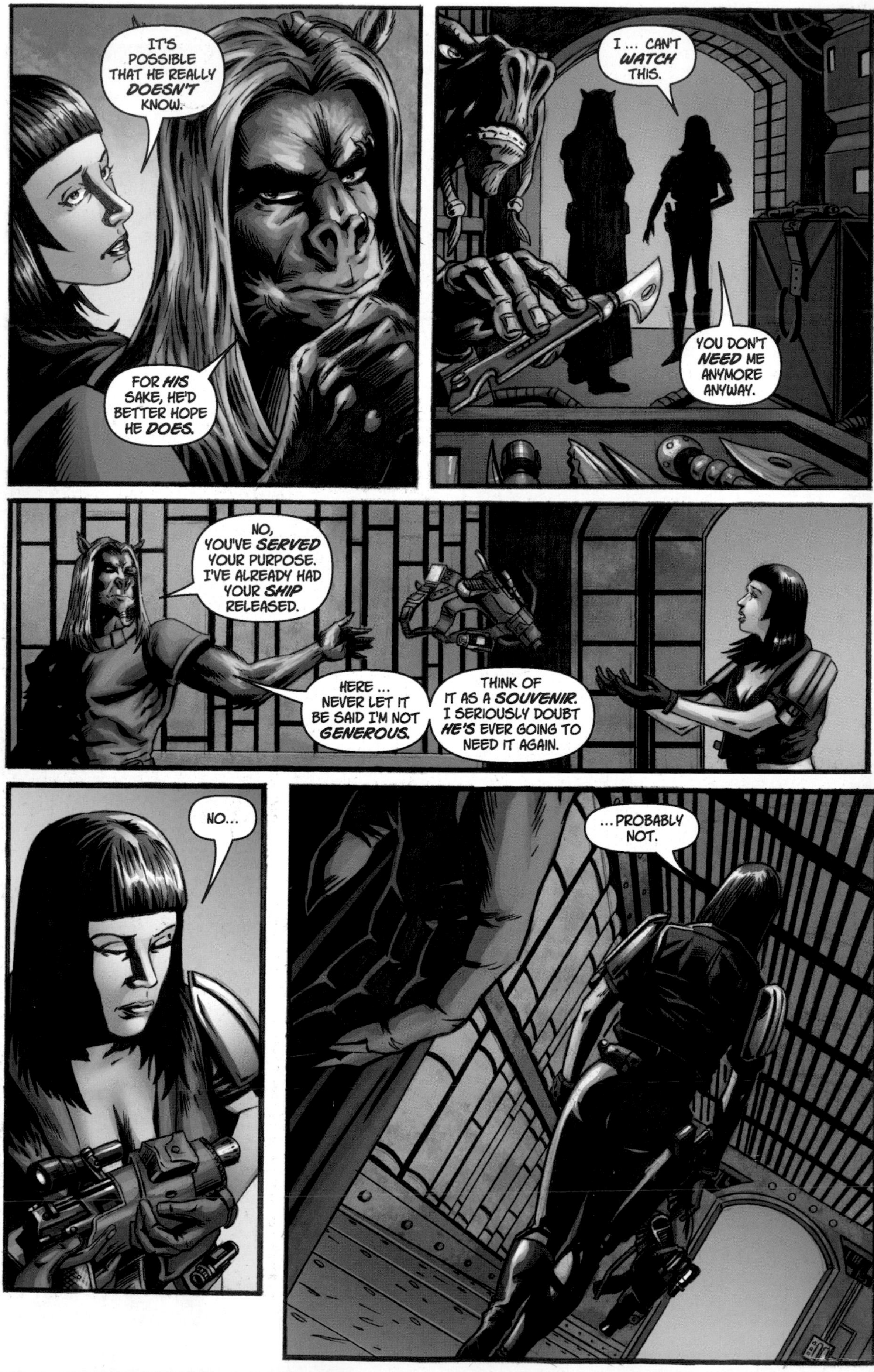
IT'S POSSIBLE THAT HE REALLY *DOESN'T* KNOW.
FOR *HIS* SAKE, HE'D BETTER HOPE HE *DOES*.
I ... CAN'T *WATCH* THIS.
YOU DON'T *NEED* ME ANYMORE ANYWAY.
NO, YOU'VE *SERVED* YOUR PURPOSE. I'VE ALREADY HAD YOUR *SHIP* RELEASED.
HERE ... NEVER LET IT BE SAID I'M NOT *GENEROUS*.
THINK OF IT AS A *SOUVENIR*. I SERIOUSLY DOUBT *HE'S* EVER GOING TO NEED IT AGAIN.
NO...
...PROBABLY NOT.

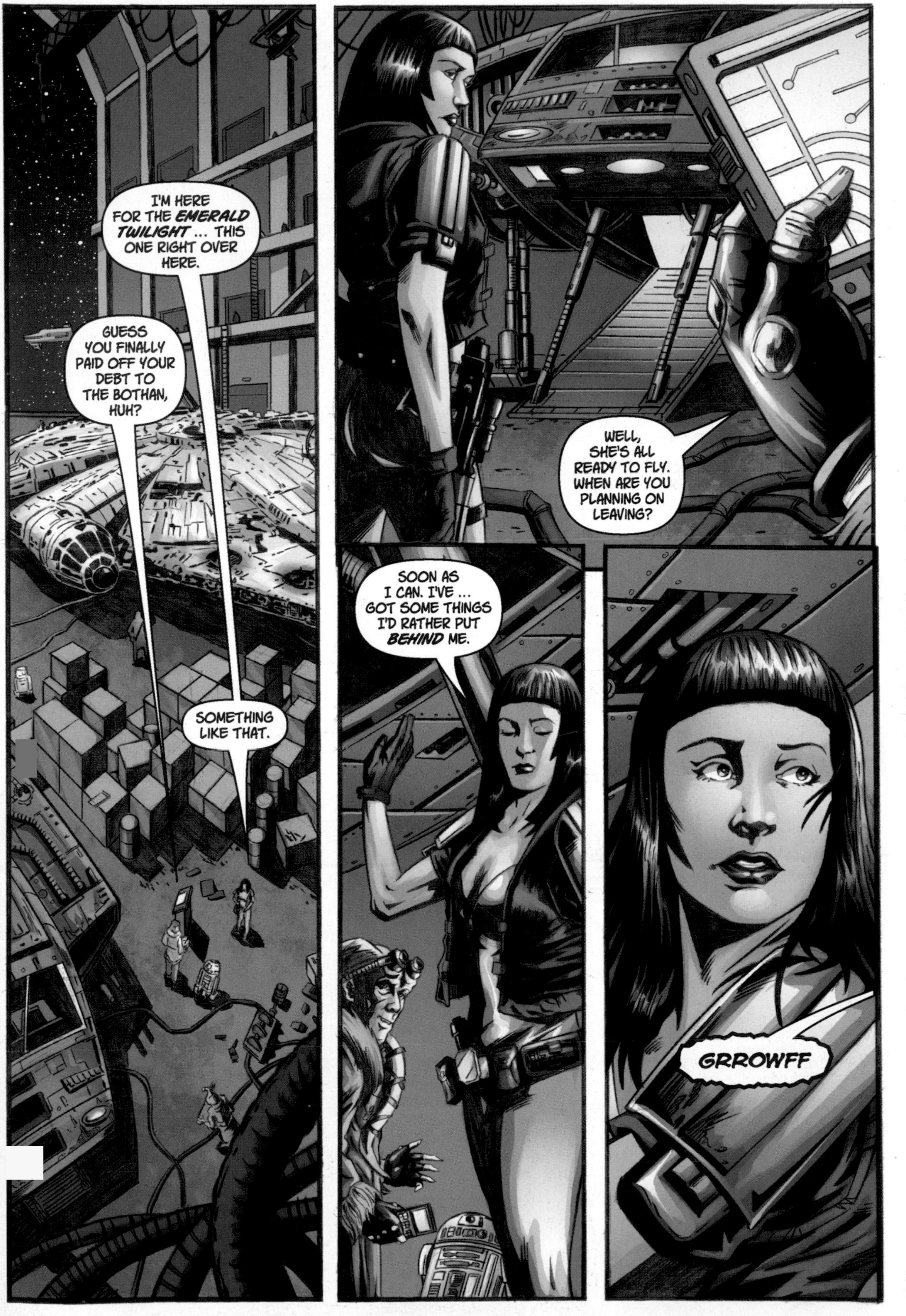
I'M HERE FOR THE *EMERALD TWILIGHT* ... THIS ONE RIGHT OVER HERE.
GUESS YOU FINALLY PAID OFF YOUR DEBT TO THE BOTHAN, HUH?
SOMETHING LIKE THAT.
WELL, SHE'S ALL READY TO FLY. WHEN ARE YOU PLANNING ON LEAVING?
SOON AS I CAN. I'VE ... GOT SOME THINGS I'D RATHER PUT *BEHIND* ME.
GRROWFF

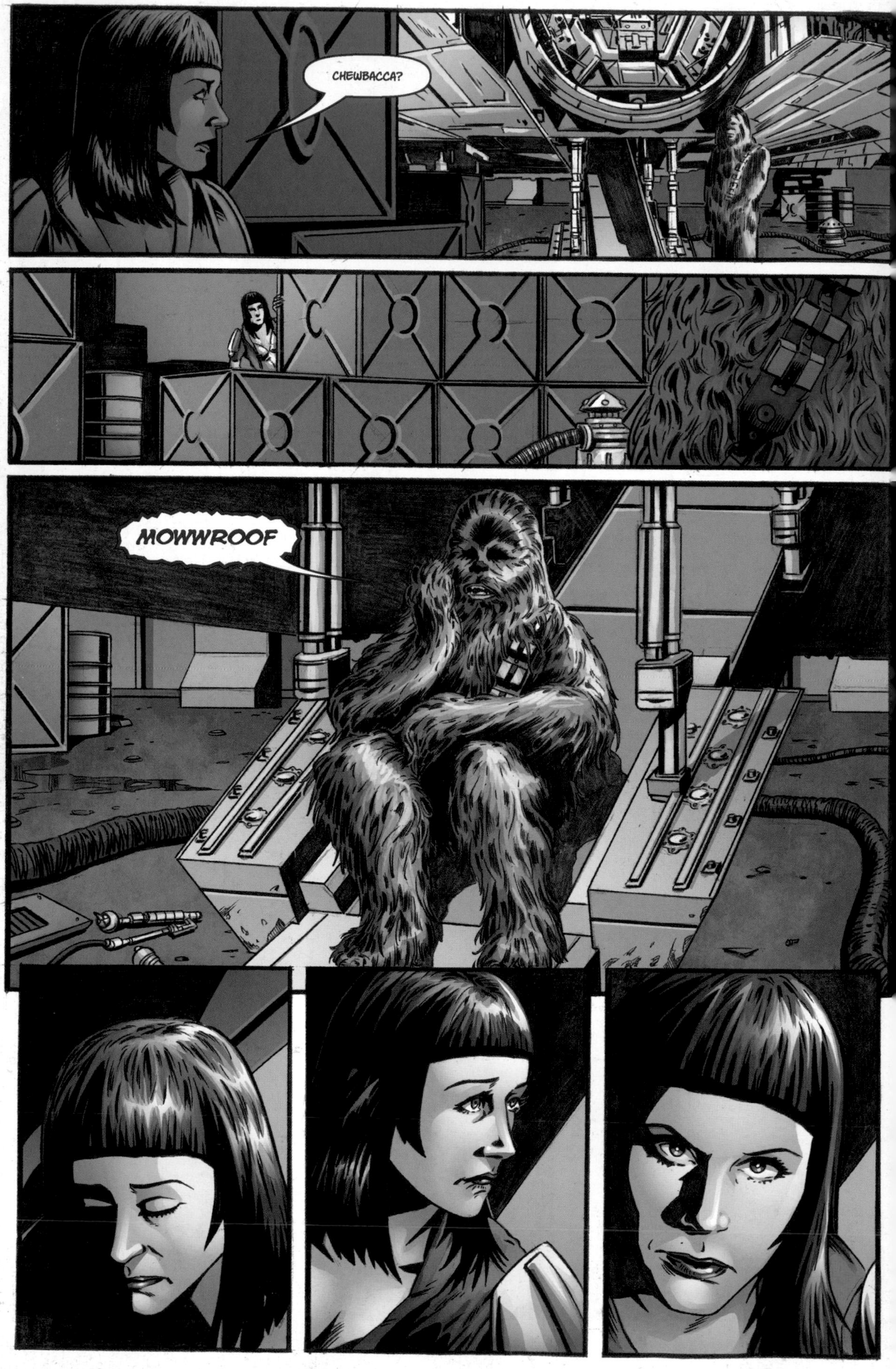
CHEWBACCA?
MOWWROOF

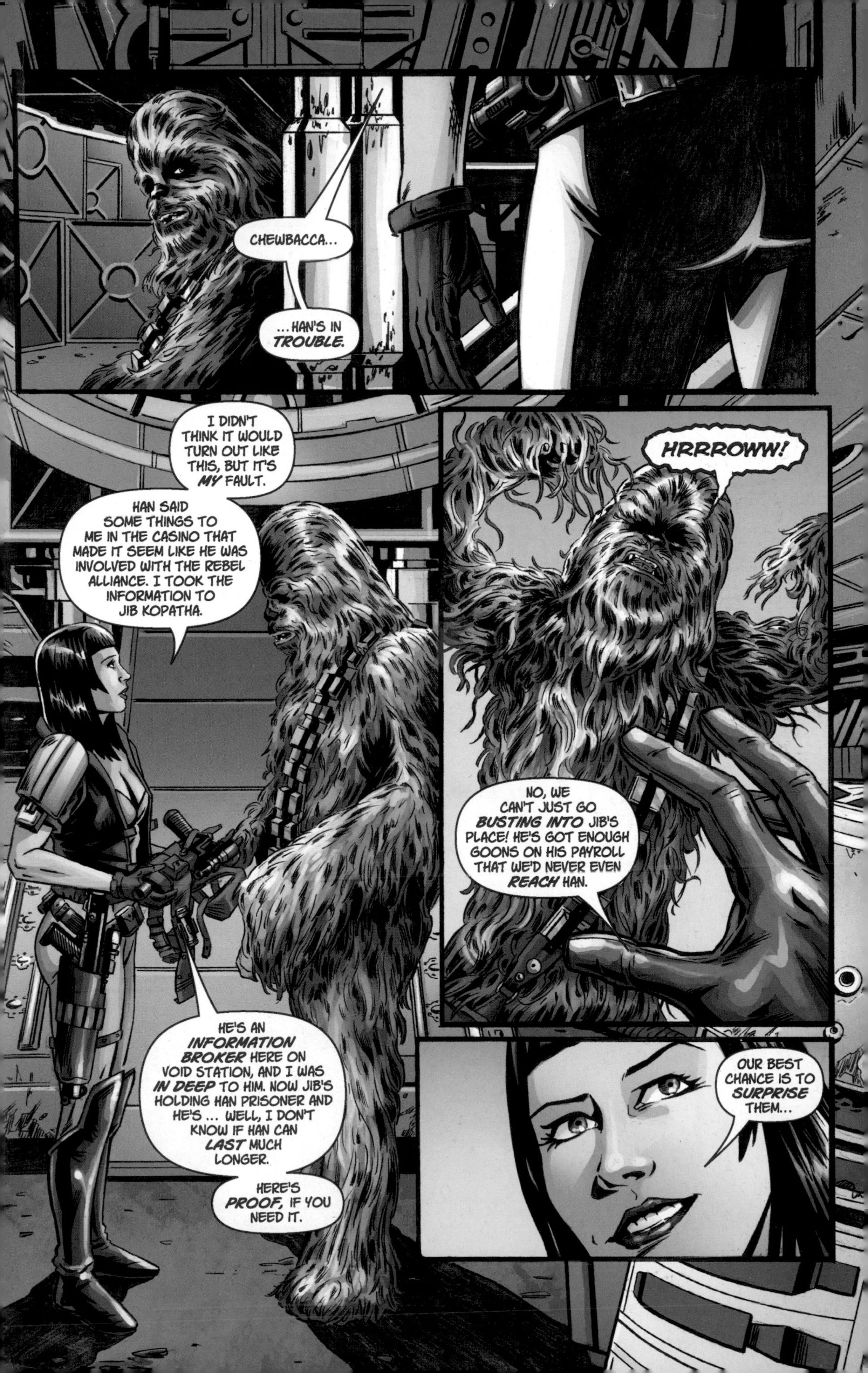
CHEWBACCA...
...HAN'S IN TROUBLE.
I DIDN'T THINK IT WOULD TURN OUT LIKE THIS, BUT IT'S MY FAULT.
HAN SAID SOME THINGS TO ME IN THE CASINO THAT MADE IT SEEM LIKE HE WAS INVOLVED WITH THE REBEL ALLIANCE. I TOOK THE INFORMATION TO JIB KOPATHA.
HE'S AN INFORMATION BROKER HERE ON VOID STATION, AND I WAS IN DEEP TO HIM. NOW JIB'S HOLDING HAN PRISONER AND HE'S ... WELL, I DON'T KNOW IF HAN CAN LAST MUCH LONGER.
HERE'S PROOF, IF YOU NEED IT.
HRRROWW!
NO, WE CAN'T JUST GO BUSTING INTO JIB'S PLACE! HE'S GOT ENOUGH GOONS ON HIS PAYROLL THAT WE'D NEVER EVEN REACH HAN.
OUR BEST CHANCE IS TO SURPRISE THEM...

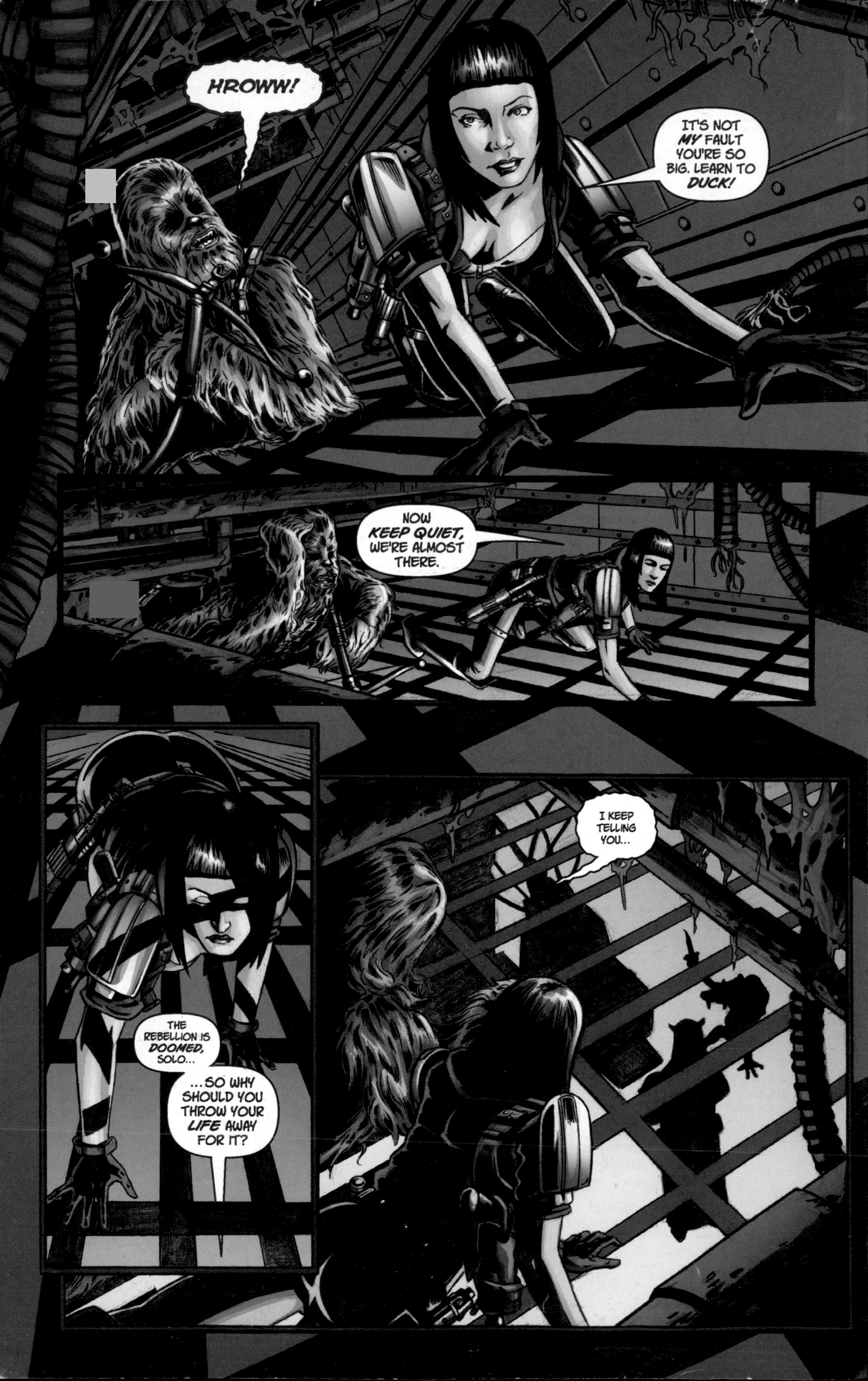
HROWW!
IT'S NOT *MY* FAULT YOU'RE SO BIG. LEARN TO *DUCK!*
NOW *KEEP QUIET,* WE'RE ALMOST THERE.
THE REBELLION IS *DOOMED,* SOLO...
...SO WHY SHOULD YOU THROW YOUR *LIFE* AWAY FOR IT?
I KEEP TELLING YOU...

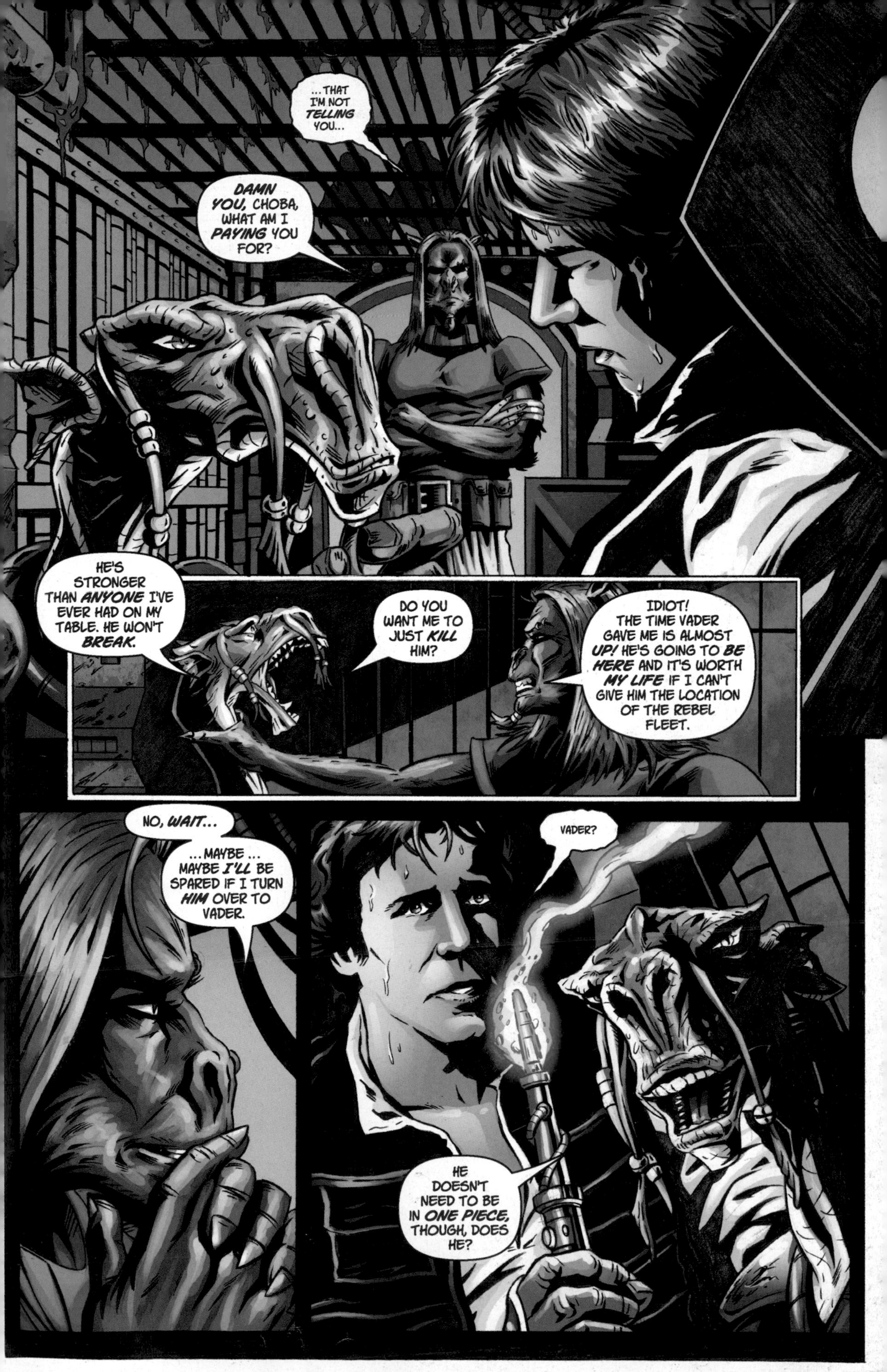
...THAT I'M NOT TELLING YOU...
DAMN YOU, CHOBA, WHAT AM I PAYING YOU FOR?
HE'S STRONGER THAN ANYONE I'VE EVER HAD ON MY TABLE. HE WON'T BREAK.
DO YOU WANT ME TO JUST KILL HIM?
IDIOT! THE TIME VADER GAVE ME IS ALMOST UP! HE'S GOING TO BE HERE AND IT'S WORTH MY LIFE IF I CAN'T GIVE HIM THE LOCATION OF THE REBEL FLEET.
NO, WAIT...
...MAYBE ... MAYBE I'LL BE SPARED IF I TURN HIM OVER TO VADER.
VADER?
HE DOESN'T NEED TO BE IN ONE PIECE, THOUGH, DOES HE?

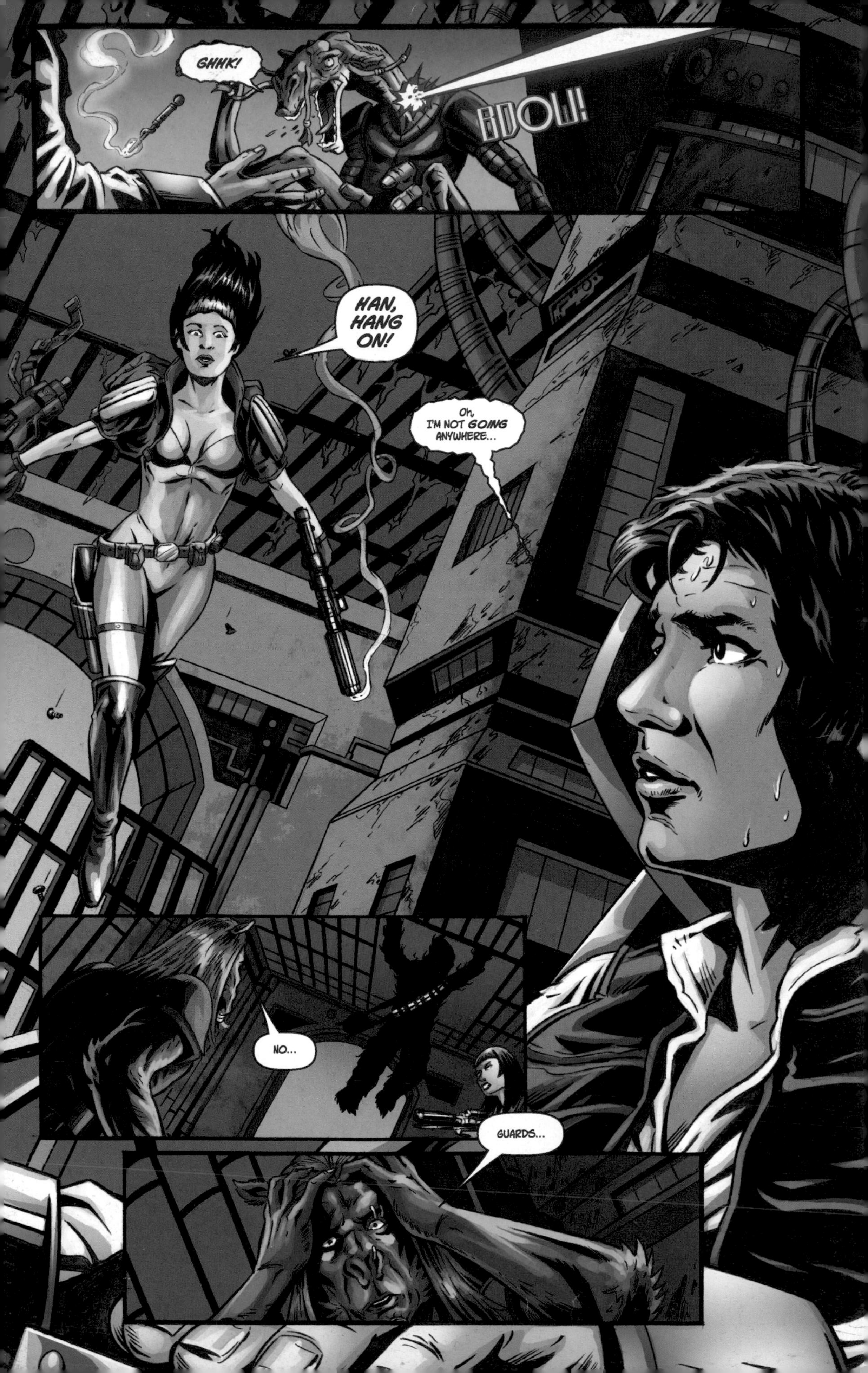
GHHK!
BDOW!
HAN, HANG ON!
Oh, I'M NOT GOING ANYWHERE...
NO...
GUARDS...

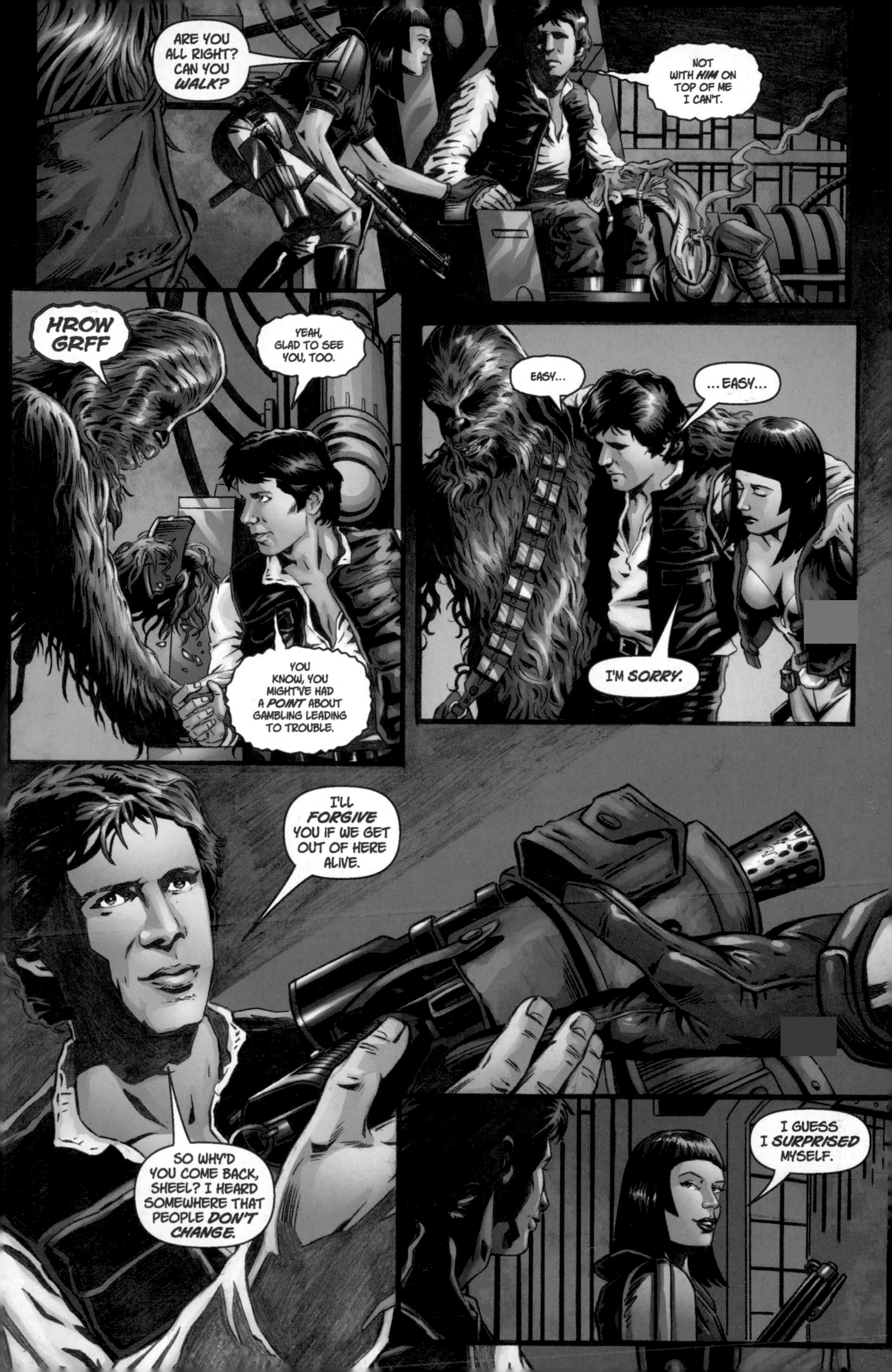
ARE YOU ALL RIGHT? CAN YOU WALK?
NOT WITH HIM ON TOP OF ME I CAN'T.
HROW GRFF
YEAH, GLAD TO SEE YOU, TOO.
YOU KNOW, YOU MIGHT'VE HAD A POINT ABOUT GAMBLING LEADING TO TROUBLE.
EASY...
...EASY...
I'M SORRY.
I'LL FORGIVE YOU IF WE GET OUT OF HERE ALIVE.
SO WHY'D YOU COME BACK, SHEEL? I HEARD SOMEWHERE THAT PEOPLE DON'T CHANGE.
I GUESS I SURPRISED MYSELF.

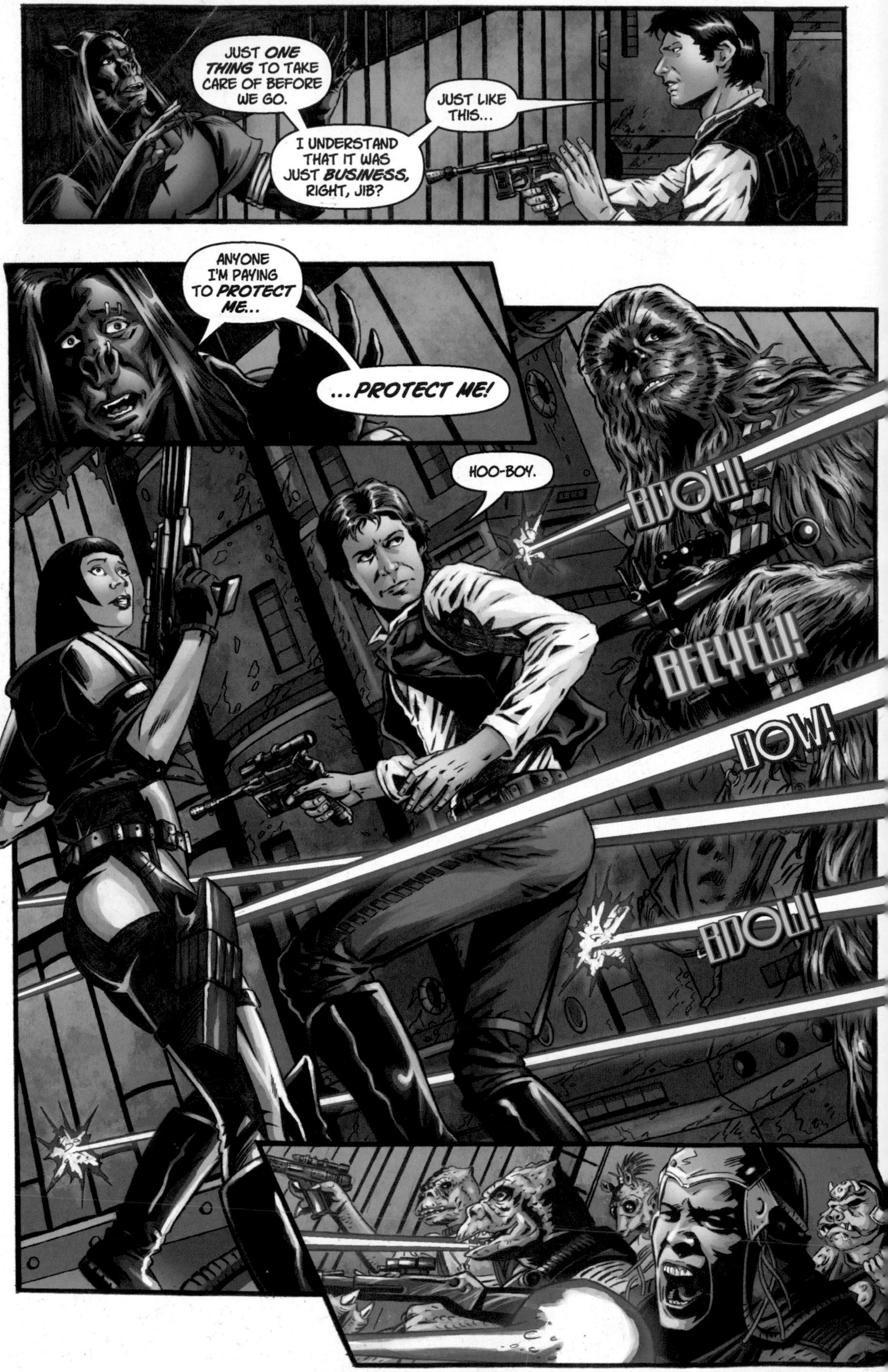
JUST ONE THING TO TAKE CARE OF BEFORE WE GO.
I UNDERSTAND THAT IT WAS JUST BUSINESS, RIGHT, JIB?
JUST LIKE THIS...
ANYONE I'M PAYING TO PROTECT ME...
...PROTECT ME!
HOO-BOY.
BDOW!
BEEYEW!
DOW!
BDOW!

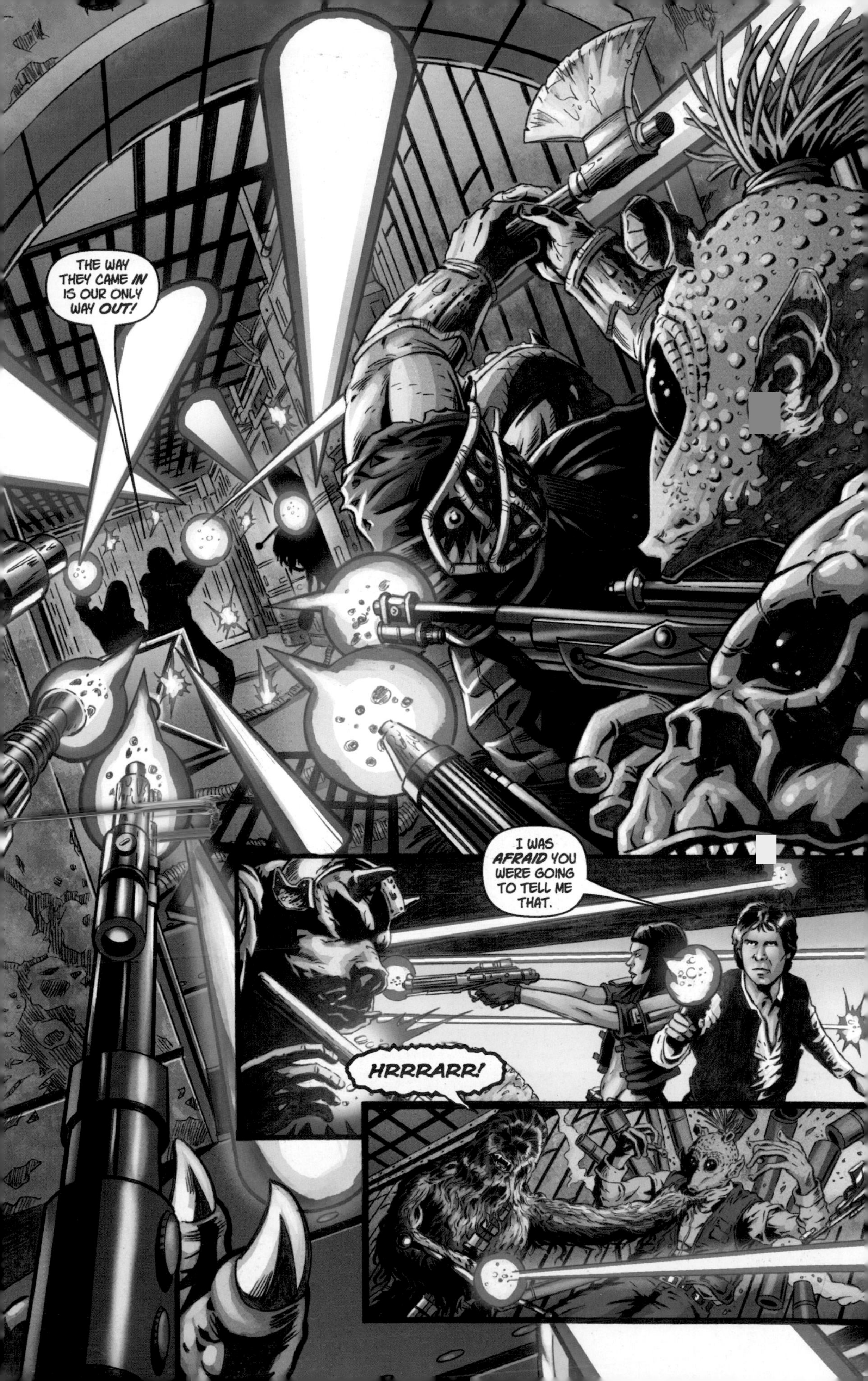
THE WAY THEY CAME IN IS OUR ONLY WAY OUT!
I WAS AFRAID YOU WERE GOING TO TELL ME THAT.
HRRRARR!

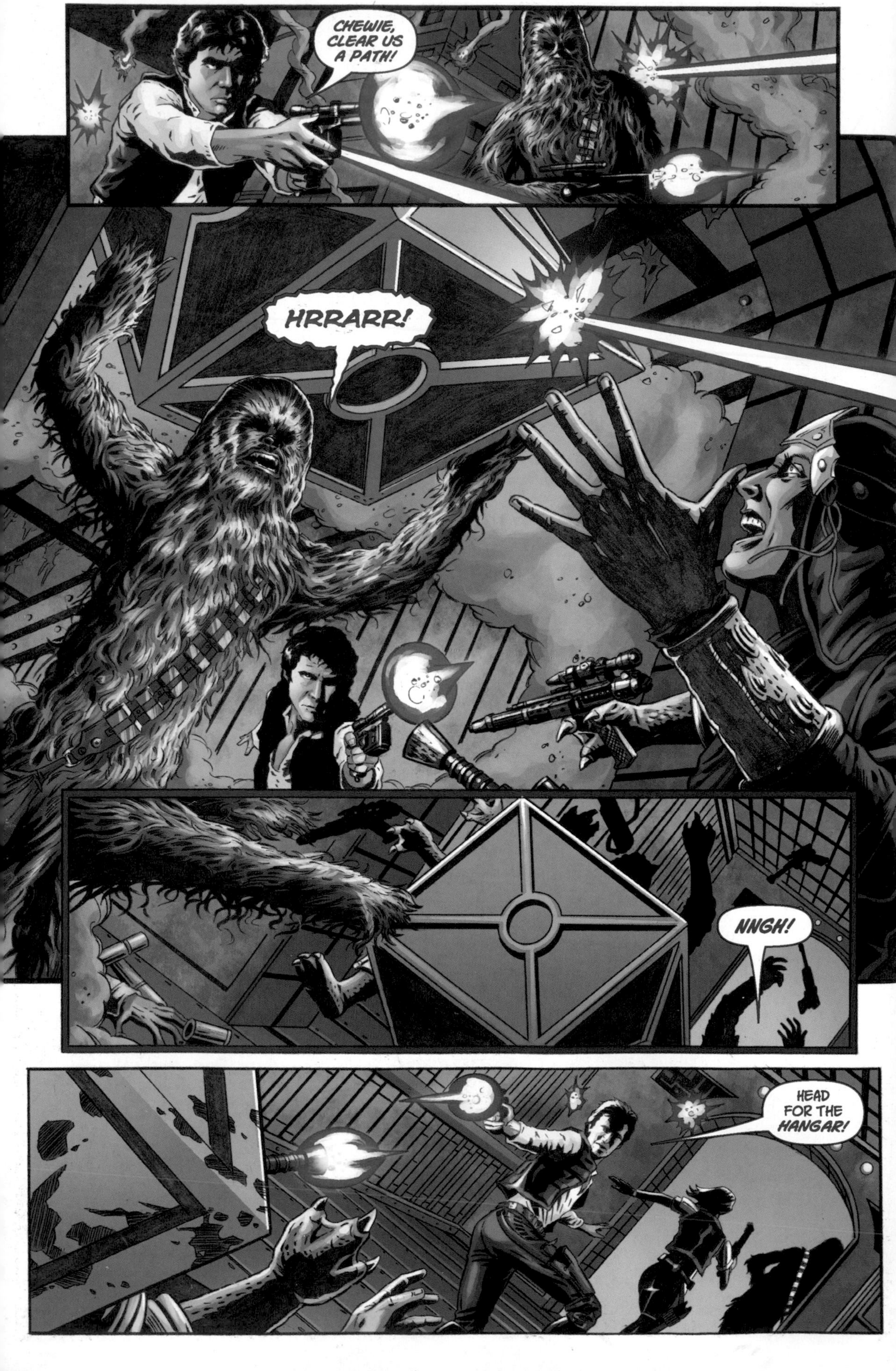
CHEWIE, CLEAR US A PATH!
HRRARR!
NNGH!
HEAD FOR THE HANGAR!

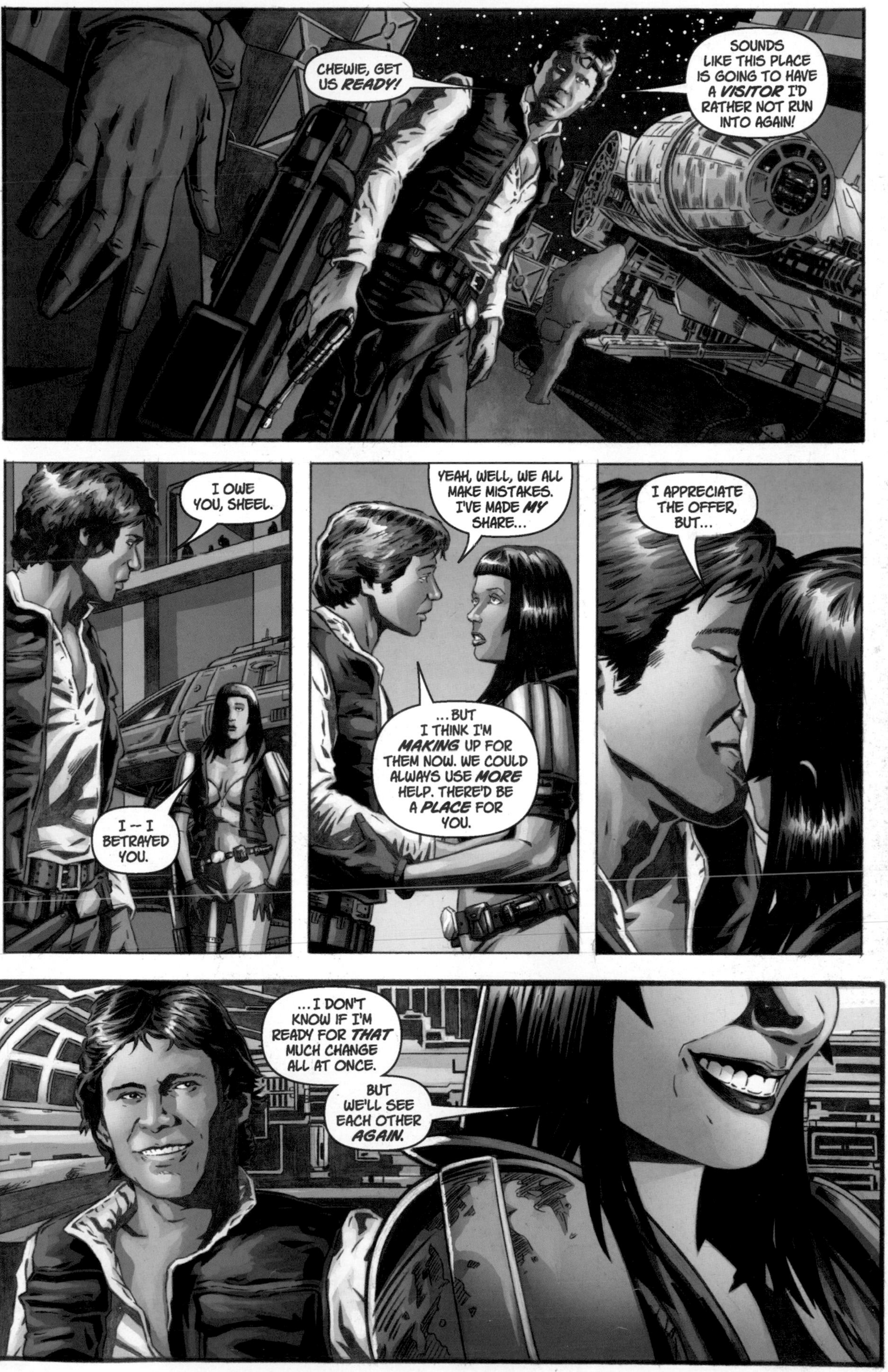
CHEWIE, GET US READY!
SOUNDS LIKE THIS PLACE IS GOING TO HAVE A VISITOR I'D RATHER NOT RUN INTO AGAIN!
I OWE YOU, SHEEL.
I -- I BETRAYED YOU.
YEAH, WELL, WE ALL MAKE MISTAKES. I'VE MADE MY SHARE...
...BUT I THINK I'M MAKING UP FOR THEM NOW. WE COULD ALWAYS USE MORE HELP. THERE'D BE A PLACE FOR YOU.
I APPRECIATE THE OFFER, BUT...
...I DON'T KNOW IF I'M READY FOR THAT MUCH CHANGE ALL AT ONCE.
BUT WE'LL SEE EACH OTHER AGAIN.

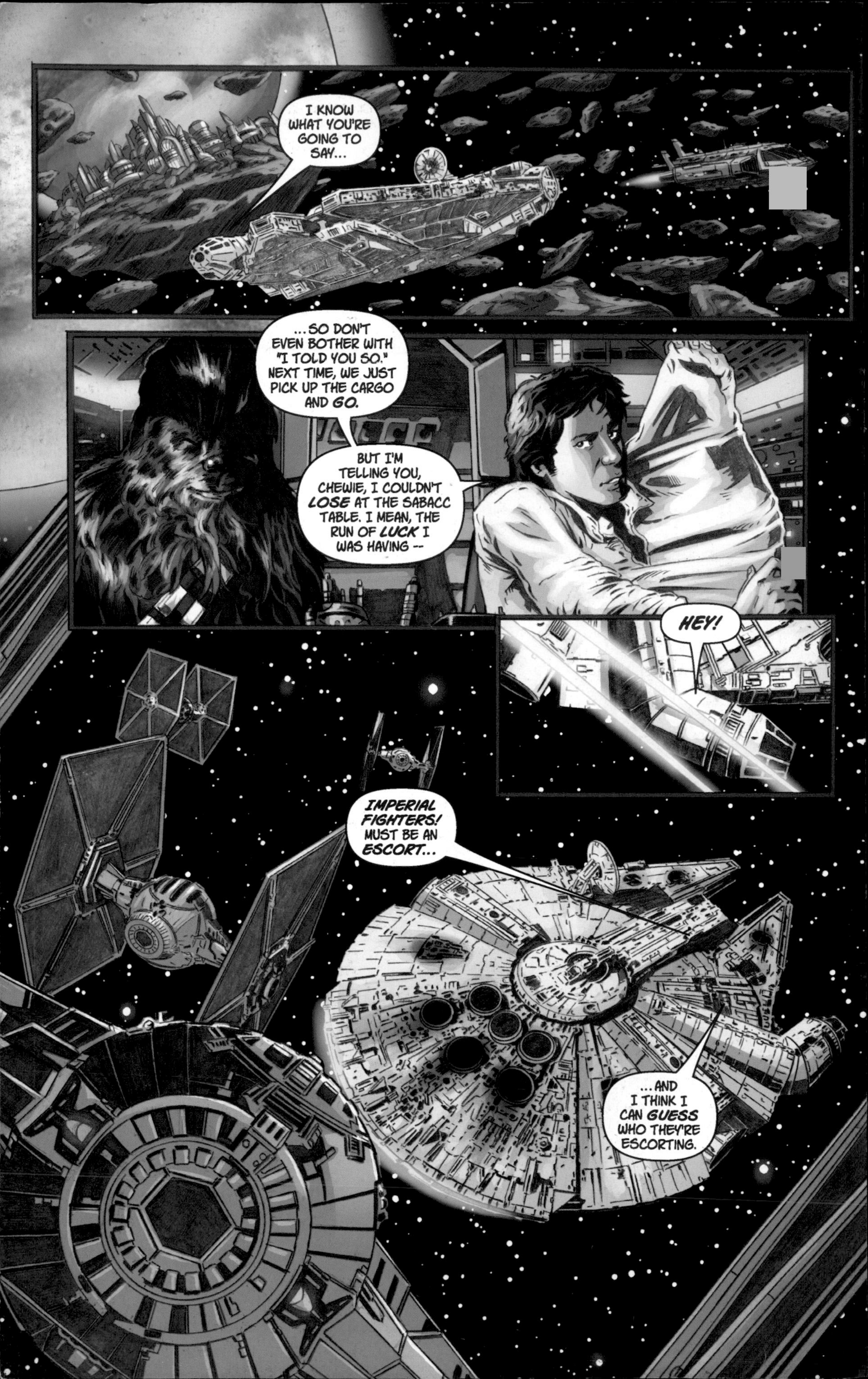
I KNOW WHAT YOU'RE GOING TO SAY...
...SO DON'T EVEN BOTHER WITH "I TOLD YOU SO." NEXT TIME, WE JUST PICK UP THE CARGO AND GO.
BUT I'M TELLING YOU, CHEWIE, I COULDN'T LOSE AT THE SABACC TABLE. I MEAN, THE RUN OF LUCK I WAS HAVING --
HEY!
IMPERIAL FIGHTERS! MUST BE AN ESCORT...
...AND I THINK I CAN GUESS WHO THEY'RE ESCORTING.

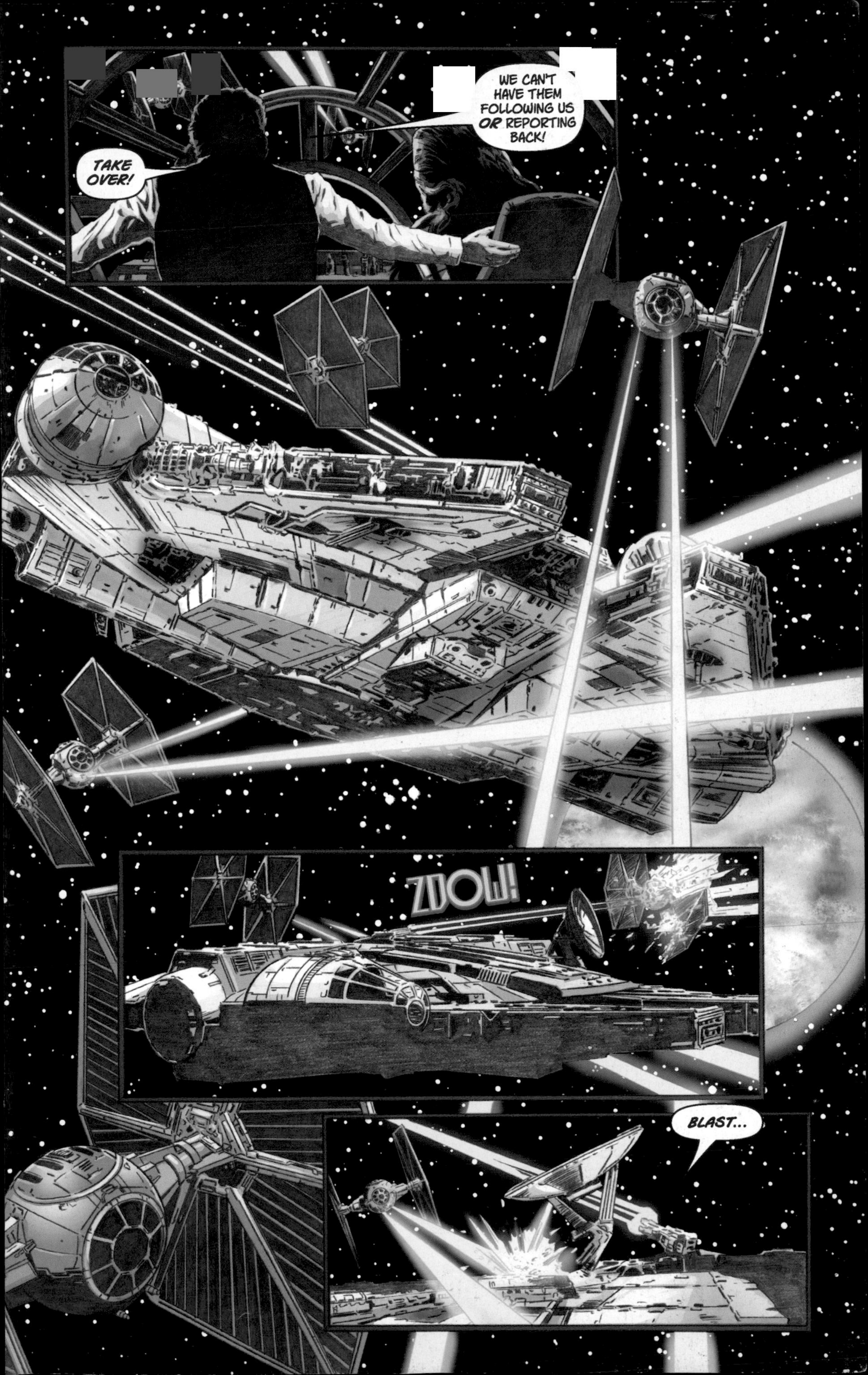
WE CAN'T HAVE THEM FOLLOWING US OR REPORTING BACK!
TAKE OVER!
ZDOW!
BLAST...

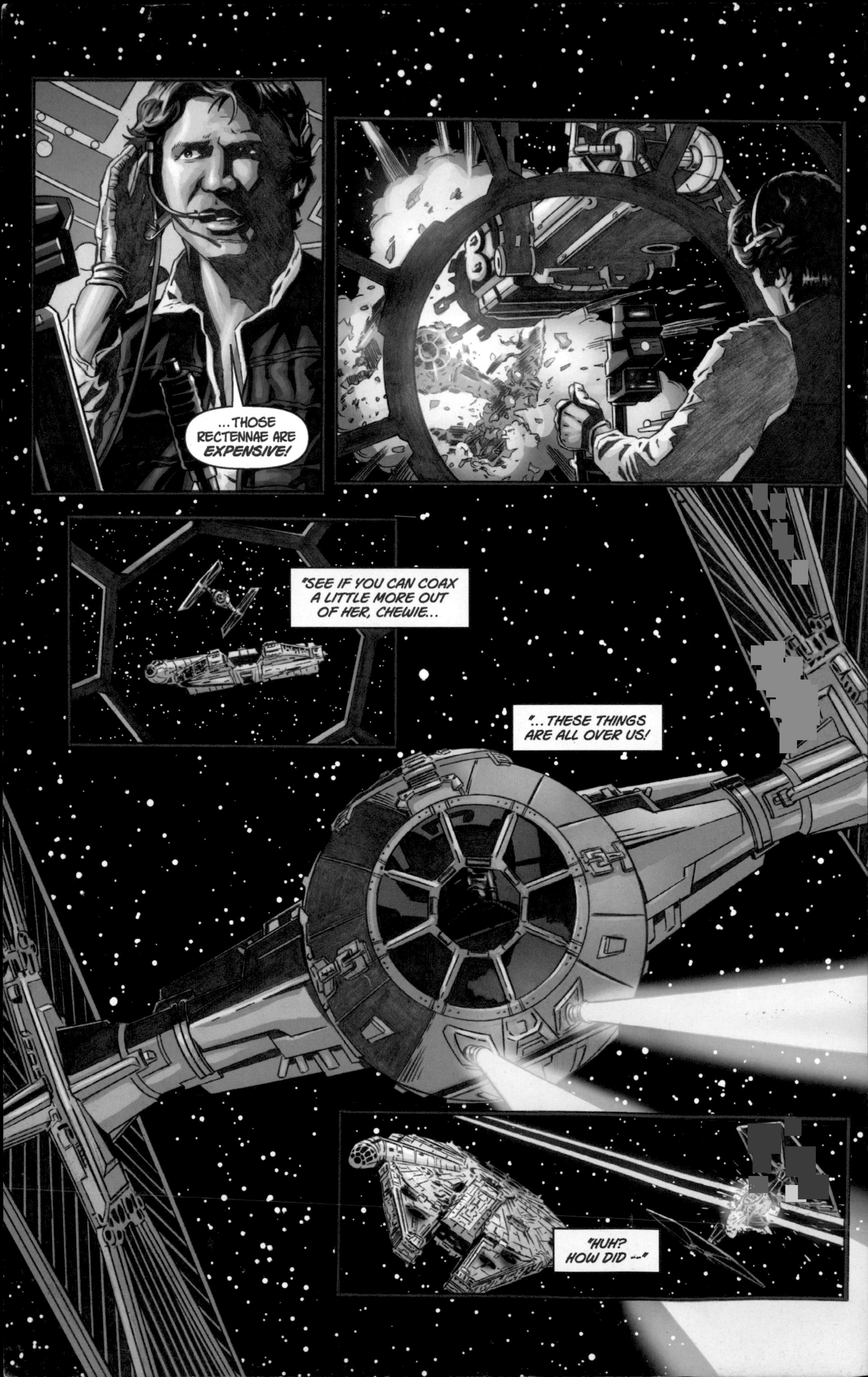
...THOSE RECTENNAE ARE EXPENSIVE!
"SEE IF YOU CAN COAX A LITTLE MORE OUT OF HER, CHEWIE...
"...THESE THINGS ARE ALL OVER US!
"HUH? HOW DID --"

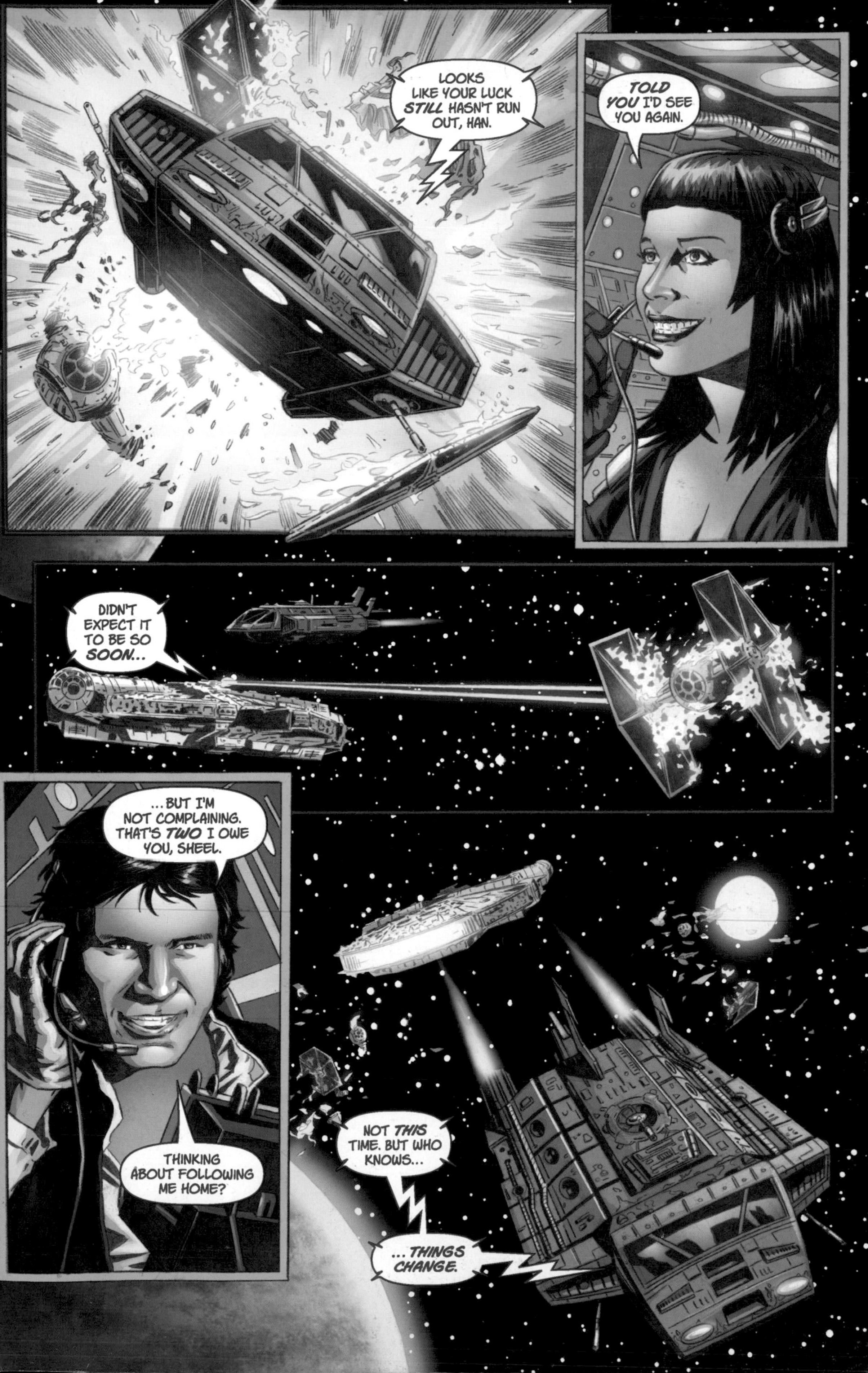
LOOKS LIKE YOUR LUCK STILL HASN'T RUN OUT, HAN.
TOLD YOU I'D SEE YOU AGAIN.
DIDN'T EXPECT IT TO BE SO SOON...
...BUT I'M NOT COMPLAINING. THAT'S TWO I OWE YOU, SHEEL.
THINKING ABOUT FOLLOWING ME HOME?
NOT THIS TIME. BUT WHO KNOWS...
...THINGS CHANGE.

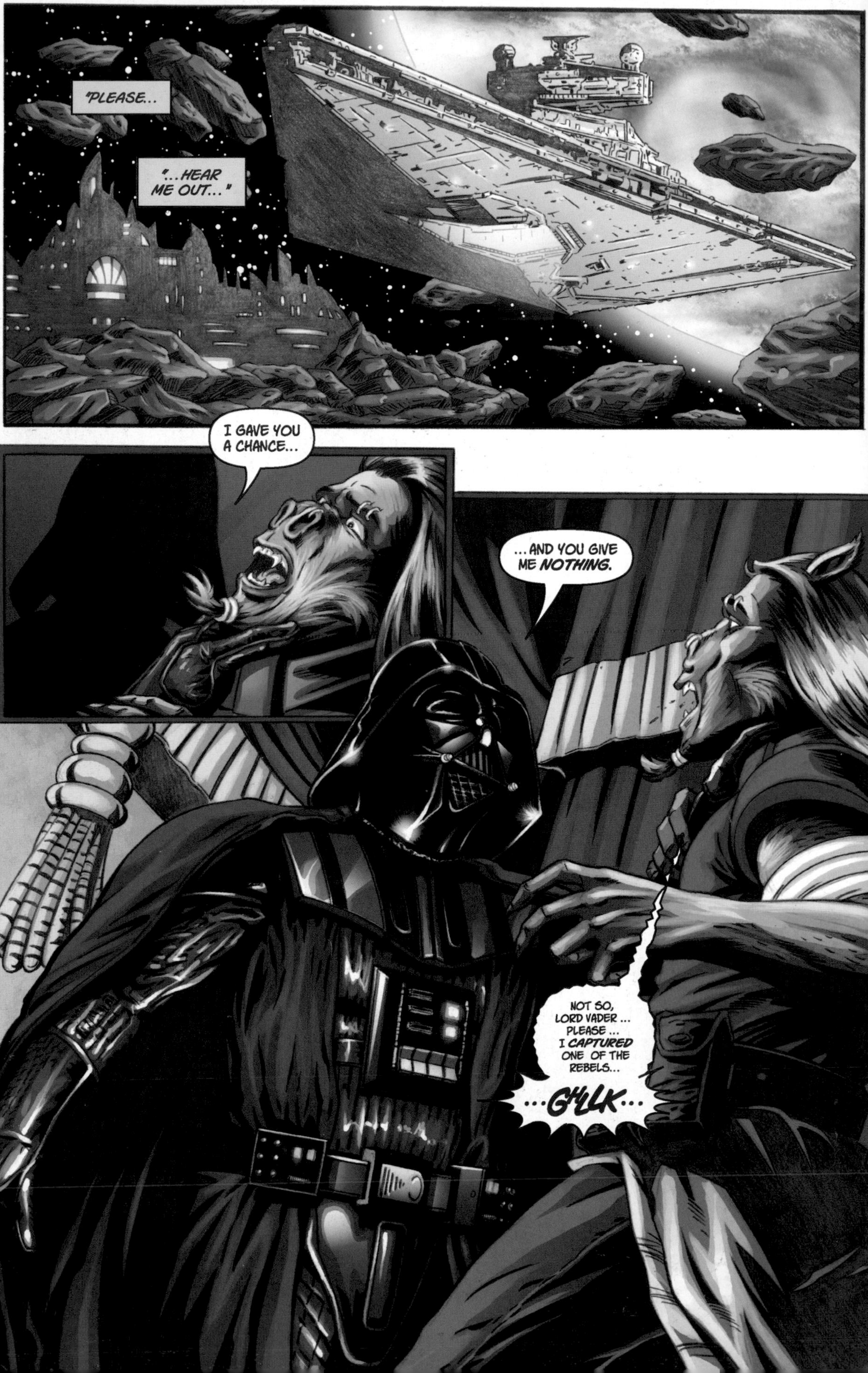
"PLEASE...
"...HEAR ME OUT..."
I GAVE YOU A CHANCE...
...AND YOU GIVE ME NOTHING.
NOT SO, LORD VADER ... PLEASE ... I CAPTURED ONE OF THE REBELS...
...GHLK...

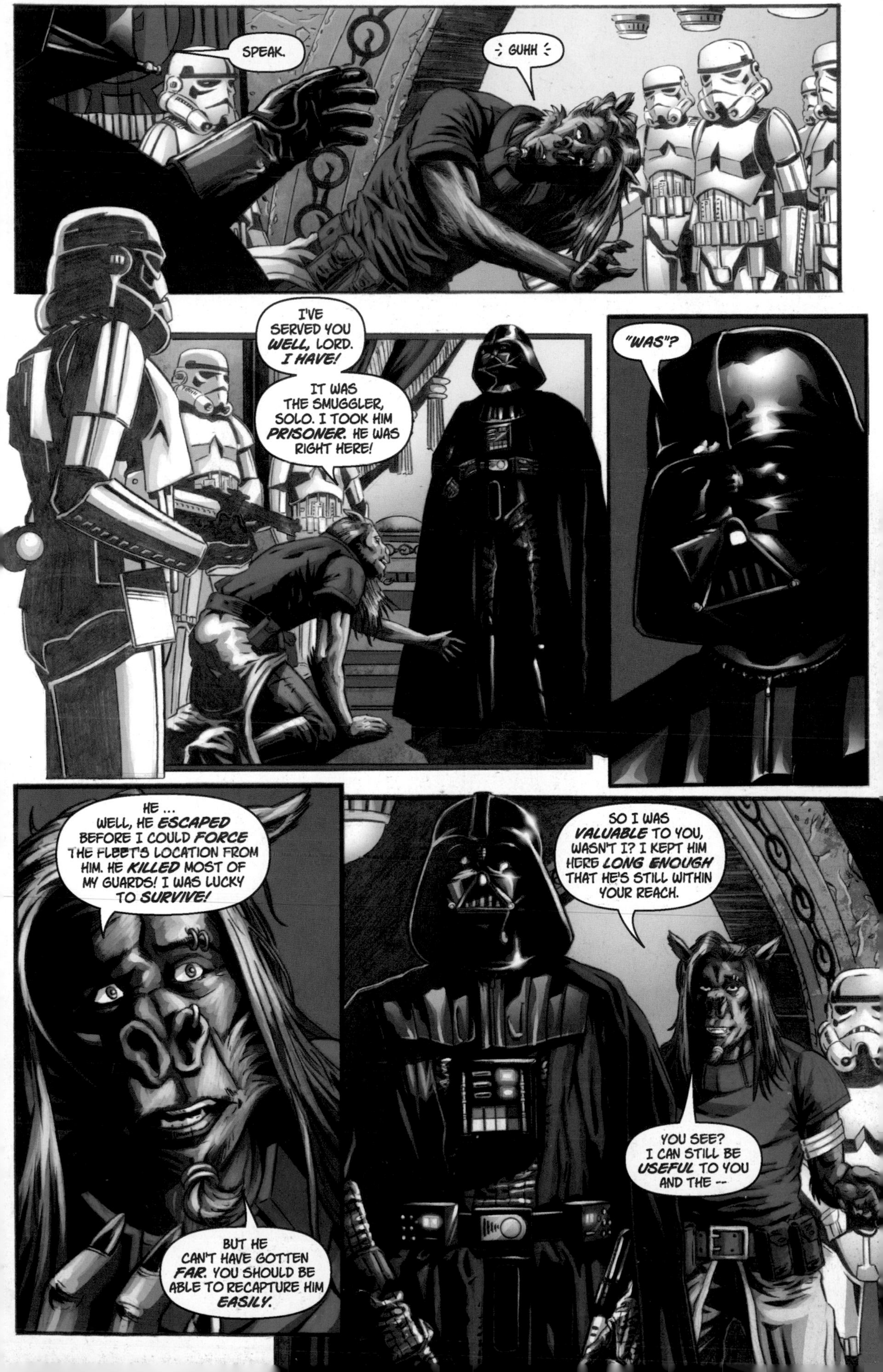
SPEAK.
GUHH
I'VE SERVED YOU WELL, LORD. I HAVE!
IT WAS THE SMUGGLER, SOLO. I TOOK HIM PRISONER. HE WAS RIGHT HERE!
"WAS"?
HE ... WELL, HE ESCAPED BEFORE I COULD FORCE THE FLEET'S LOCATION FROM HIM. HE KILLED MOST OF MY GUARDS! I WAS LUCKY TO SURVIVE!
BUT HE CAN'T HAVE GOTTEN FAR. YOU SHOULD BE ABLE TO RECAPTURE HIM EASILY.
SO I WAS VALUABLE TO YOU, WASN'T I? I KEPT HIM HERE LONG ENOUGH THAT HE'S STILL WITHIN YOUR REACH.
YOU SEE? I CAN STILL BE USEFUL TO YOU AND THE --

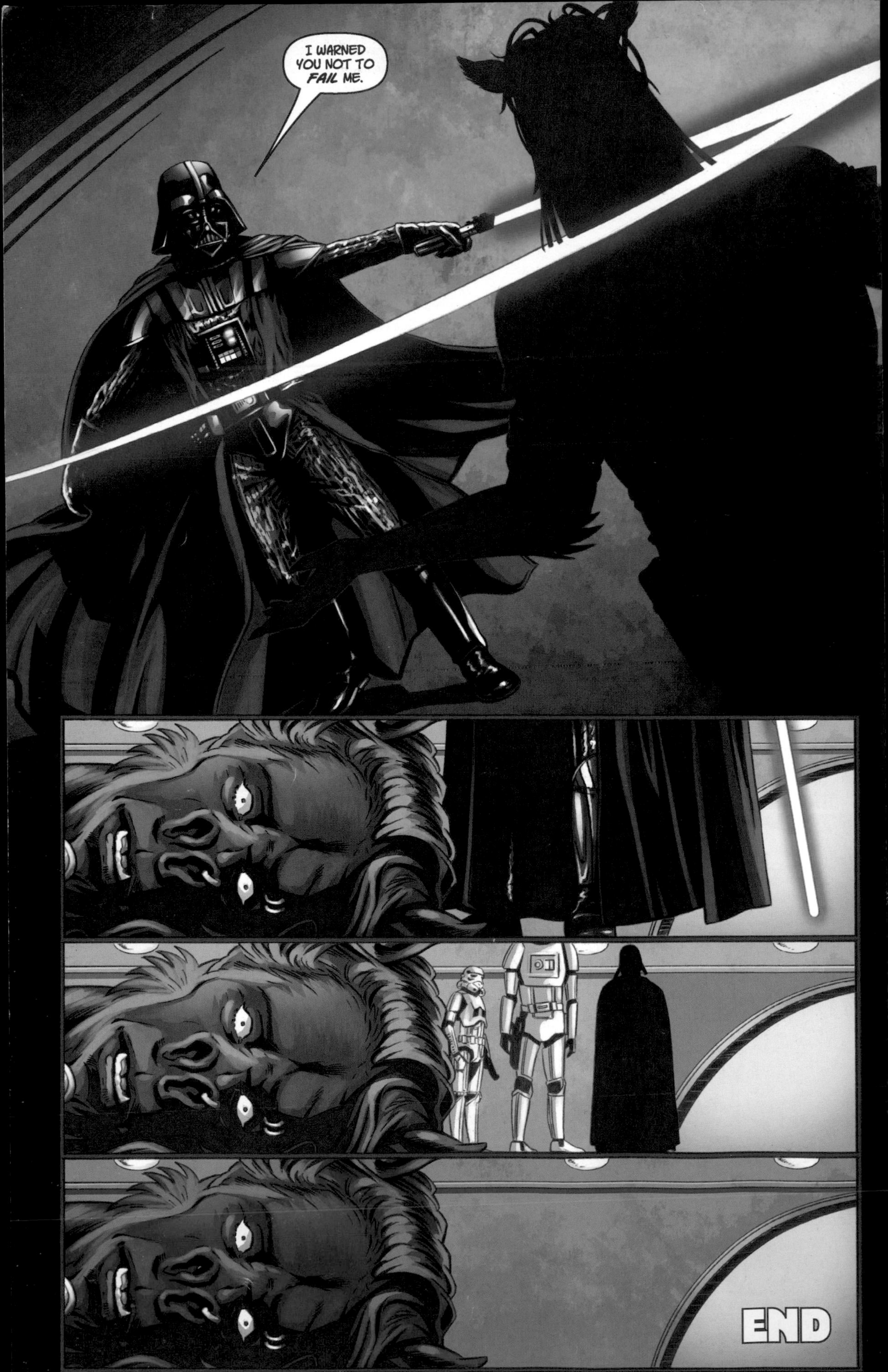
I WARNED YOU NOT TO FAIL ME.
END

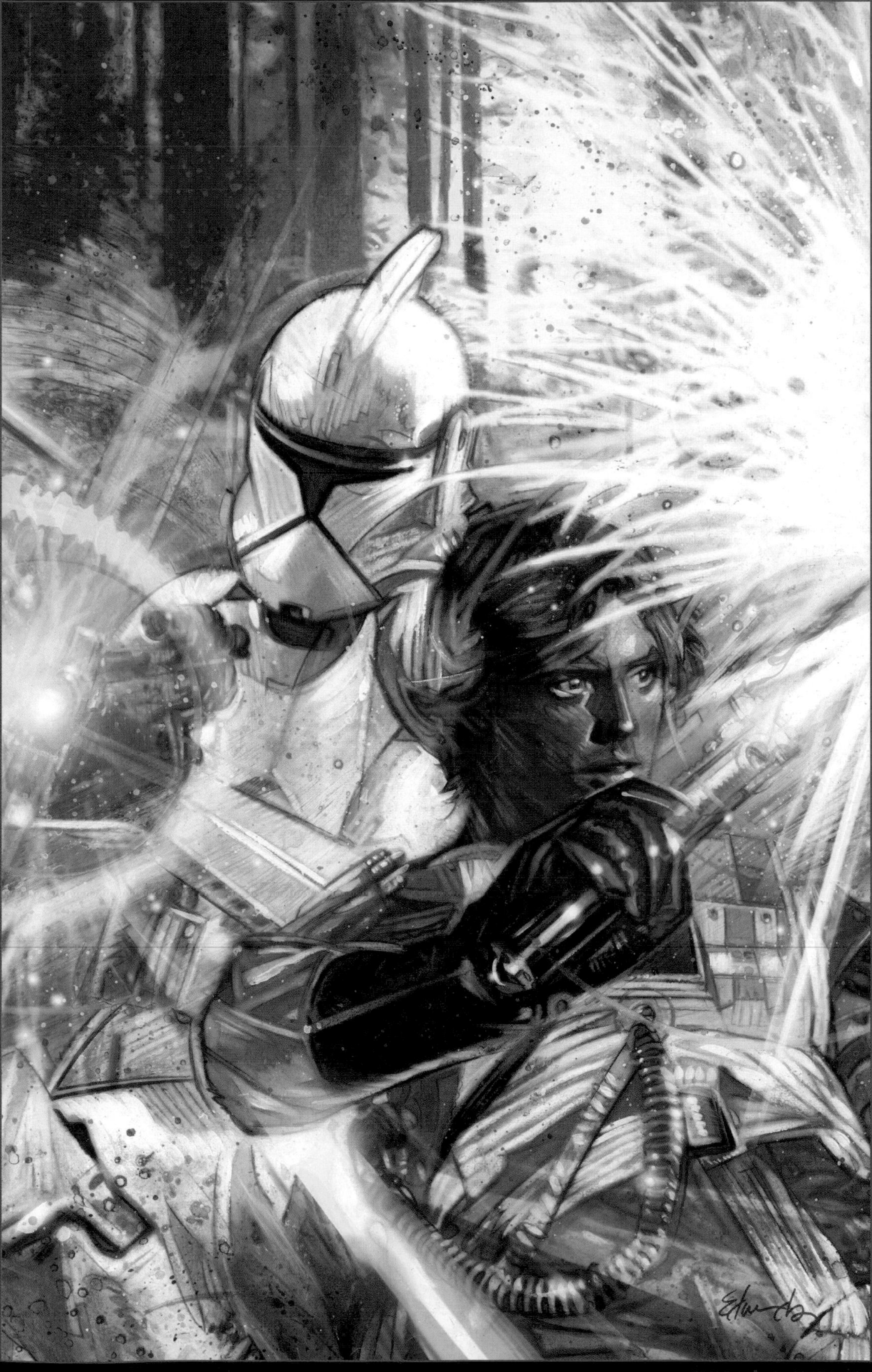

TOMMY LEE EDWARDS

"GENERAL" SKYWALKER

Script RON MARZ
Art ADRIANA MELO AND NICOLA SCOTT
Colors MICHAEL ATIYEH

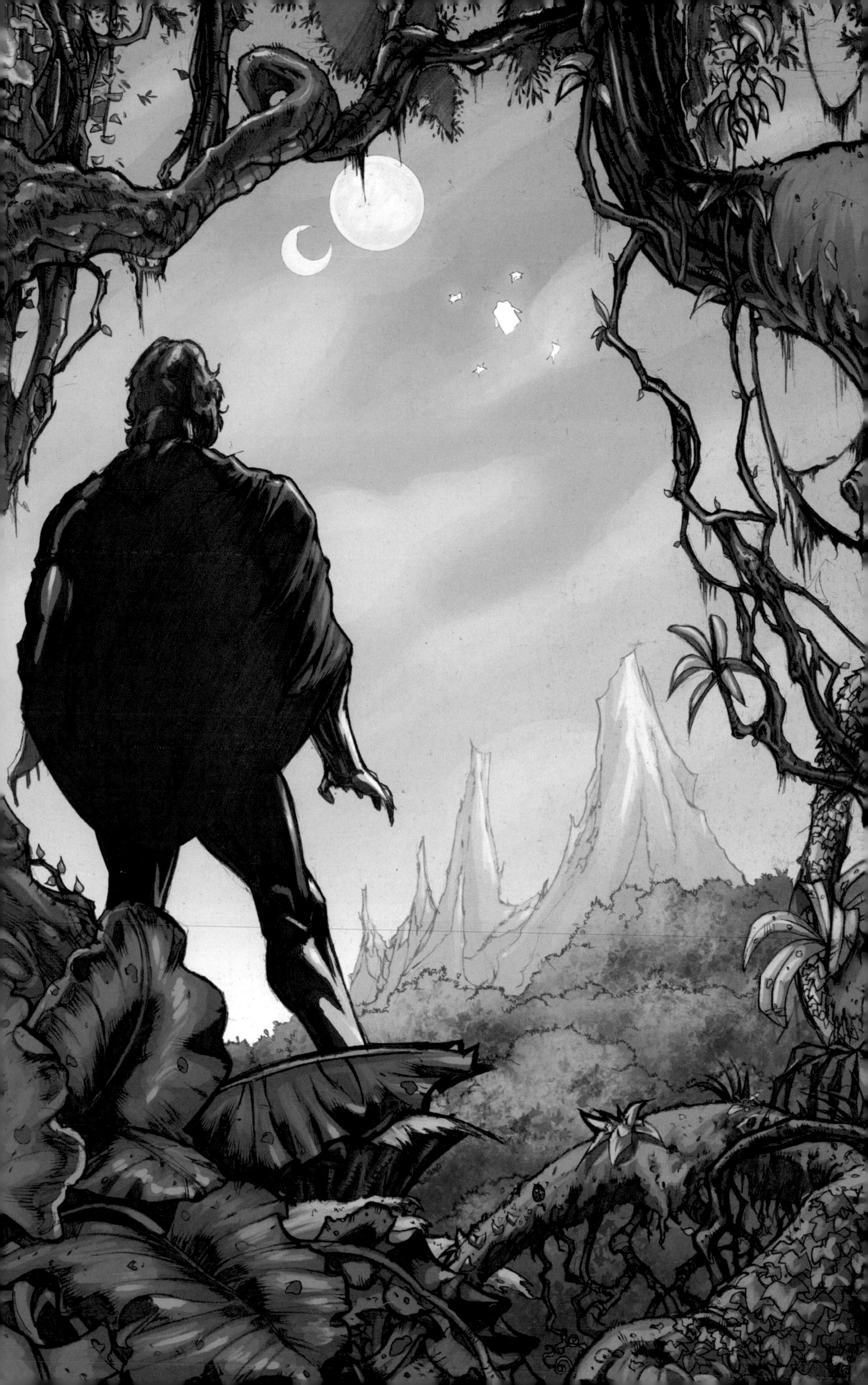

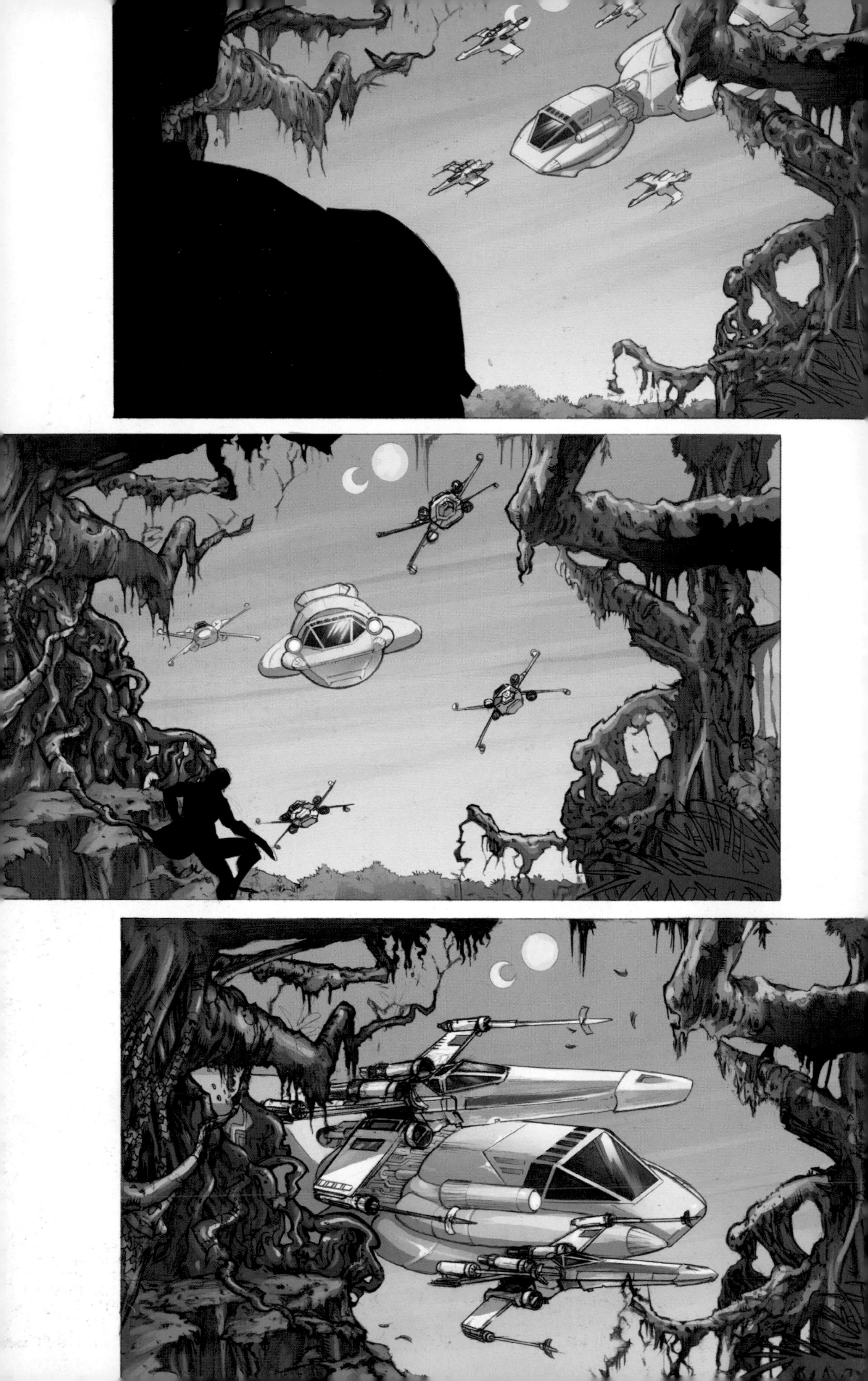

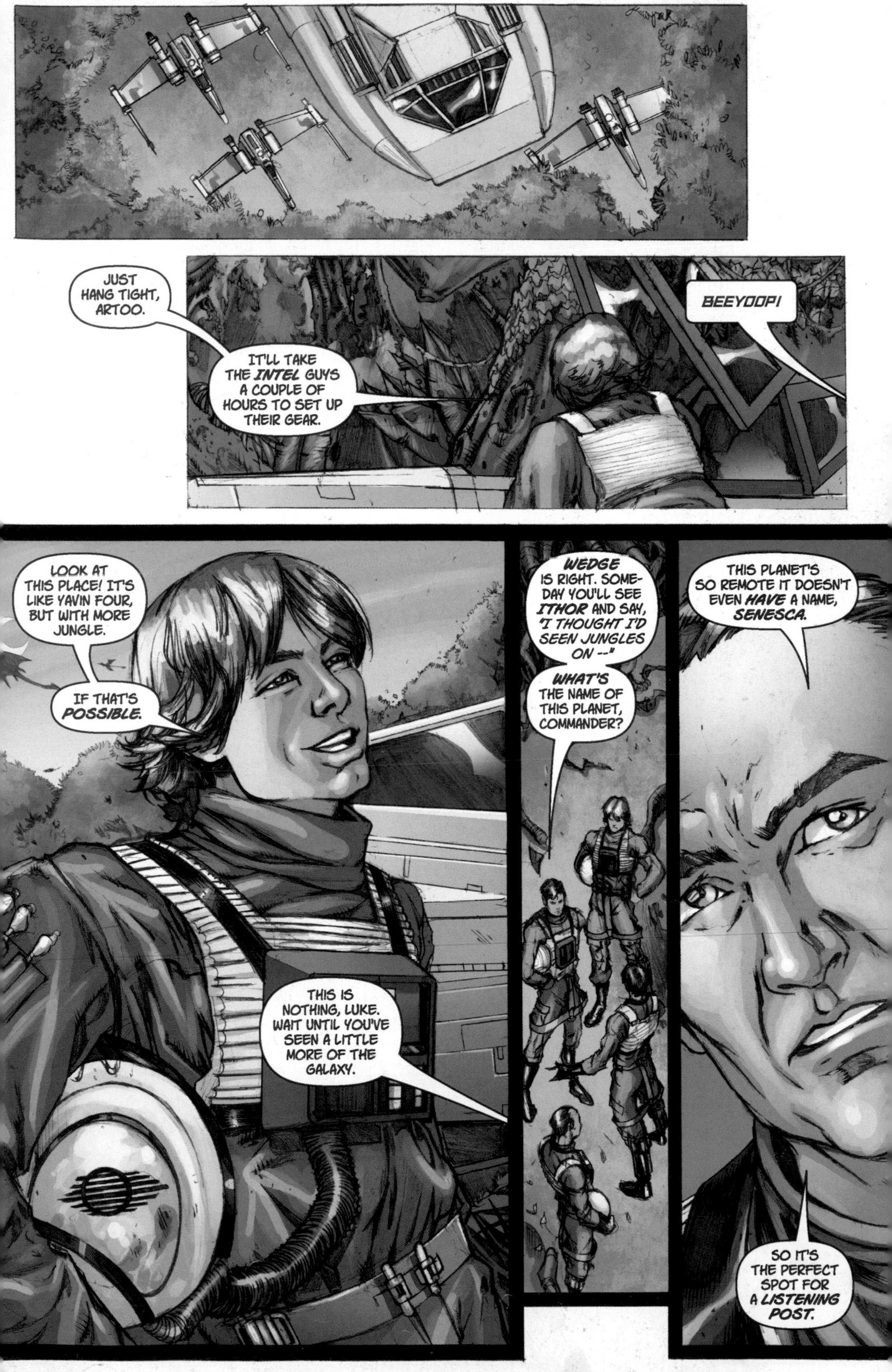
JUST HANG TIGHT, ARTOO.
IT'LL TAKE THE INTEL GUYS A COUPLE OF HOURS TO SET UP THEIR GEAR.
BEEYOOP!
LOOK AT THIS PLACE! IT'S LIKE YAVIN FOUR, BUT WITH MORE JUNGLE.
IF THAT'S POSSIBLE.
THIS IS NOTHING, LUKE. WAIT UNTIL YOU'VE SEEN A LITTLE MORE OF THE GALAXY.
WEDGE IS RIGHT. SOMEDAY YOU'LL SEE ITHOR AND SAY, "I THOUGHT I'D SEEN JUNGLES ON --"
WHAT'S THE NAME OF THIS PLANET, COMMANDER?
THIS PLANET'S SO REMOTE IT DOESN'T EVEN HAVE A NAME, SENESCA.
SO IT'S THE PERFECT SPOT FOR A LISTENING POST.

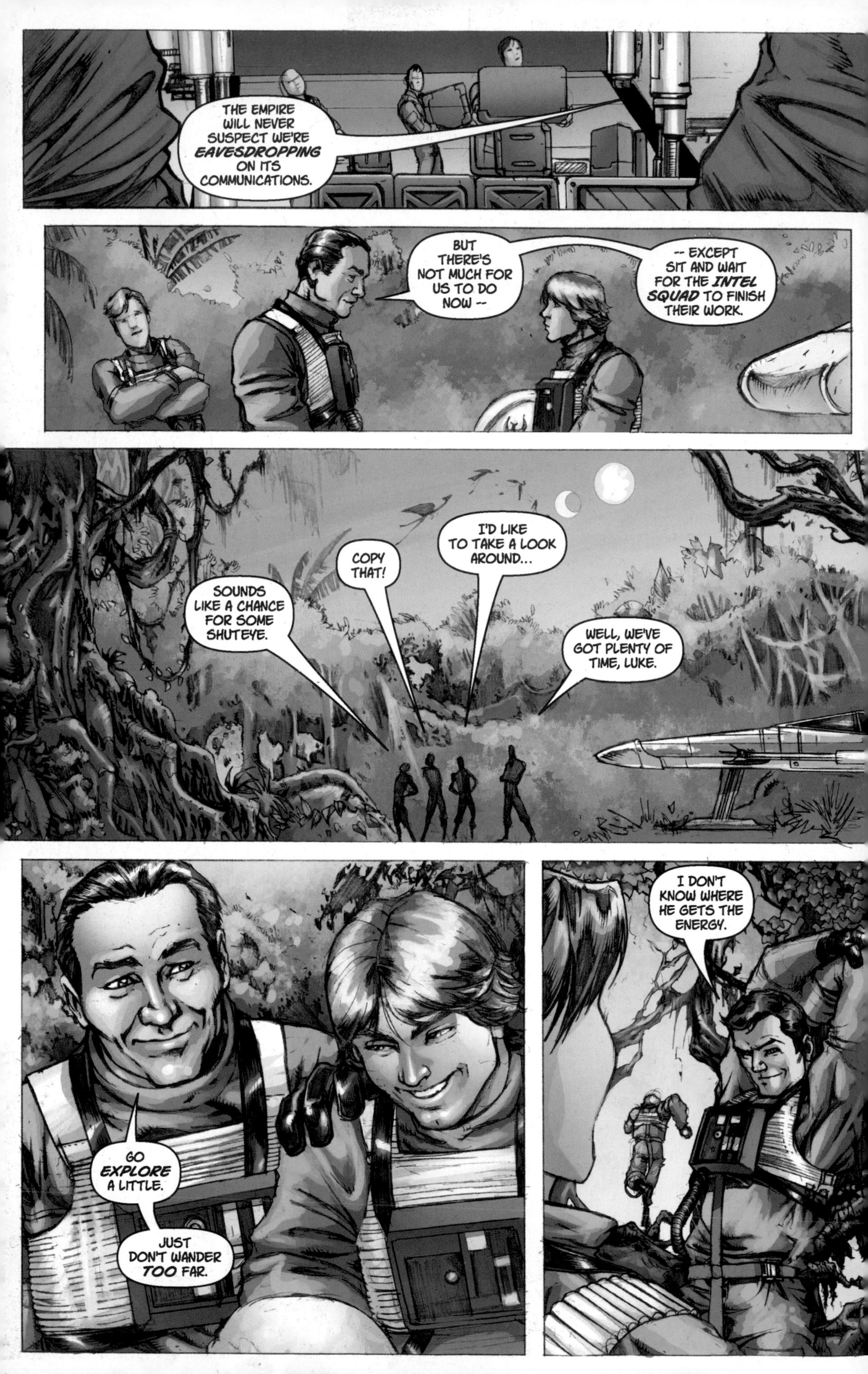
THE EMPIRE WILL NEVER SUSPECT WE'RE EAVESDROPPING ON ITS COMMUNICATIONS.
BUT THERE'S NOT MUCH FOR US TO DO NOW --
-- EXCEPT SIT AND WAIT FOR THE INTEL SQUAD TO FINISH THEIR WORK.
SOUNDS LIKE A CHANCE FOR SOME SHUTEYE.
COPY THAT!
I'D LIKE TO TAKE A LOOK AROUND...
WELL, WE'VE GOT PLENTY OF TIME, LUKE.
GO EXPLORE A LITTLE.
JUST DON'T WANDER TOO FAR.
I DON'T KNOW WHERE HE GETS THE ENERGY.

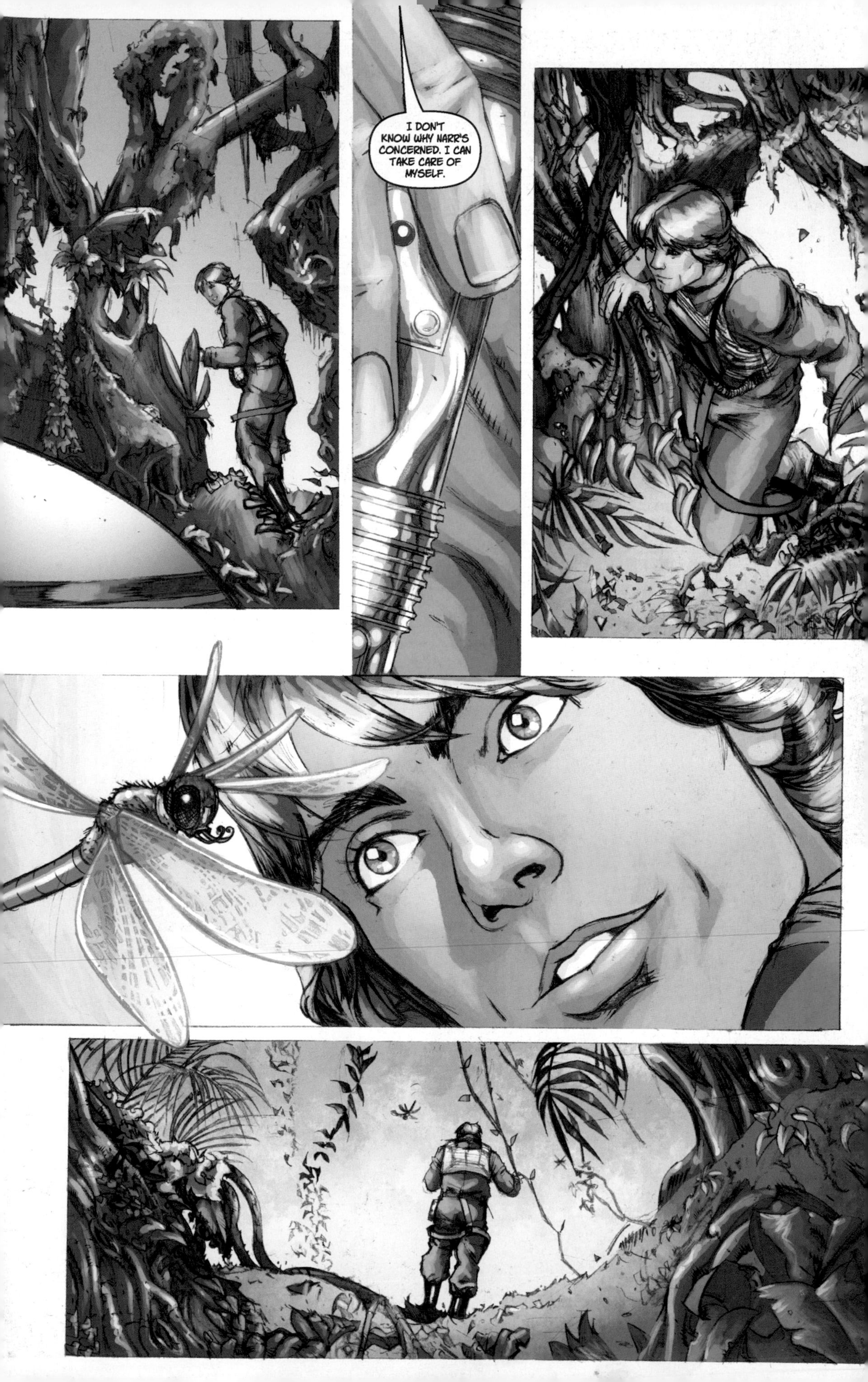
I DON'T KNOW WHY NARR'S CONCERNED. I CAN TAKE CARE OF MYSELF.

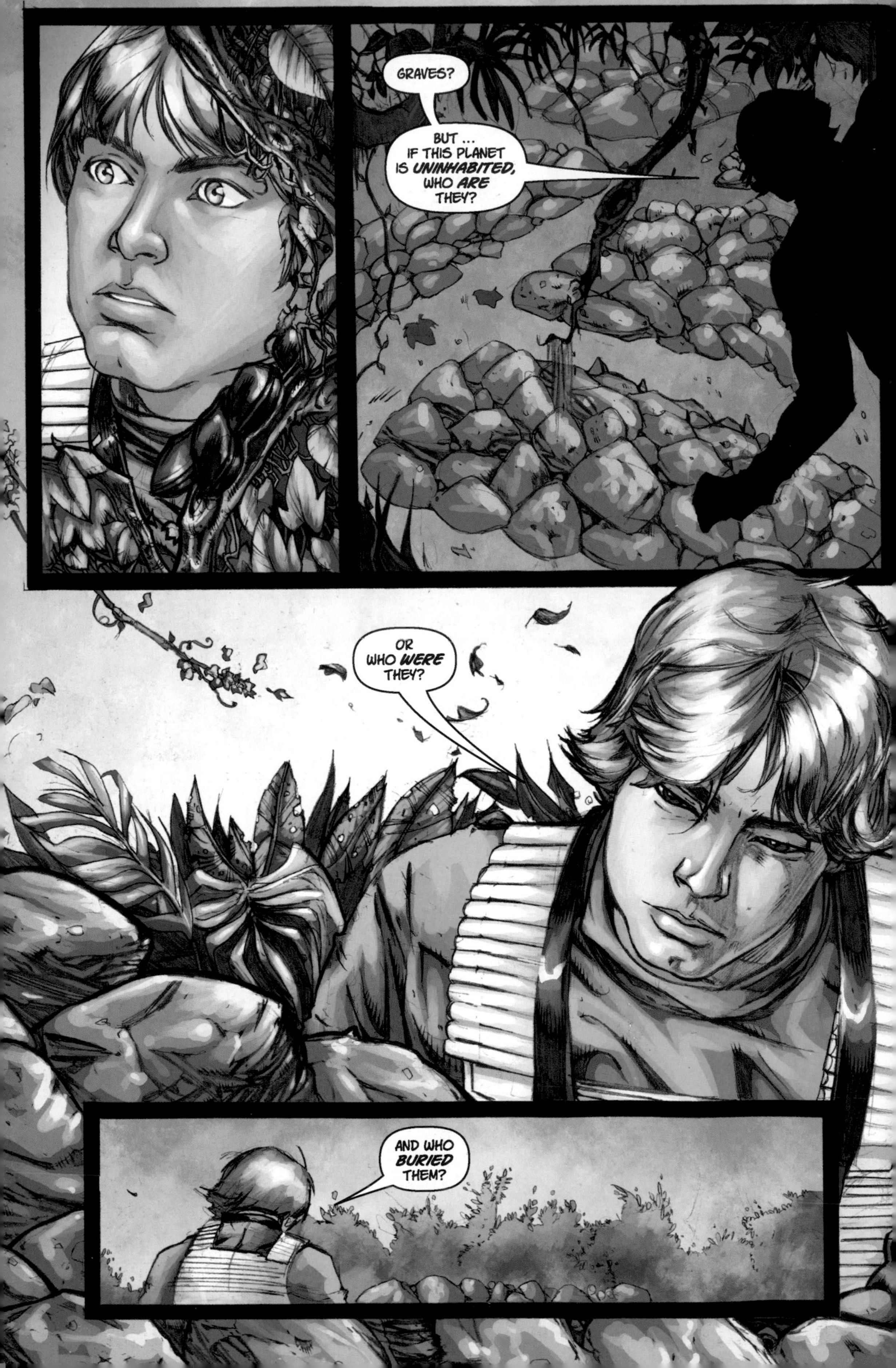
GRAVES?
BUT ... IF THIS PLANET IS UNINHABITED, WHO ARE THEY?
OR WHO WERE THEY?
AND WHO BURIED THEM?

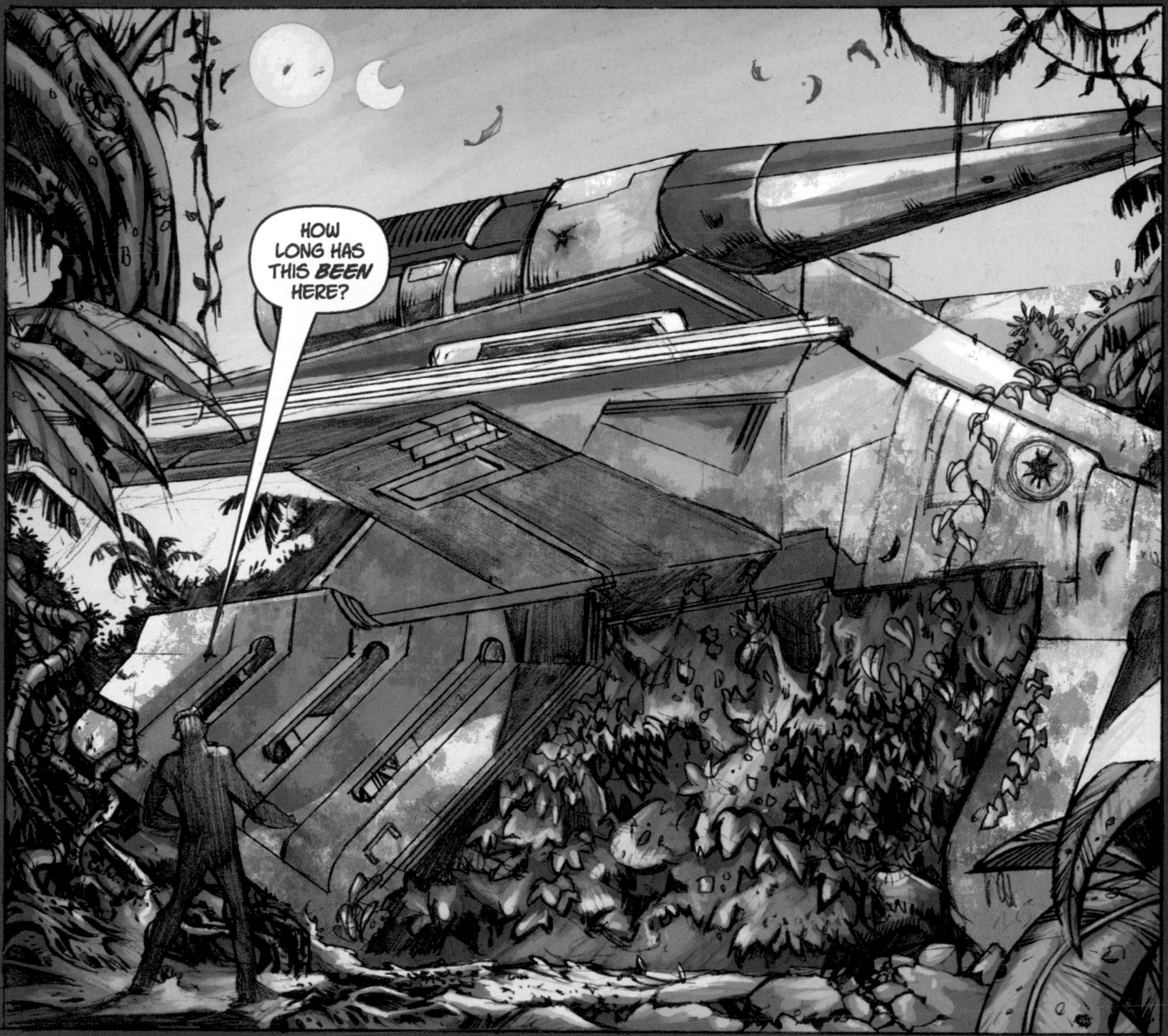
HOW LONG HAS THIS *BEEN* HERE?

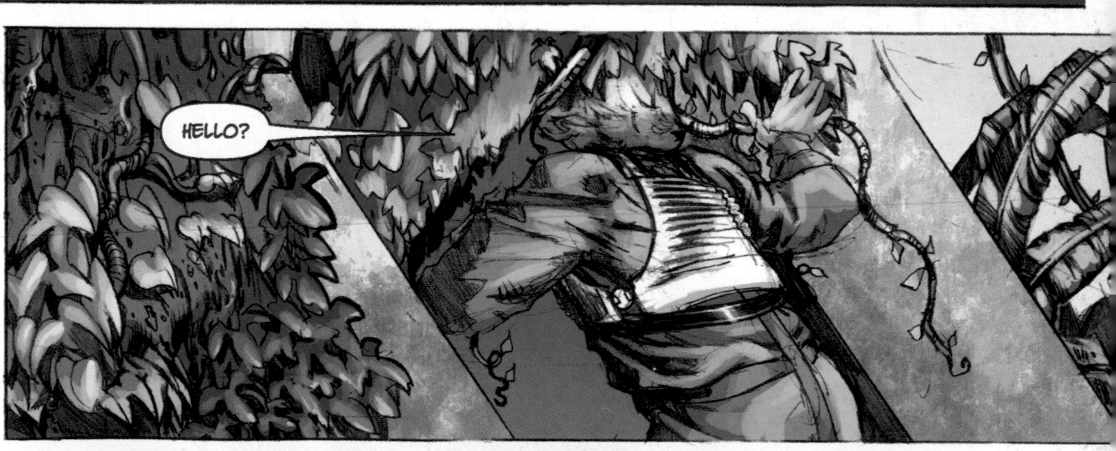
HELLO?

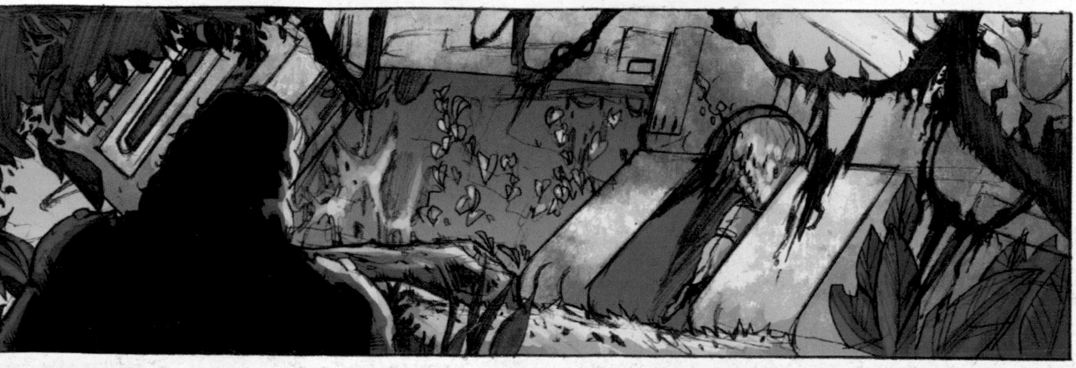

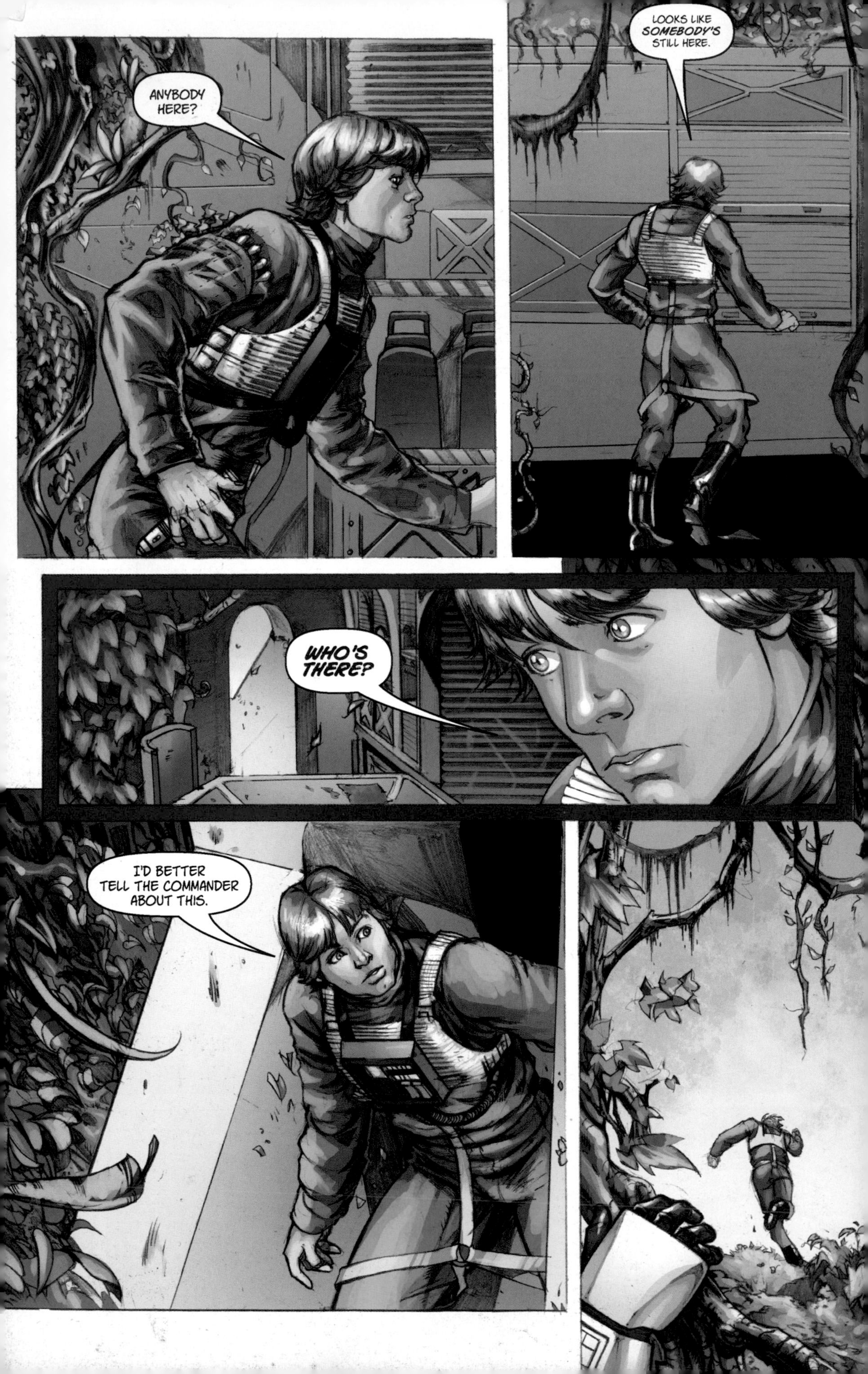
ANYBODY HERE?
LOOKS LIKE SOMEBODY'S STILL HERE.
WHO'S THERE?
I'D BETTER TELL THE COMMANDER ABOUT THIS.

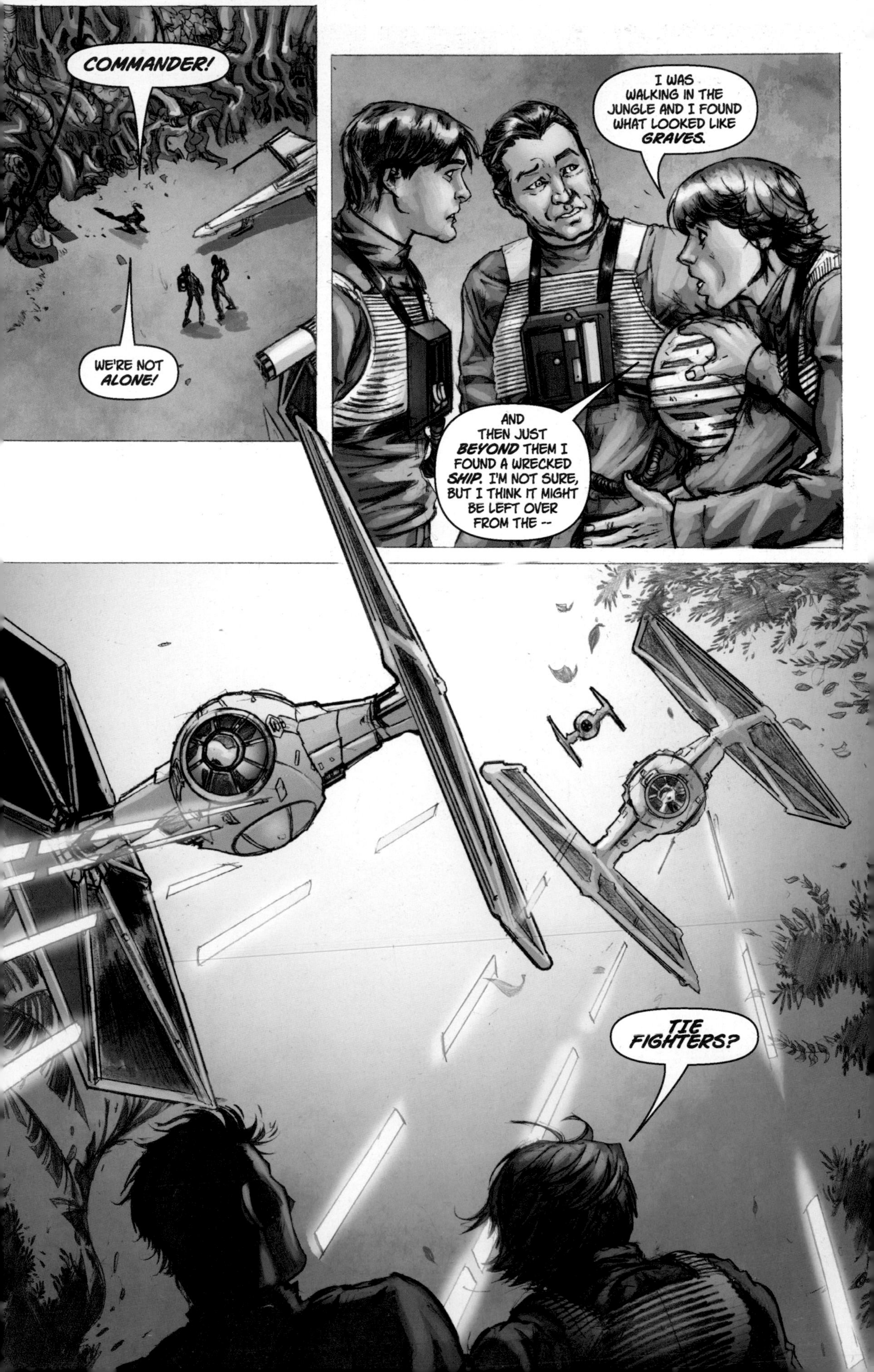
COMMANDER!
WE'RE NOT ALONE!
I WAS WALKING IN THE JUNGLE AND I FOUND WHAT LOOKED LIKE GRAVES.
AND THEN JUST BEYOND THEM I FOUND A WRECKED SHIP. I'M NOT SURE, BUT I THINK IT MIGHT BE LEFT OVER FROM THE --
TIE FIGHTERS?

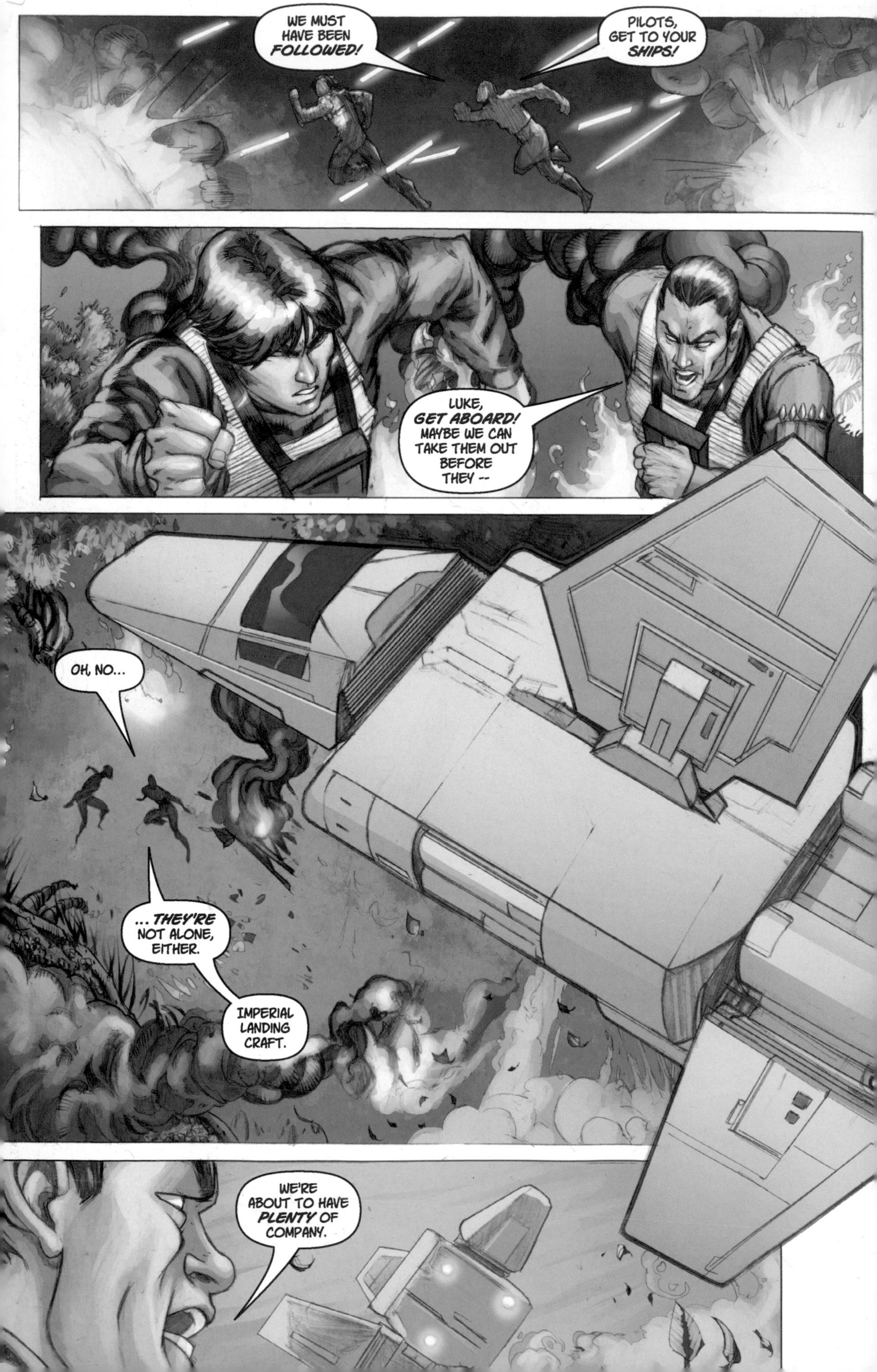
WE MUST HAVE BEEN FOLLOWED!
PILOTS, GET TO YOUR SHIPS!
LUKE, GET ABOARD! MAYBE WE CAN TAKE THEM OUT BEFORE THEY --
OH, NO...
...THEY'RE NOT ALONE, EITHER.
IMPERIAL LANDING CRAFT.
WE'RE ABOUT TO HAVE PLENTY OF COMPANY.

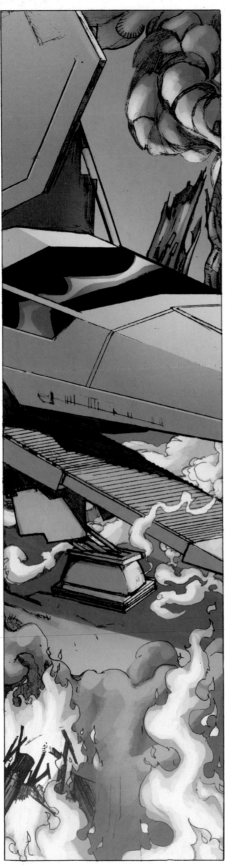

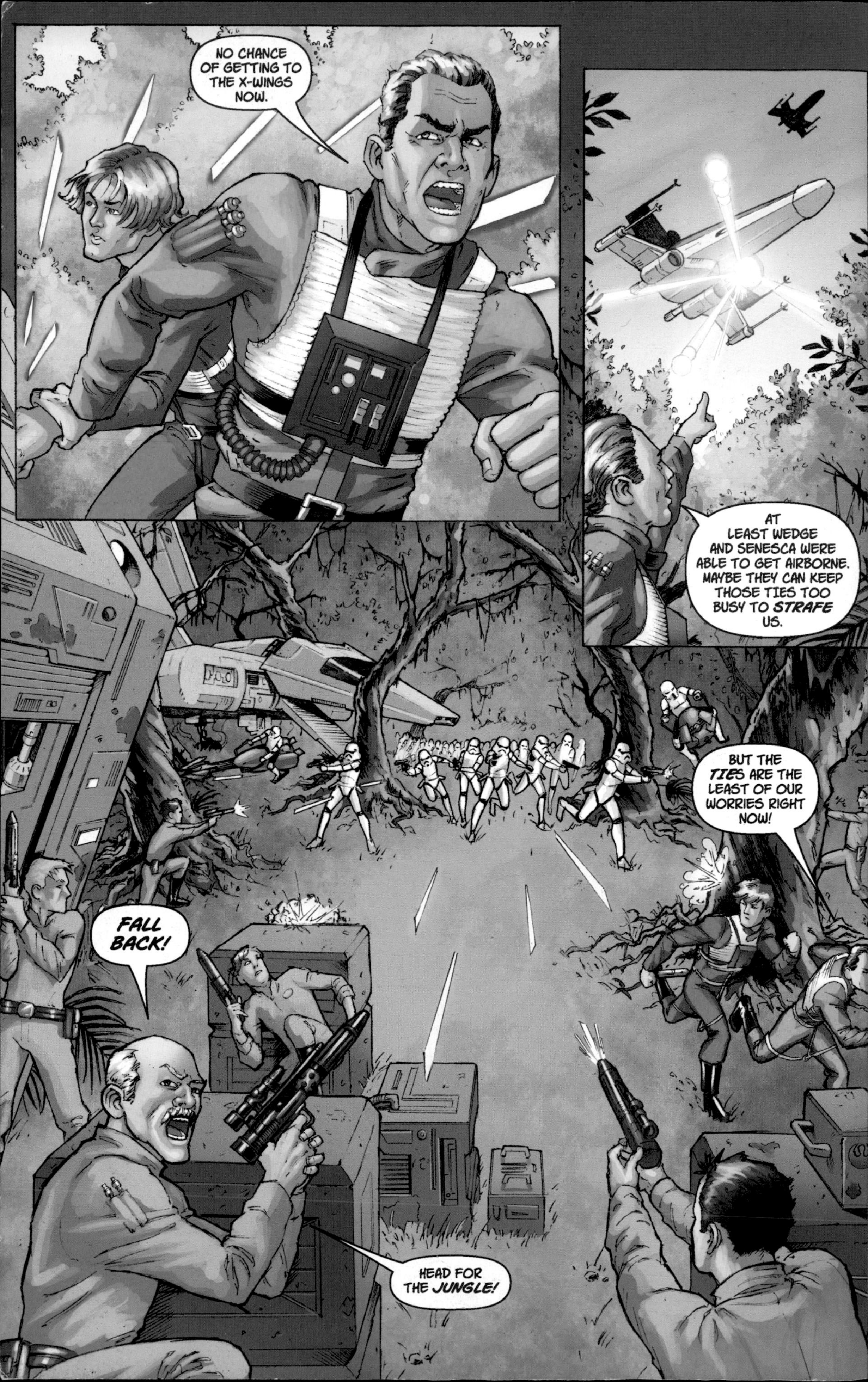
NO CHANCE OF GETTING TO THE X-WINGS NOW.
AT LEAST WEDGE AND SENESCA WERE ABLE TO GET AIRBORNE. MAYBE THEY CAN KEEP THOSE TIES TOO BUSY TO *STRAFE* US.
BUT THE *TIES* ARE THE LEAST OF OUR WORRIES RIGHT NOW!
FALL BACK!
HEAD FOR THE *JUNGLE!*

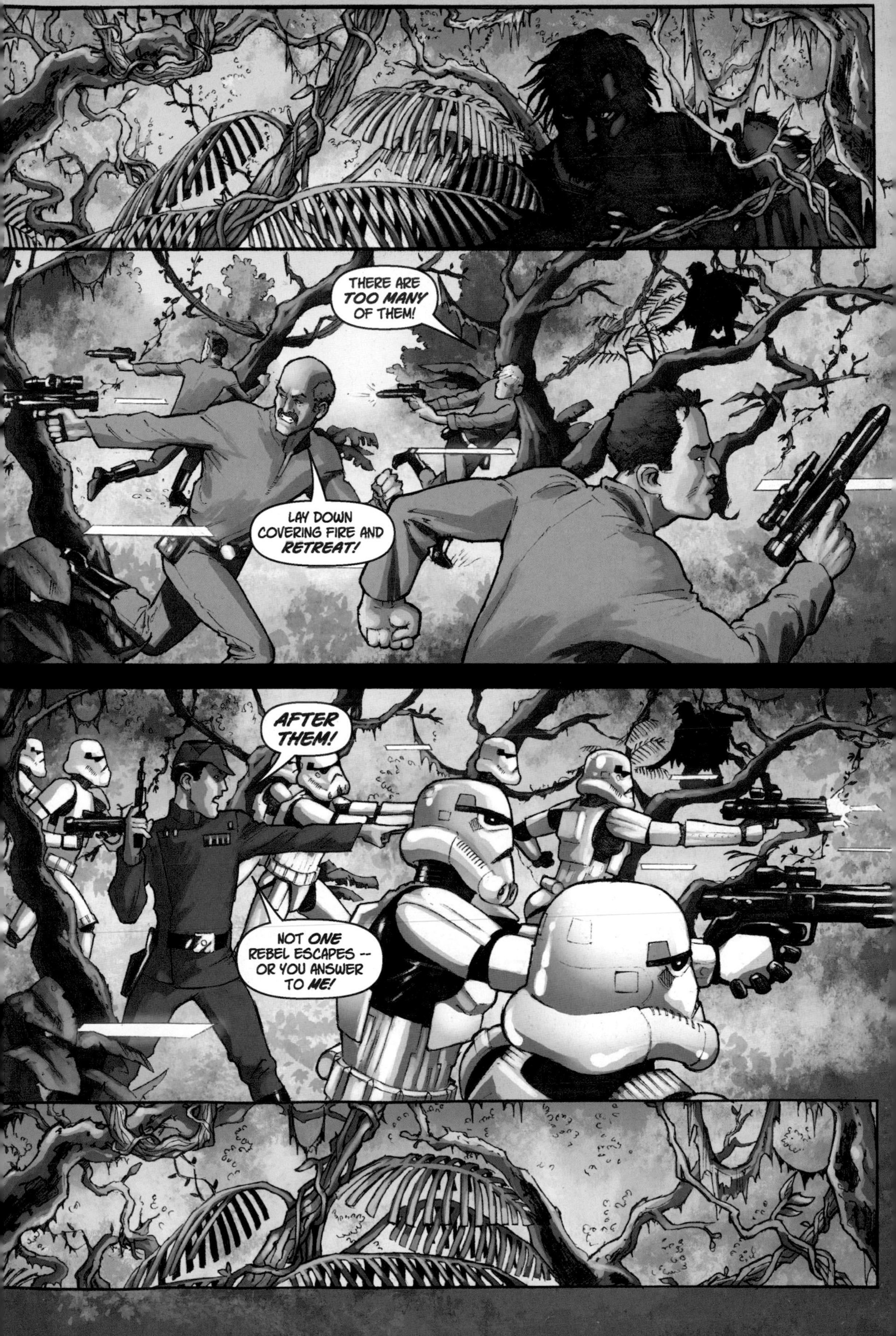
THERE ARE TOO MANY OF THEM!
LAY DOWN COVERING FIRE AND RETREAT!
AFTER THEM!
NOT ONE REBEL ESCAPES -- OR YOU ANSWER TO ME!

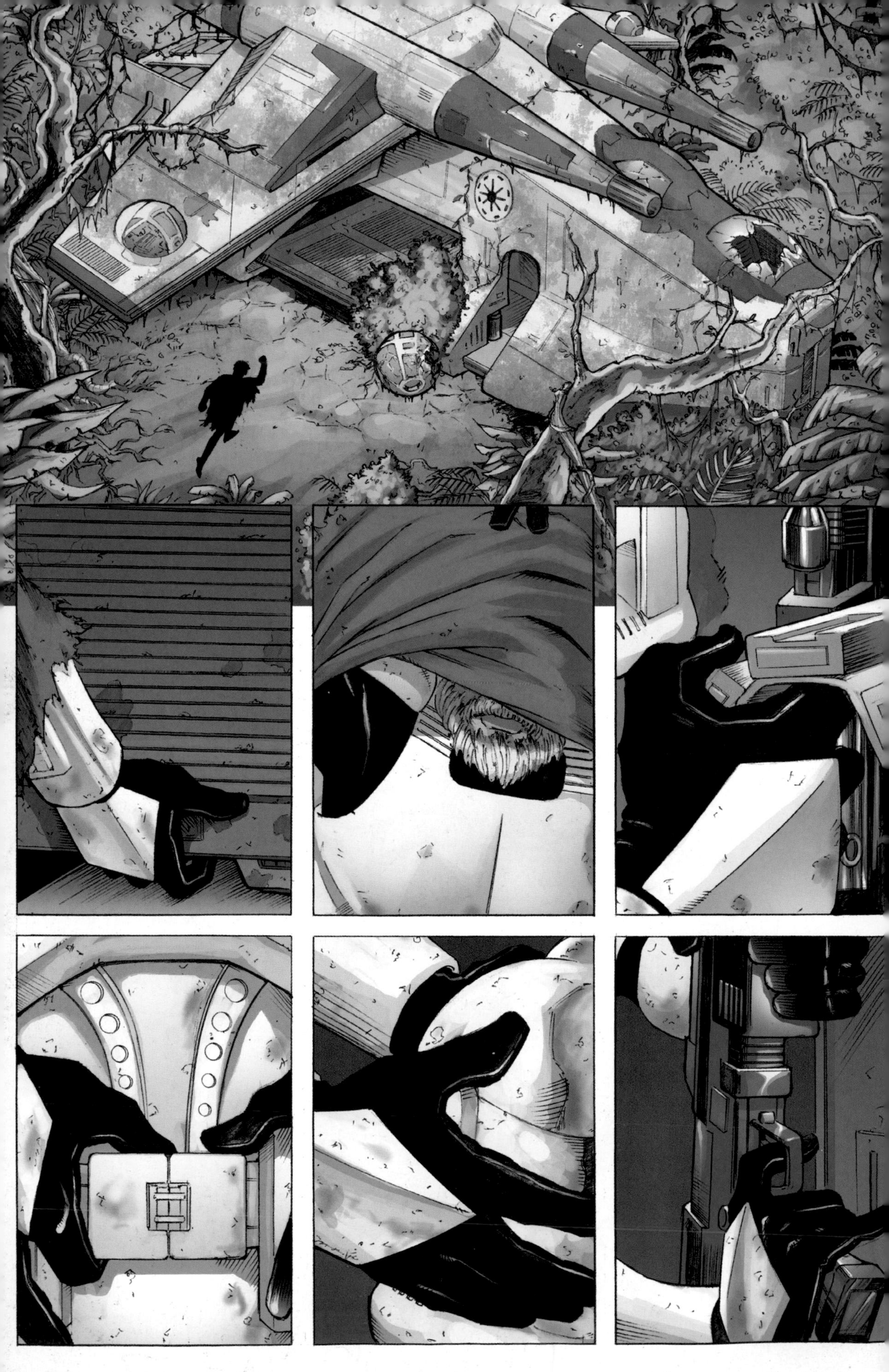

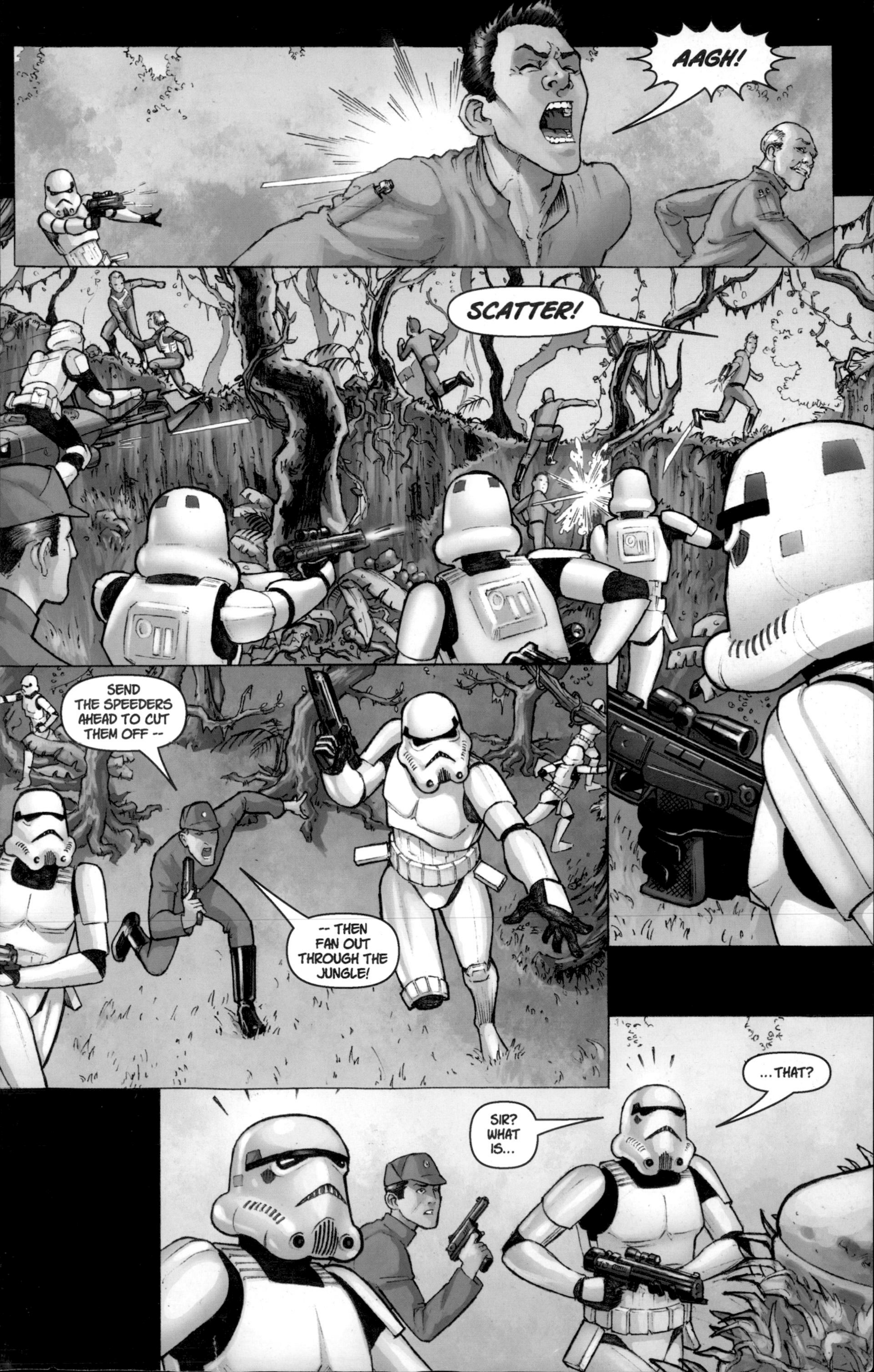
AAGH!
SCATTER!
SEND THE SPEEDERS AHEAD TO CUT THEM OFF --
-- THEN FAN OUT THROUGH THE JUNGLE!
SIR? WHAT IS...
...THAT?

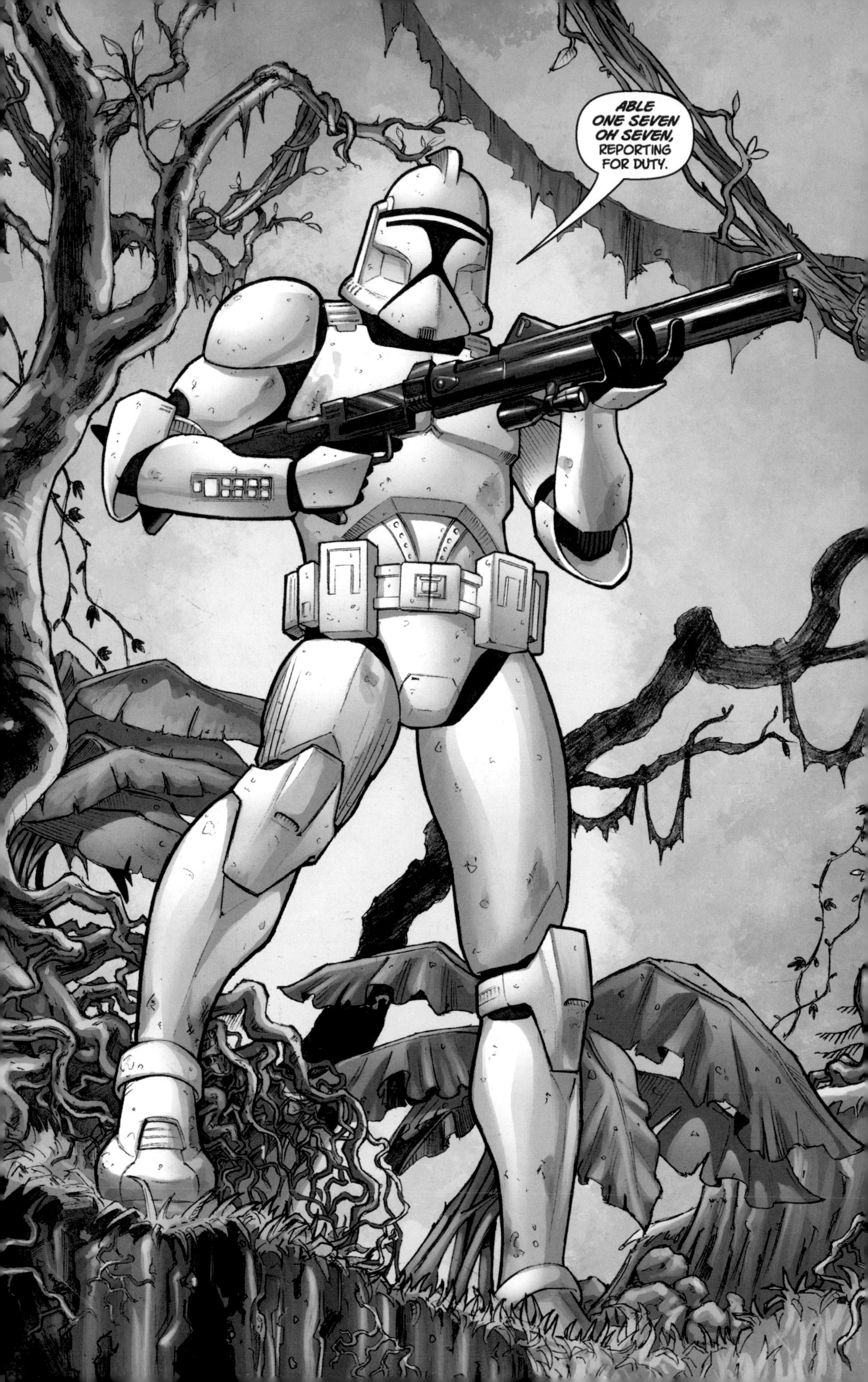
ABLE ONE SEVEN OH SEVEN, REPORTING FOR DUTY.

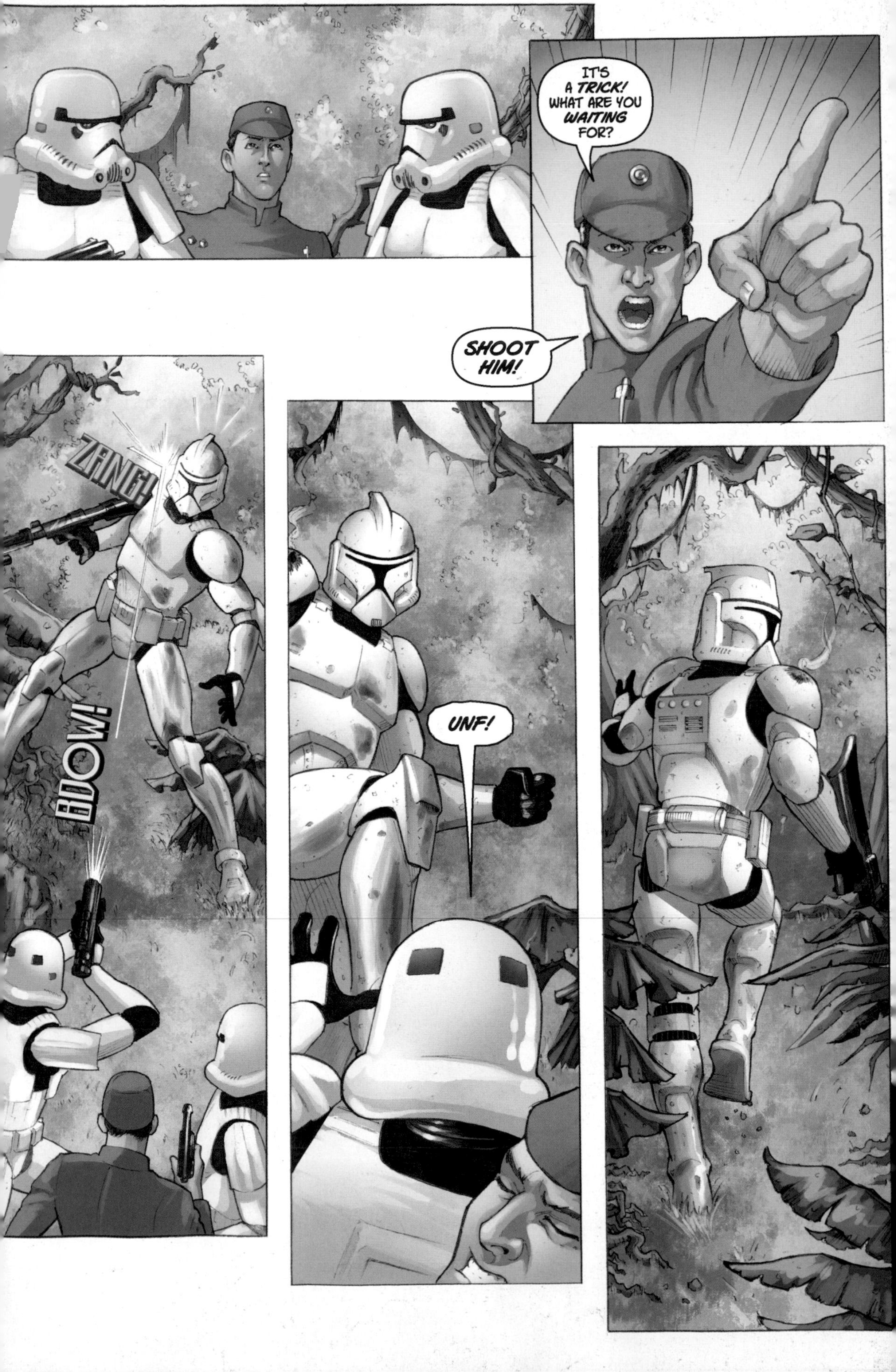
IT'S A TRICK! WHAT ARE YOU WAITING FOR?
SHOOT HIM!
ZANG!
BDOW!
UNF!

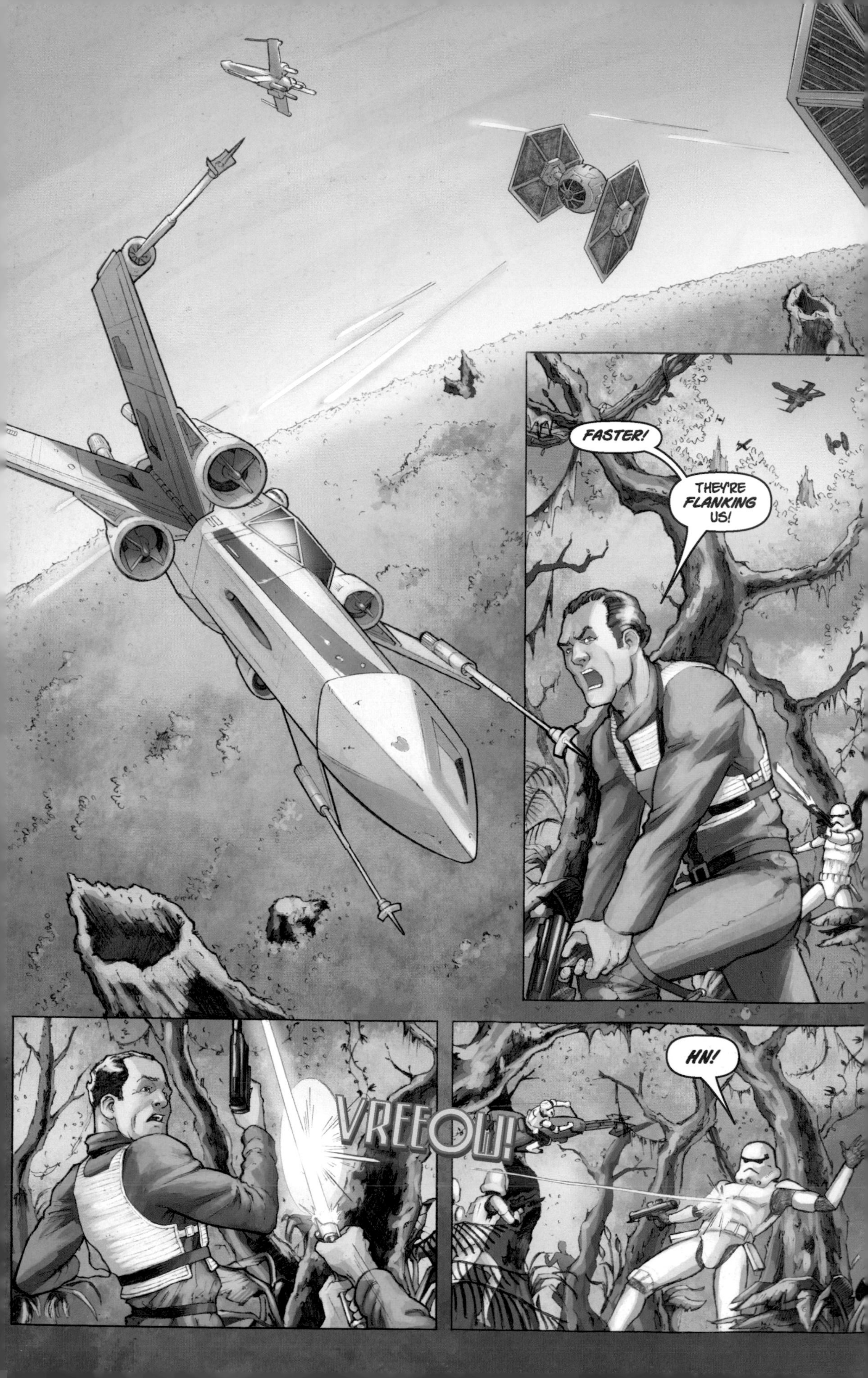
FASTER!
THEY'RE FLANKING US!
VREEOW!
HN!

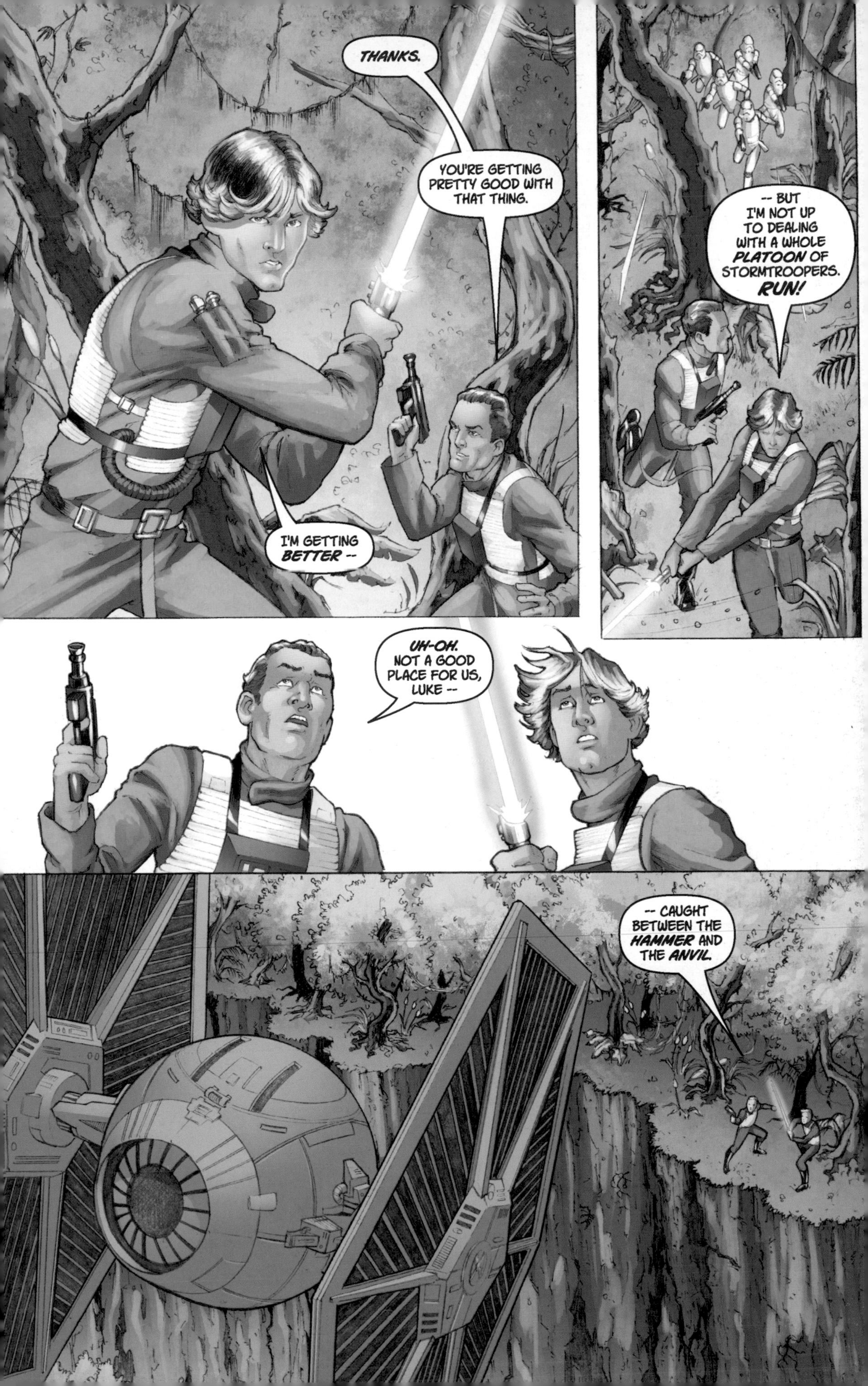
THANKS.
YOU'RE GETTING PRETTY GOOD WITH THAT THING.
I'M GETTING BETTER --
-- BUT I'M NOT UP TO DEALING WITH A WHOLE PLATOON OF STORMTROOPERS. RUN!
UH-OH. NOT A GOOD PLACE FOR US, LUKE --
-- CAUGHT BETWEEN THE HAMMER AND THE ANVIL.

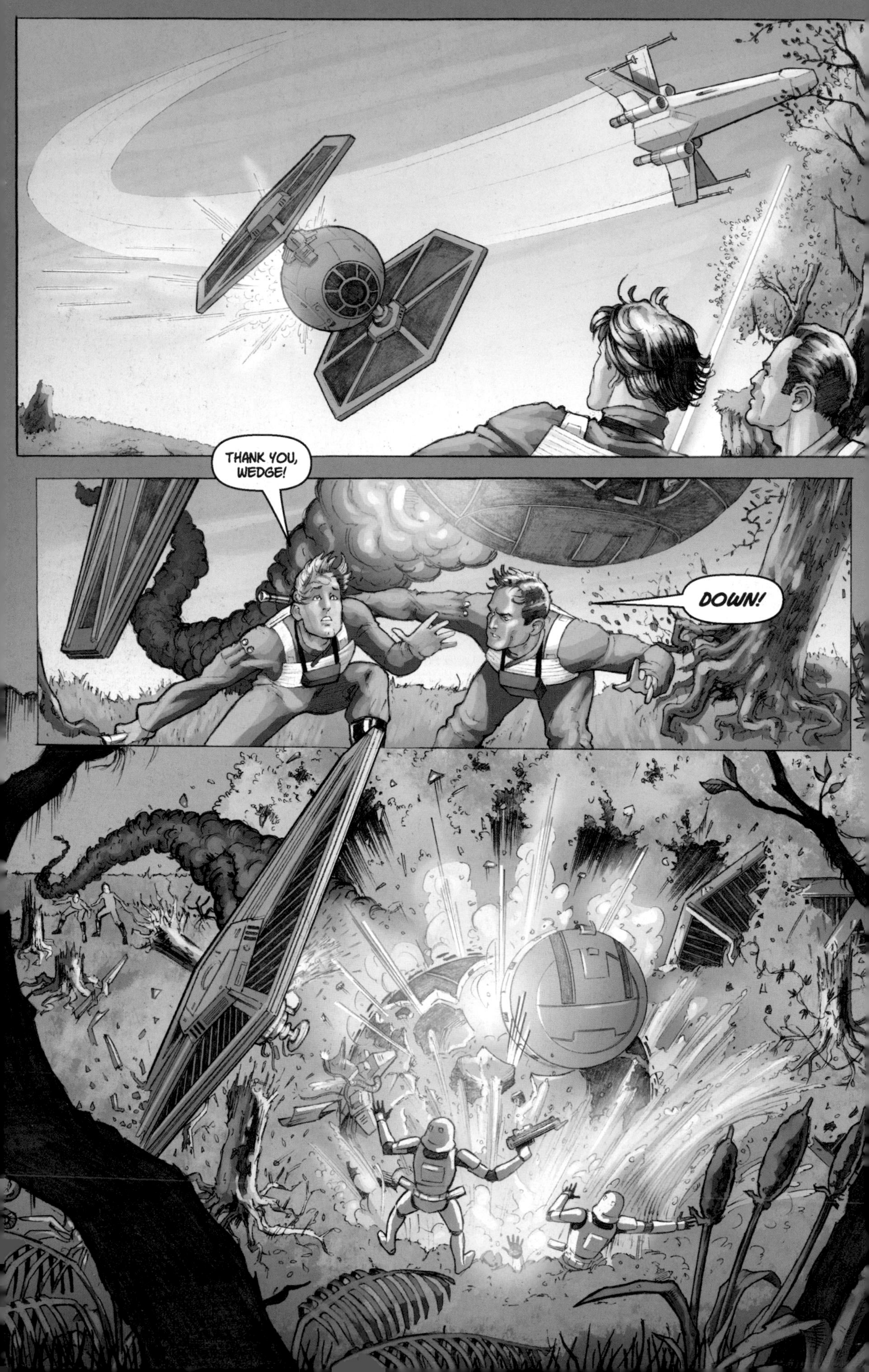
THANK YOU, WEDGE!
DOWN!

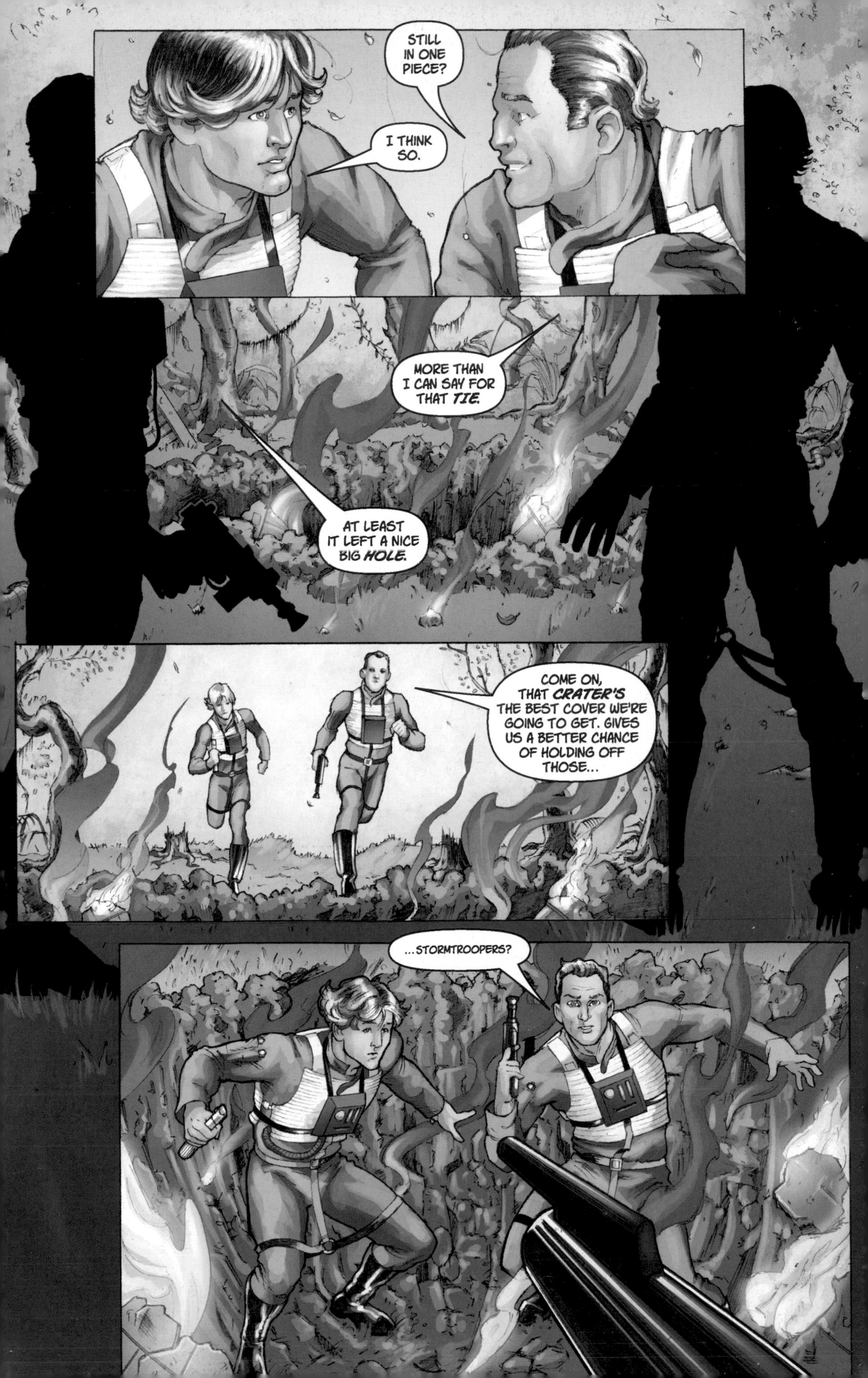
STILL IN ONE PIECE?
I THINK SO.
MORE THAN I CAN SAY FOR THAT *TIE*.
AT LEAST IT LEFT A NICE BIG *HOLE*.
COME ON, THAT *CRATER'S* THE BEST COVER WE'RE GOING TO GET. GIVES US A BETTER CHANCE OF HOLDING OFF THOSE...
...STORMTROOPERS?

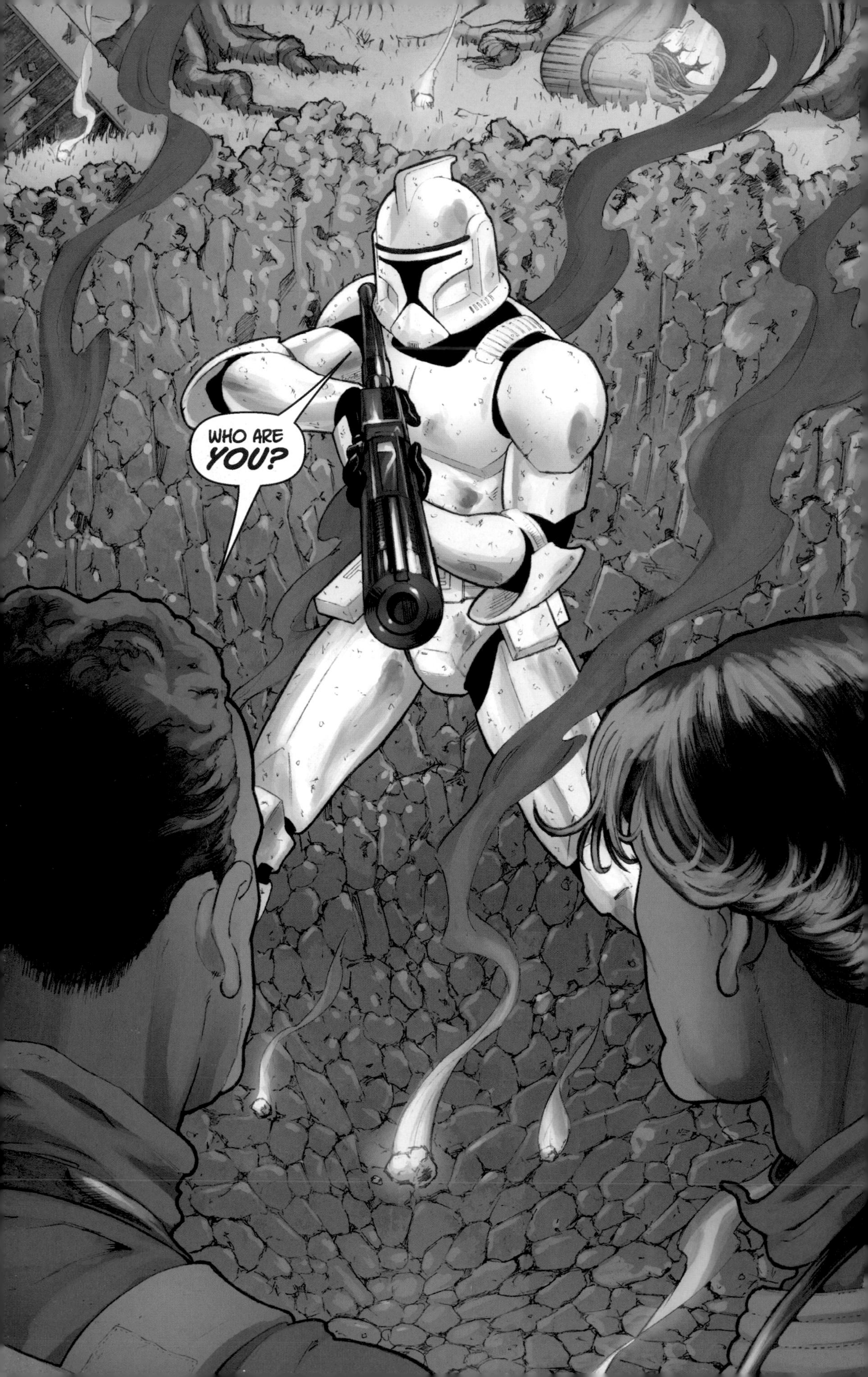
WHO ARE YOU?

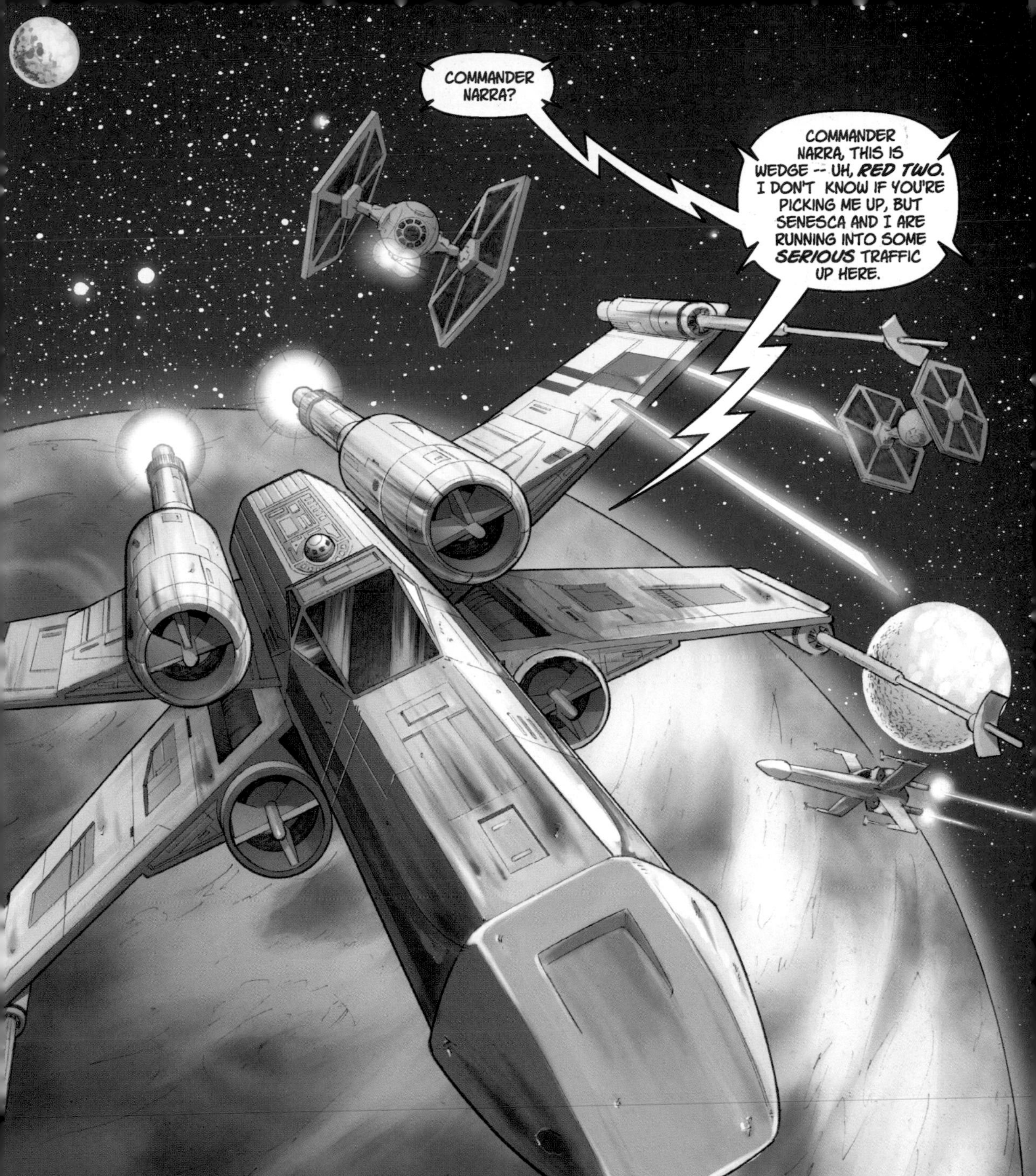
COMMANDER NARRA?
COMMANDER NARRA, THIS IS WEDGE -- UH, RED TWO. I DON'T KNOW IF YOU'RE PICKING ME UP, BUT SENESCA AND I ARE RUNNING INTO SOME SERIOUS TRAFFIC UP HERE.

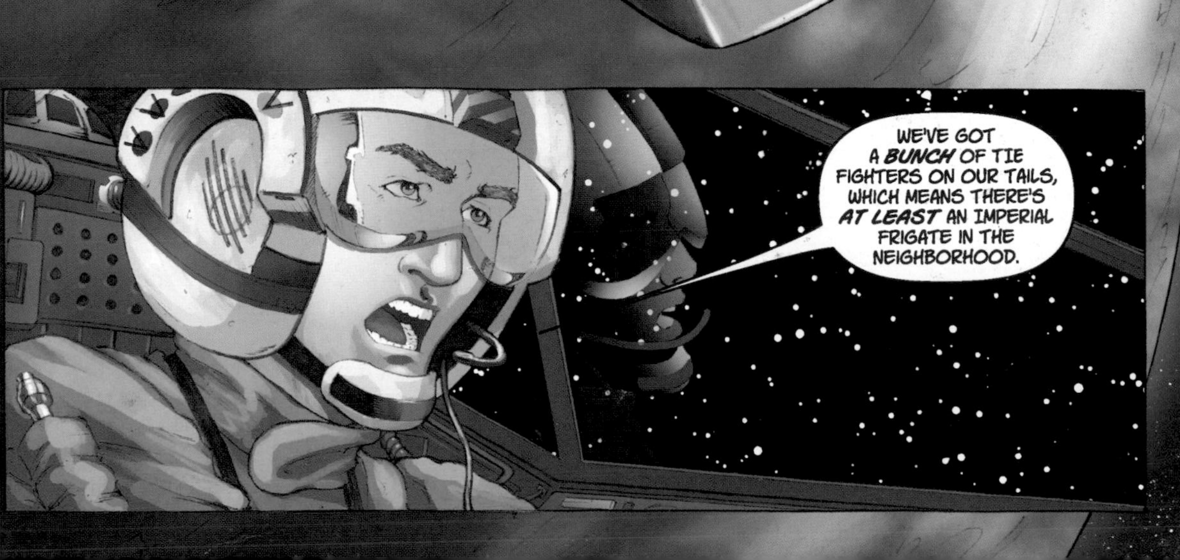
WE'VE GOT A BUNCH OF TIE FIGHTERS ON OUR TAILS, WHICH MEANS THERE'S AT LEAST AN IMPERIAL FRIGATE IN THE NEIGHBORHOOD.

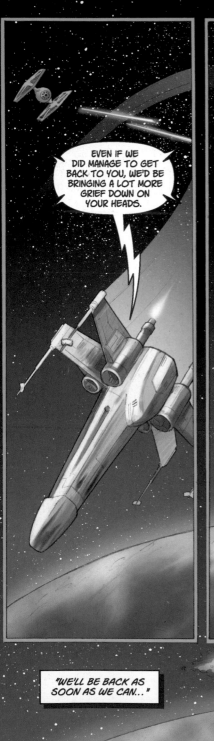

EVEN IF WE DID MANAGE TO GET BACK TO YOU, WE'D BE BRINGING A LOT MORE GRIEF DOWN ON YOUR HEADS.

CAN'T RISK BEING FOLLOWED BACK TO THE FLEET...

...SO WE'RE GOING TO TRY DUCKING AROUND TO THE OTHER SIDE OF THE PLANET --

-- AND KEEP OUR HEADS LOW.

"WE'LL BE BACK AS SOON AS WE CAN..."

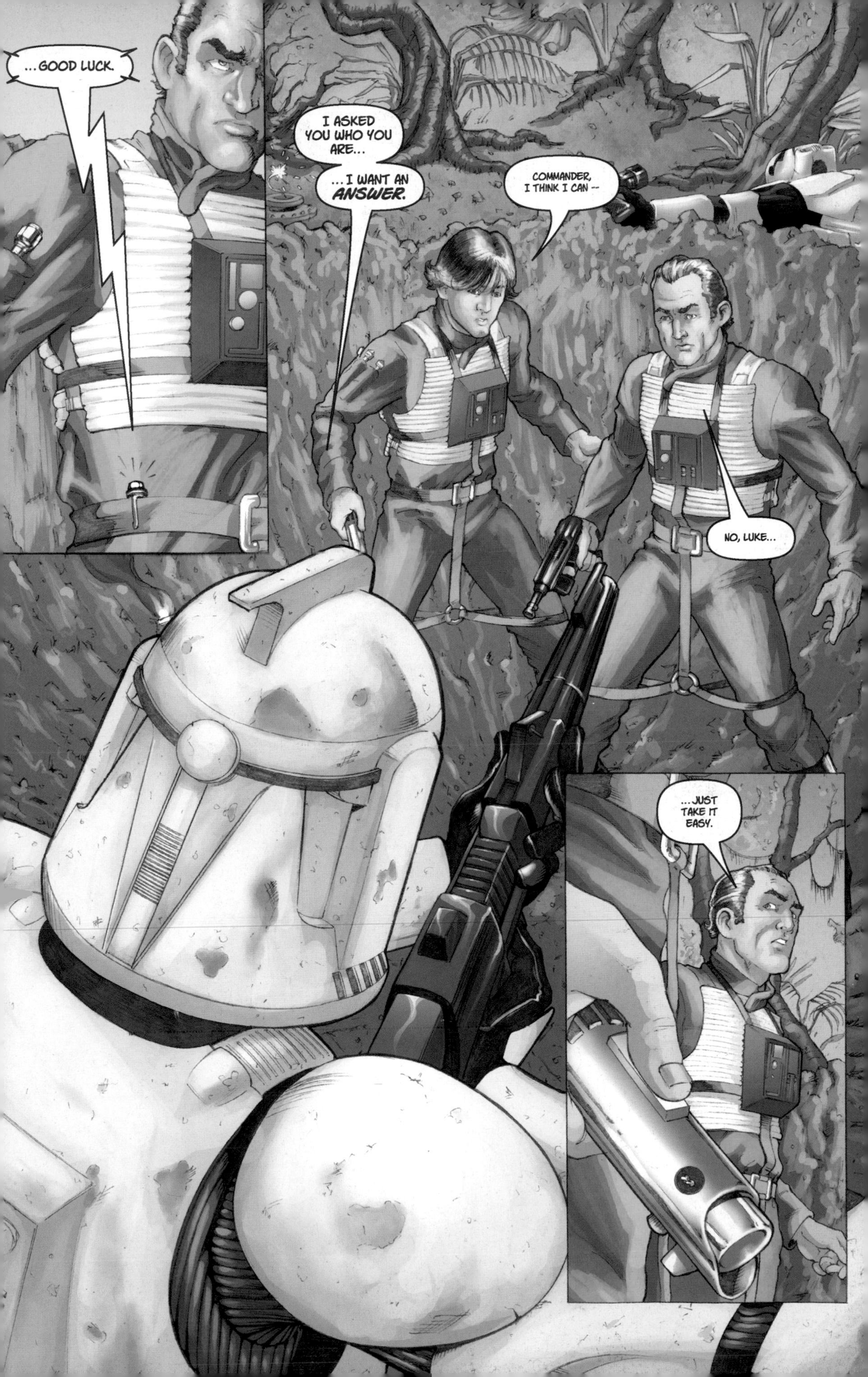
...GOOD LUCK.
I ASKED YOU WHO YOU ARE...
...I WANT AN ANSWER.
COMMANDER, I THINK I CAN --
NO, LUKE...
...JUST TAKE IT EASY.

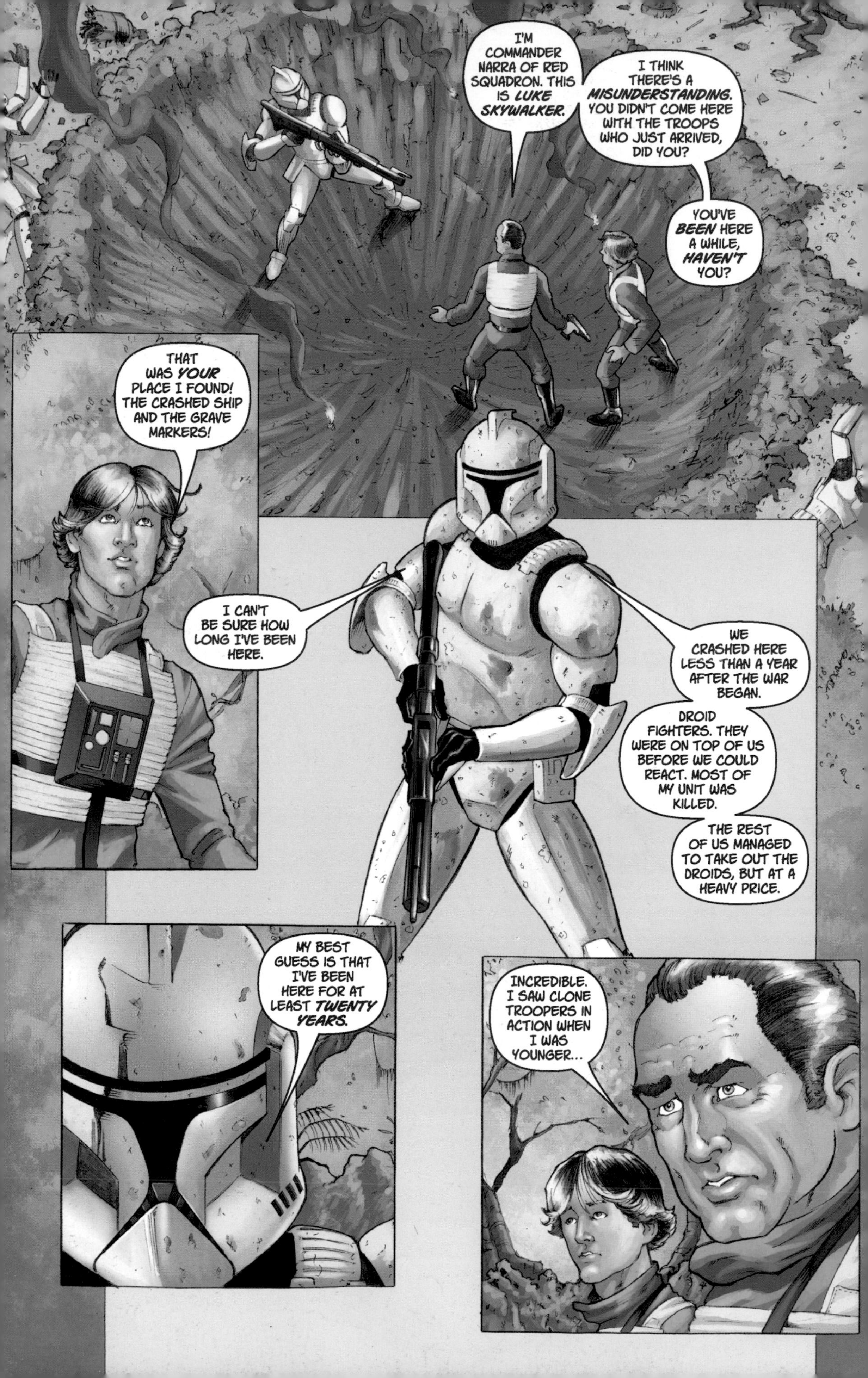

I'M COMMANDER NARRA OF RED SQUADRON. THIS IS LUKE SKYWALKER.
I THINK THERE'S A MISUNDERSTANDING. YOU DIDN'T COME HERE WITH THE TROOPS WHO JUST ARRIVED, DID YOU?
YOU'VE BEEN HERE A WHILE, HAVEN'T YOU?
THAT WAS YOUR PLACE I FOUND! THE CRASHED SHIP AND THE GRAVE MARKERS!
I CAN'T BE SURE HOW LONG I'VE BEEN HERE.
WE CRASHED HERE LESS THAN A YEAR AFTER THE WAR BEGAN.
DROID FIGHTERS. THEY WERE ON TOP OF US BEFORE WE COULD REACT. MOST OF MY UNIT WAS KILLED.
THE REST OF US MANAGED TO TAKE OUT THE DROIDS, BUT AT A HEAVY PRICE.
MY BEST GUESS IS THAT I'VE BEEN HERE FOR AT LEAST TWENTY YEARS.
INCREDIBLE. I SAW CLONE TROOPERS IN ACTION WHEN I WAS YOUNGER...

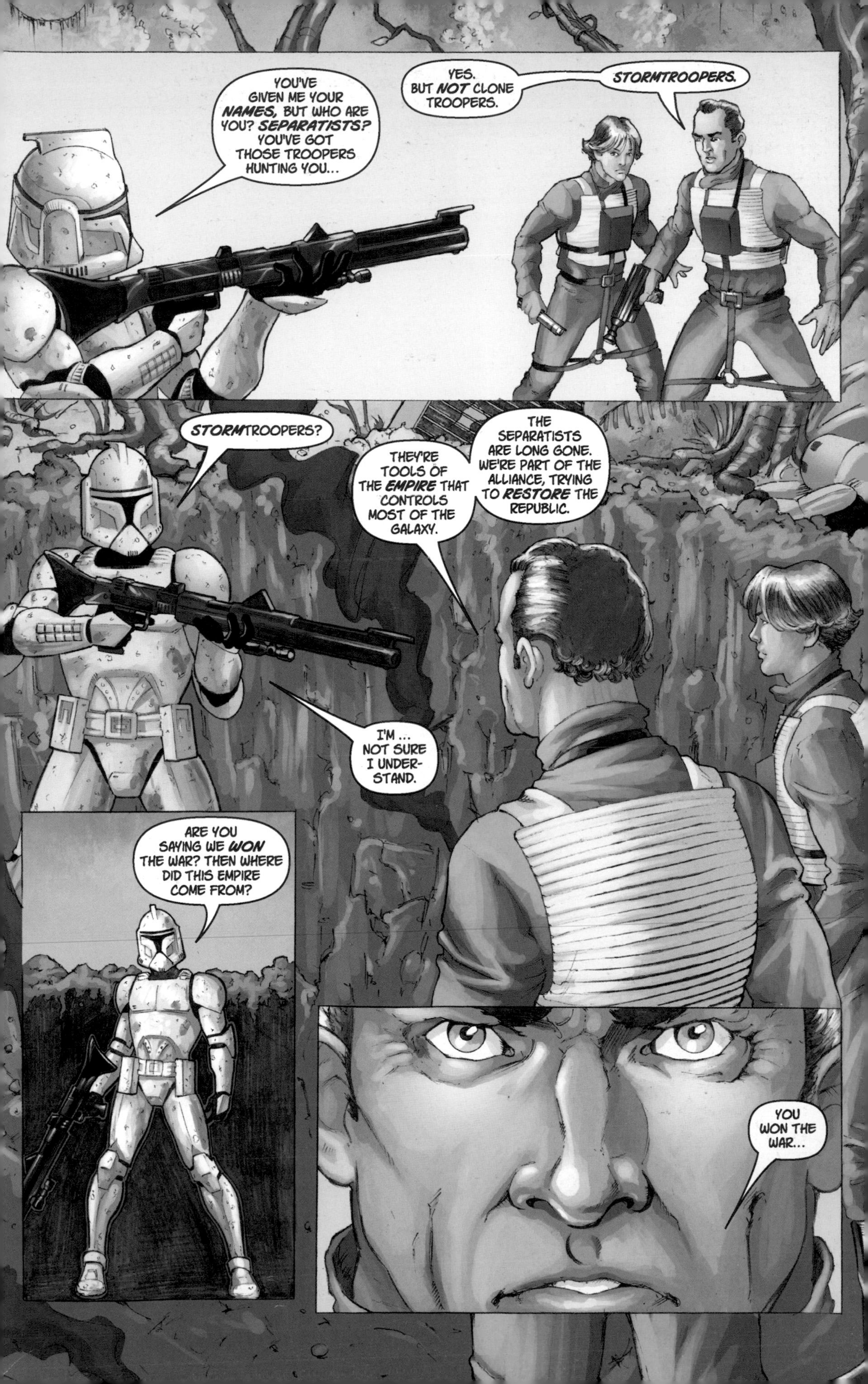
YOU'VE GIVEN ME YOUR NAMES, BUT WHO ARE YOU? SEPARATISTS? YOU'VE GOT THOSE TROOPERS HUNTING YOU...
YES. BUT NOT CLONE TROOPERS.
STORMTROOPERS.
STORMTROOPERS?
THEY'RE TOOLS OF THE EMPIRE THAT CONTROLS MOST OF THE GALAXY.
THE SEPARATISTS ARE LONG GONE. WE'RE PART OF THE ALLIANCE, TRYING TO RESTORE THE REPUBLIC.
I'M ... NOT SURE I UNDER-STAND.
ARE YOU SAYING WE WON THE WAR? THEN WHERE DID THIS EMPIRE COME FROM?
YOU WON THE WAR...

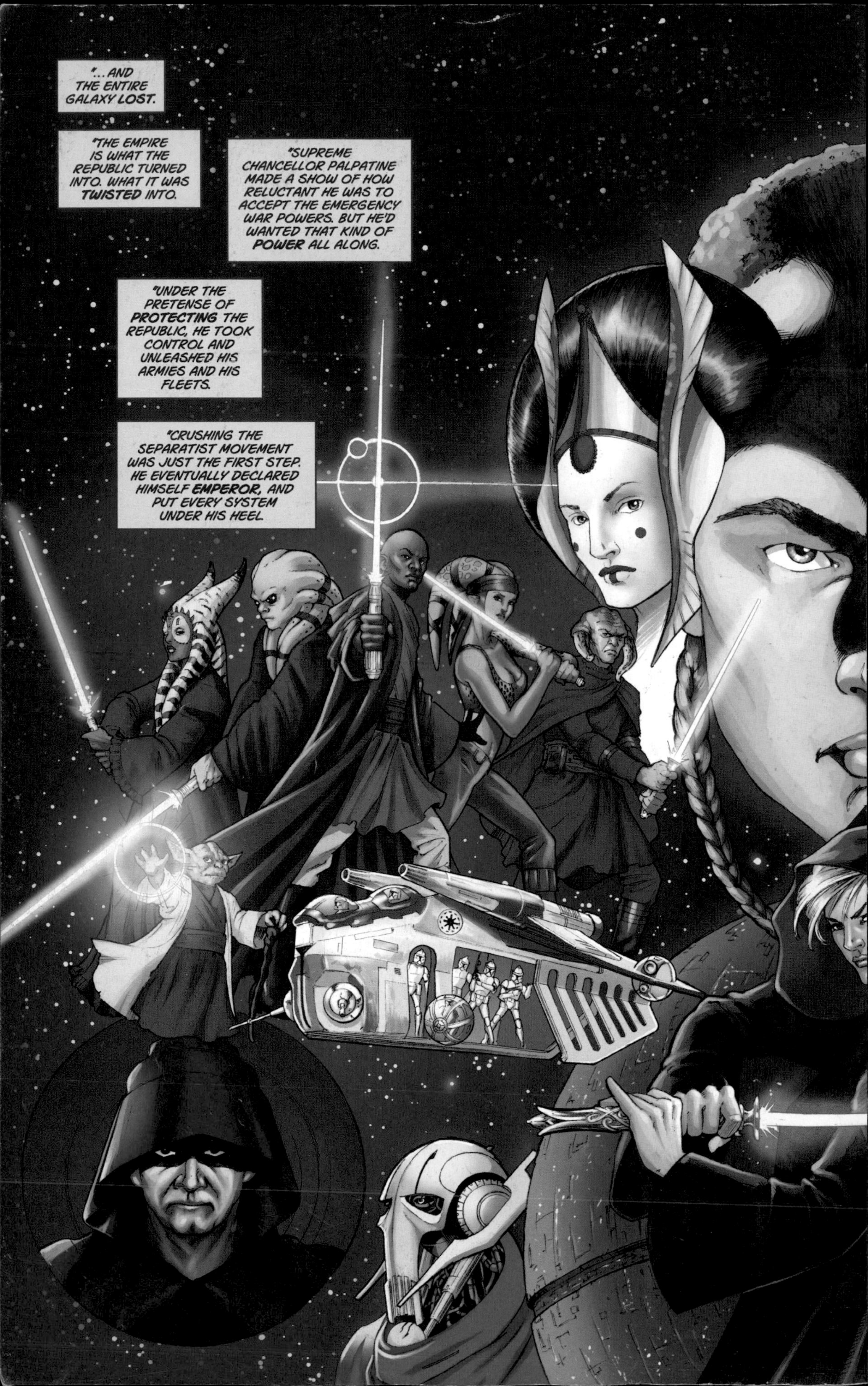
"... AND THE ENTIRE GALAXY LOST.
"THE EMPIRE IS WHAT THE REPUBLIC TURNED INTO. WHAT IT WAS TWISTED INTO.
"SUPREME CHANCELLOR PALPATINE MADE A SHOW OF HOW RELUCTANT HE WAS TO ACCEPT THE EMERGENCY WAR POWERS. BUT HE'D WANTED THAT KIND OF POWER ALL ALONG.
"UNDER THE PRETENSE OF PROTECTING THE REPUBLIC, HE TOOK CONTROL AND UNLEASHED HIS ARMIES AND HIS FLEETS.
"CRUSHING THE SEPARATIST MOVEMENT WAS JUST THE FIRST STEP. HE EVENTUALLY DECLARED HIMSELF EMPEROR, AND PUT EVERY SYSTEM UNDER HIS HEEL.

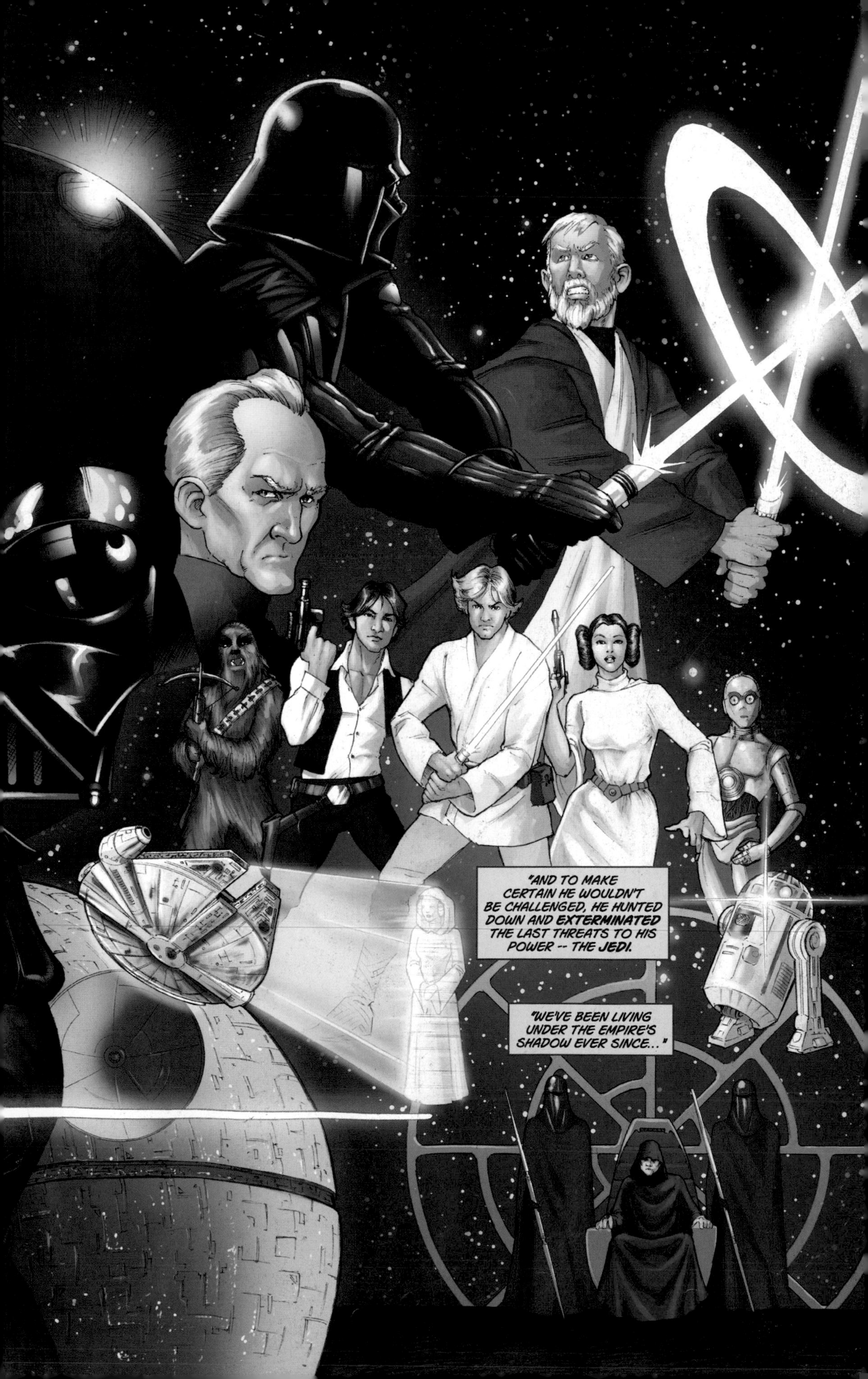
"AND TO MAKE CERTAIN HE WOULDN'T BE CHALLENGED, HE HUNTED DOWN AND **EXTERMINATED** THE LAST THREATS TO HIS POWER -- THE **JEDI**.
"WE'VE BEEN LIVING UNDER THE EMPIRE'S SHADOW EVER SINCE..."

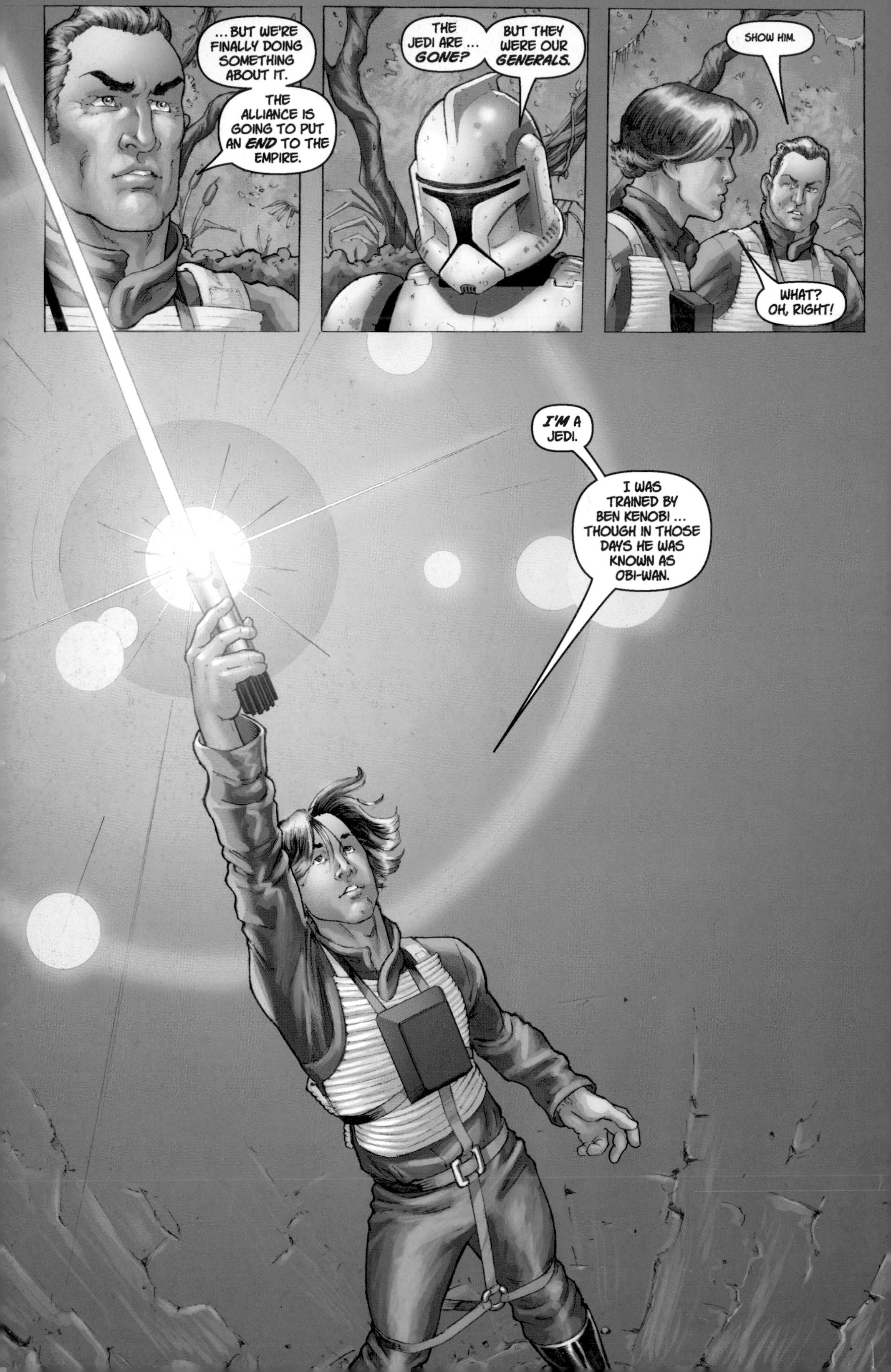
... BUT WE'RE FINALLY DOING SOMETHING ABOUT IT.
THE ALLIANCE IS GOING TO PUT AN *END* TO THE EMPIRE.
THE JEDI ARE ... *GONE?*
BUT THEY WERE OUR *GENERALS.*
SHOW HIM.
WHAT? OH, RIGHT!
I'M A JEDI.
I WAS TRAINED BY BEN KENOBI ... THOUGH IN THOSE DAYS HE WAS KNOWN AS OBI-WAN.

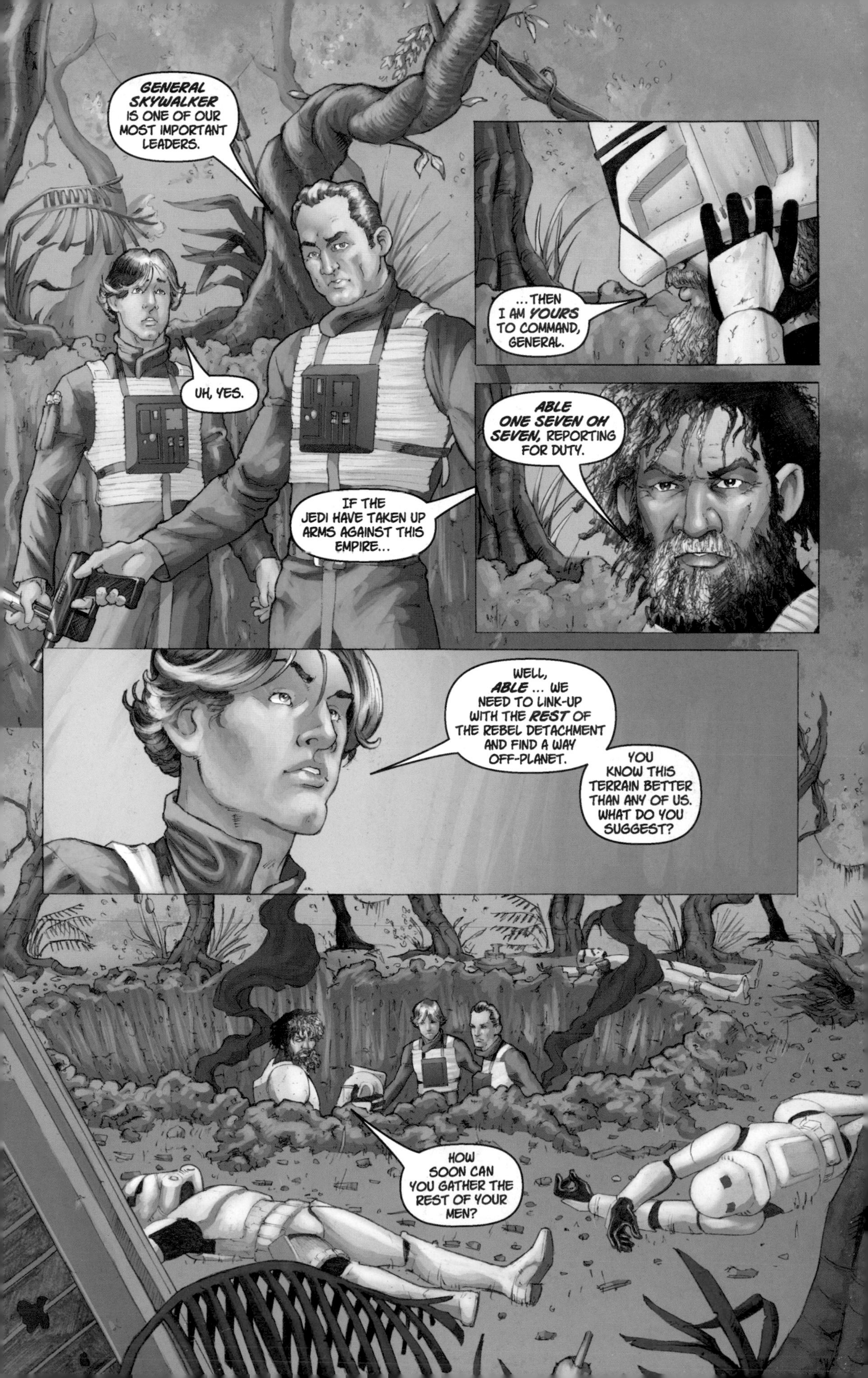
GENERAL SKYWALKER IS ONE OF OUR MOST IMPORTANT LEADERS.
UH, YES.
IF THE JEDI HAVE TAKEN UP ARMS AGAINST THIS EMPIRE...
...THEN I AM YOURS TO COMMAND, GENERAL.
ABLE ONE SEVEN OH SEVEN, REPORTING FOR DUTY.
WELL, ABLE ... WE NEED TO LINK-UP WITH THE REST OF THE REBEL DETACHMENT AND FIND A WAY OFF-PLANET.
YOU KNOW THIS TERRAIN BETTER THAN ANY OF US. WHAT DO YOU SUGGEST?
HOW SOON CAN YOU GATHER THE REST OF YOUR MEN?

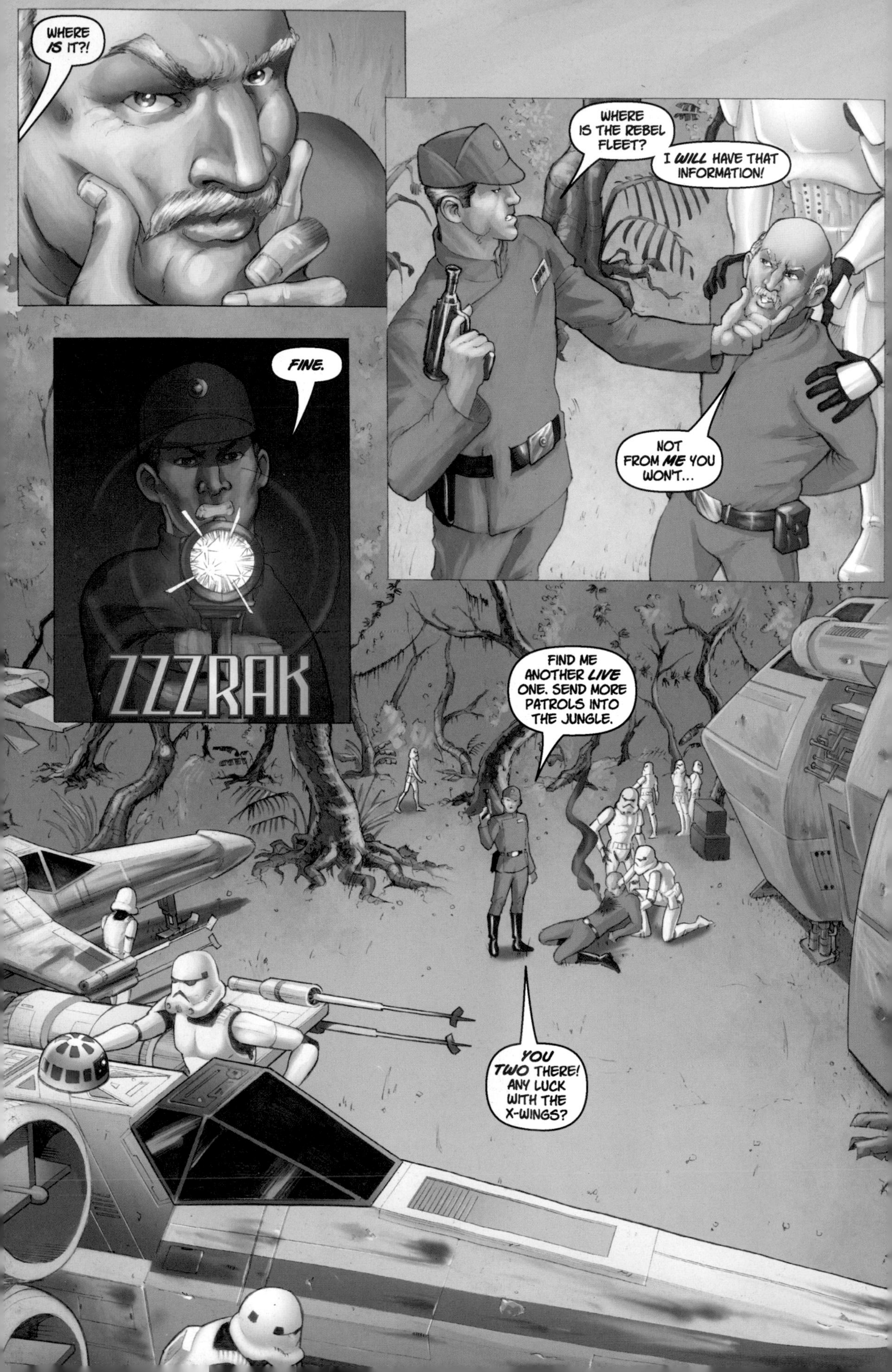
WHERE IS IT?!
WHERE IS THE REBEL FLEET?
I WILL HAVE THAT INFORMATION!
NOT FROM ME YOU WON'T...
FINE.
ZZZRAK
FIND ME ANOTHER LIVE ONE. SEND MORE PATROLS INTO THE JUNGLE.
YOU TWO THERE! ANY LUCK WITH THE X-WINGS?

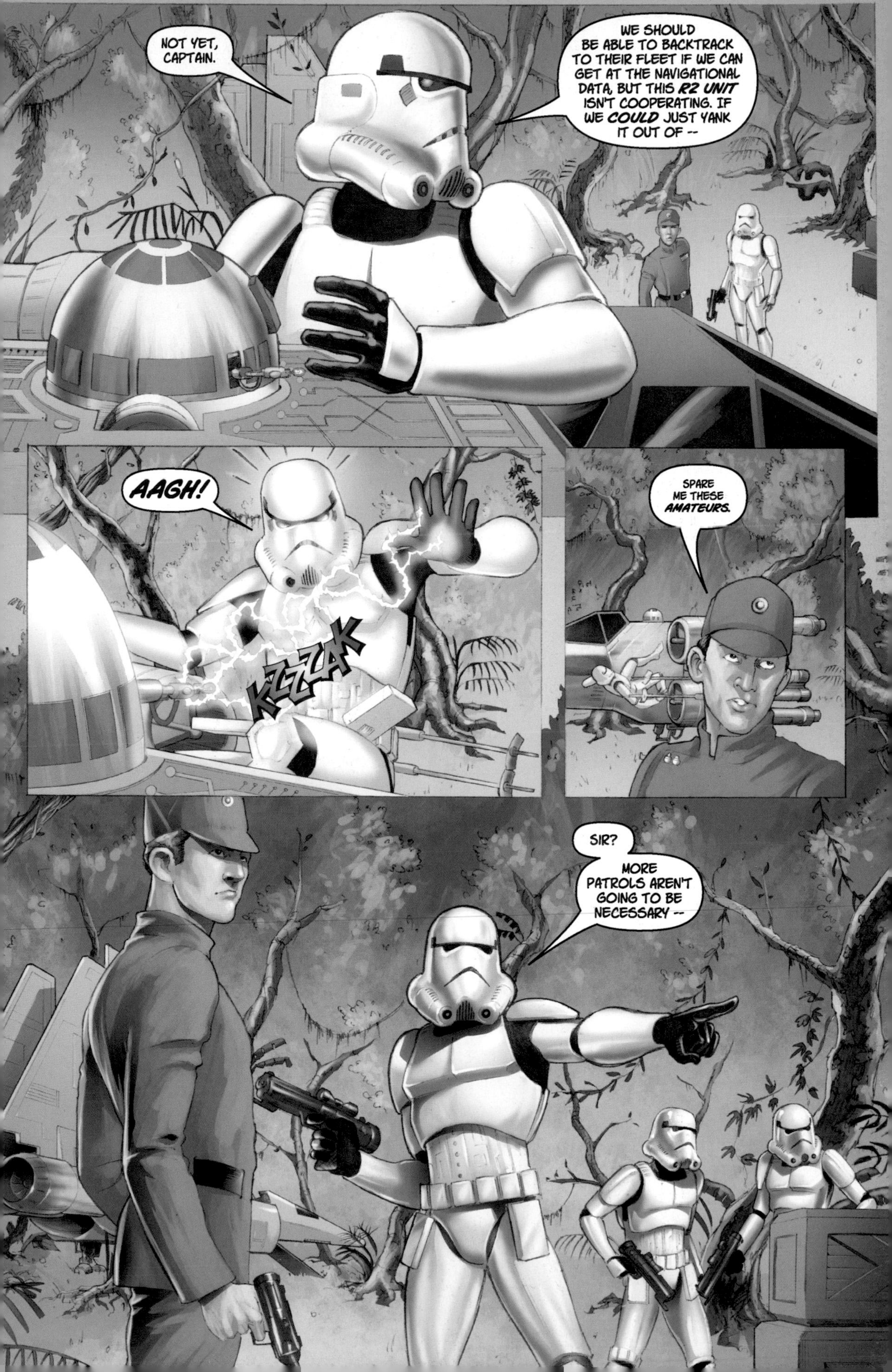
NOT YET, CAPTAIN.
WE SHOULD BE ABLE TO BACKTRACK TO THEIR FLEET IF WE CAN GET AT THE NAVIGATIONAL DATA, BUT THIS R2 UNIT ISN'T COOPERATING. IF WE COULD JUST YANK IT OUT OF --
AAGH!
KZZZAK
SPARE ME THESE AMATEURS.
SIR?
MORE PATROLS AREN'T GOING TO BE NECESSARY --

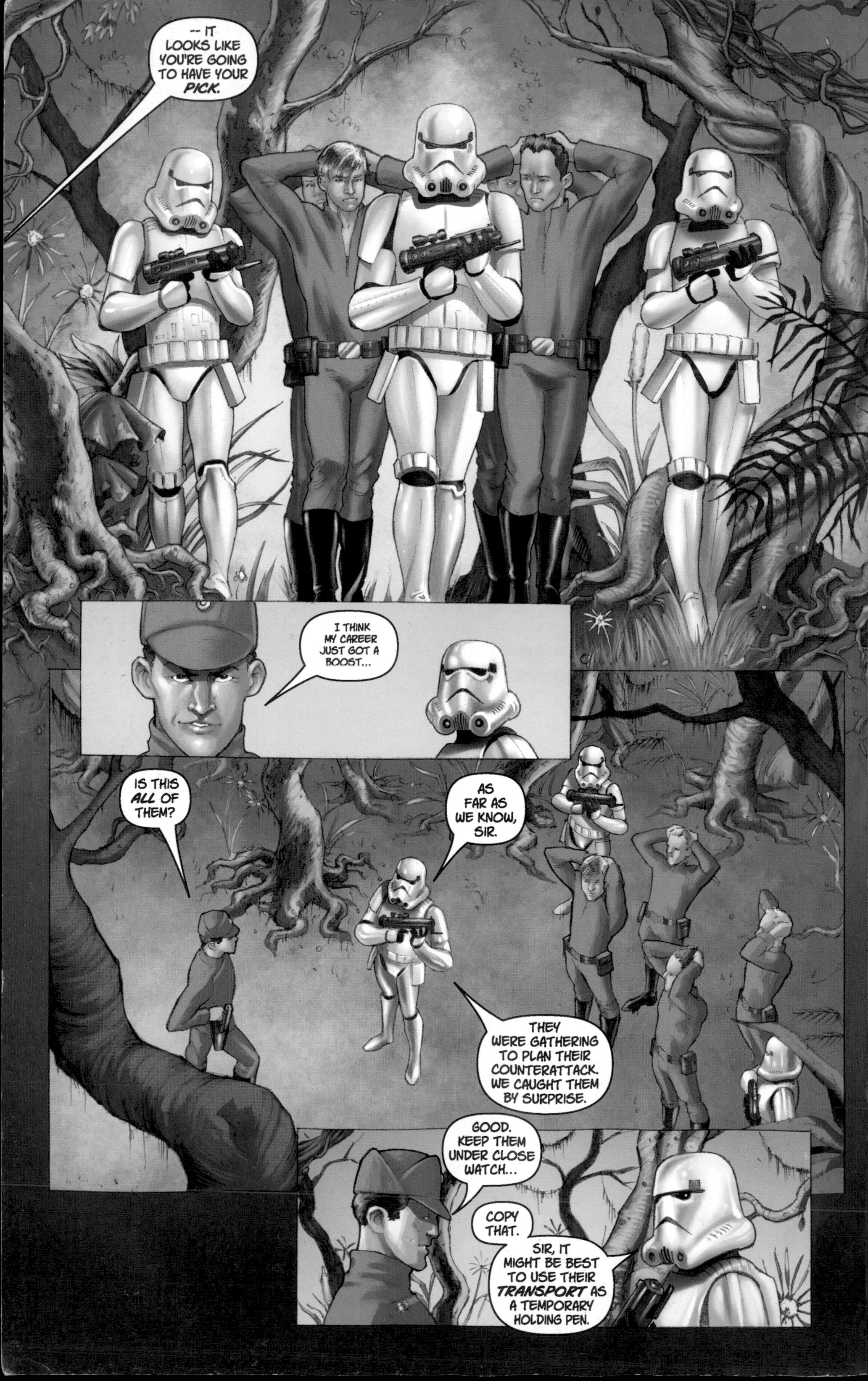
-- IT LOOKS LIKE YOU'RE GOING TO HAVE YOUR *PICK*.
I THINK MY CAREER JUST GOT A BOOST...
IS THIS *ALL* OF THEM?
AS FAR AS WE KNOW, SIR.
THEY WERE GATHERING TO PLAN THEIR COUNTERATTACK. WE CAUGHT THEM BY SURPRISE.
GOOD. KEEP THEM UNDER CLOSE WATCH...
COPY THAT.
SIR, IT MIGHT BE BEST TO USE THEIR *TRANSPORT* AS A TEMPORARY HOLDING PEN.

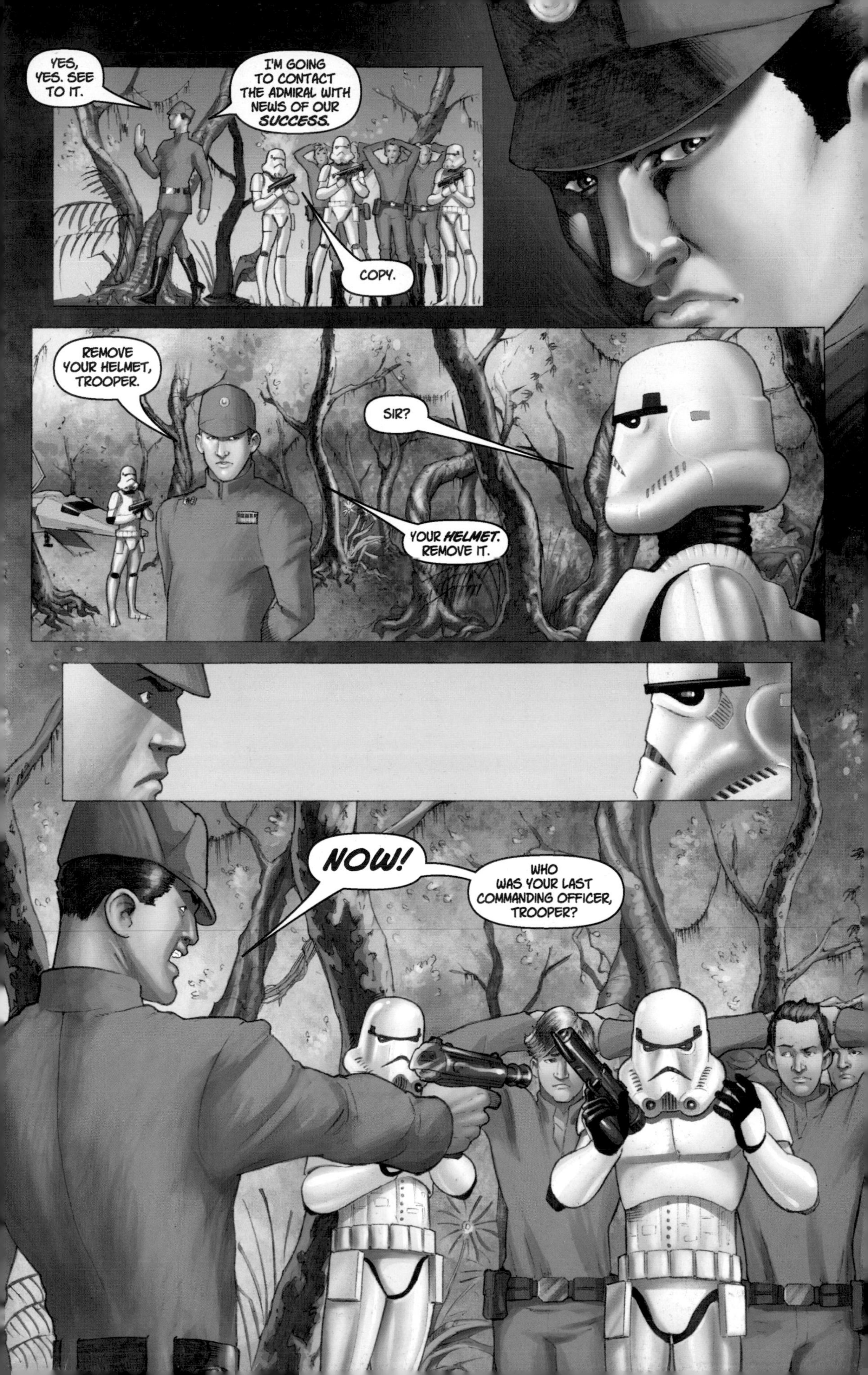
YES, YES. SEE TO IT.
I'M GOING TO CONTACT THE ADMIRAL WITH NEWS OF OUR SUCCESS.
COPY.
REMOVE YOUR HELMET, TROOPER.
SIR?
YOUR HELMET. REMOVE IT.
NOW!
WHO WAS YOUR LAST COMMANDING OFFICER, TROOPER?

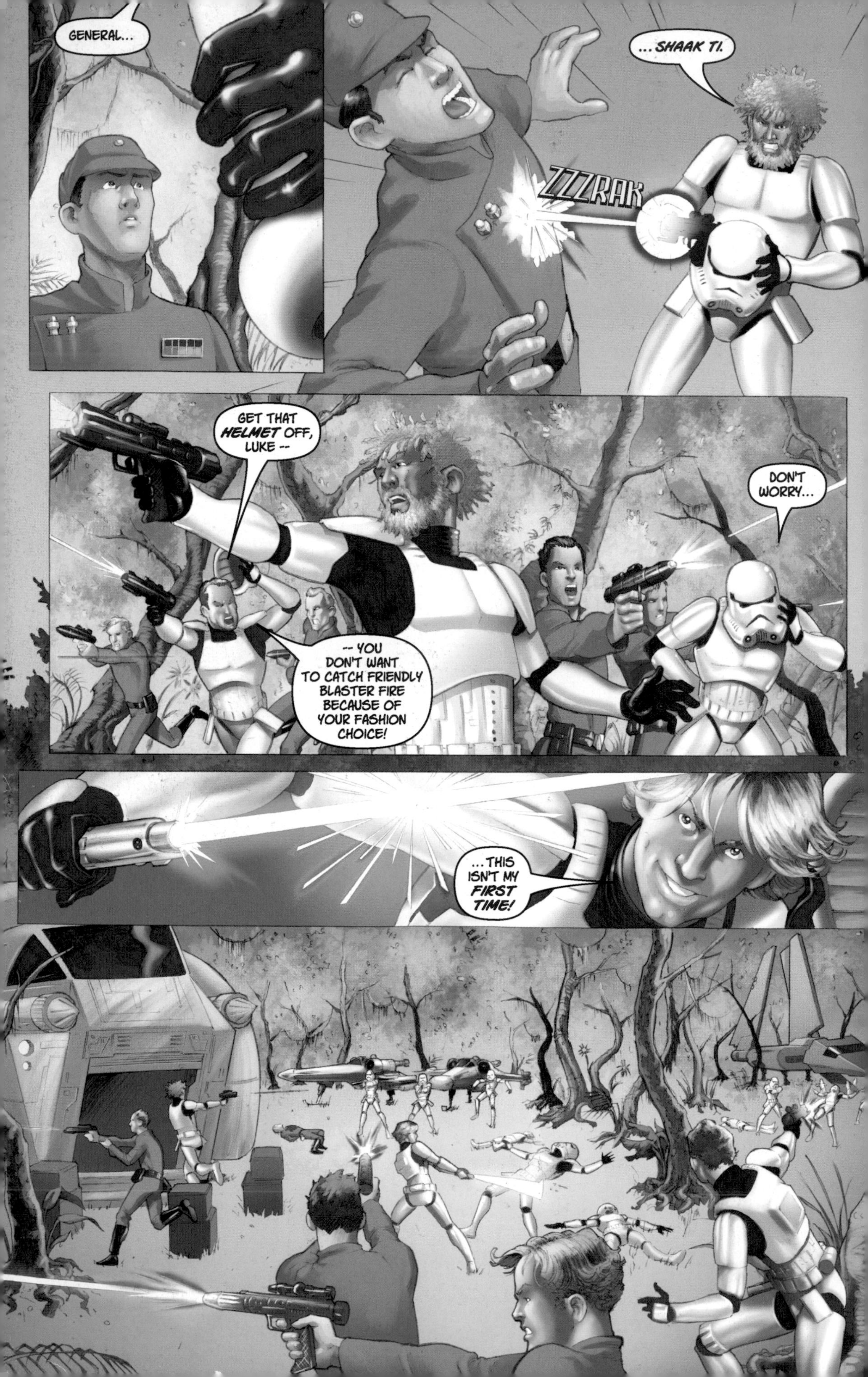

GENERAL...
...SHAAK TI.
ZZZRAK
GET THAT HELMET OFF, LUKE --
-- YOU DON'T WANT TO CATCH FRIENDLY BLASTER FIRE BECAUSE OF YOUR FASHION CHOICE!
DON'T WORRY...
...THIS ISN'T MY FIRST TIME!

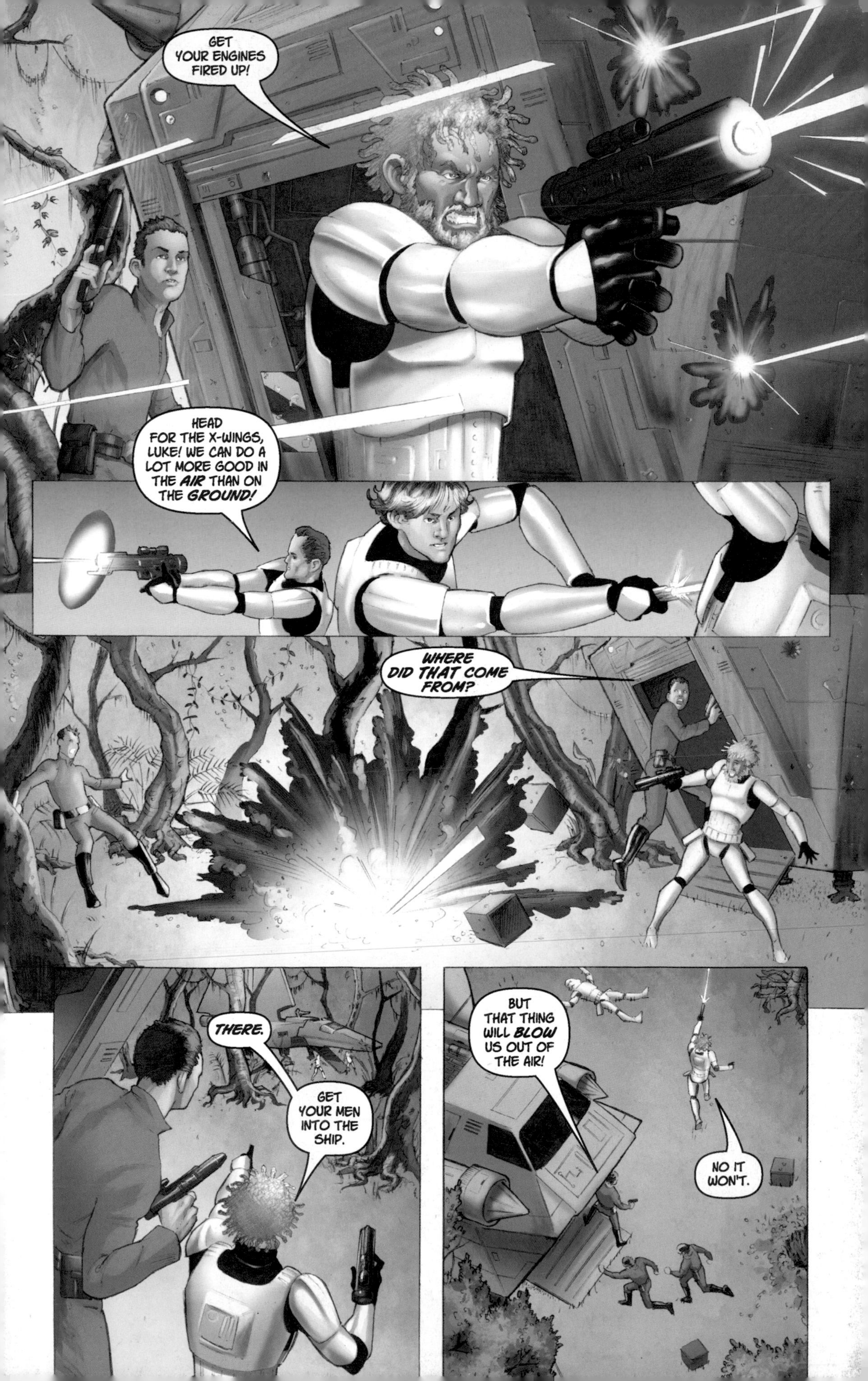
GET YOUR ENGINES FIRED UP!
HEAD FOR THE X-WINGS, LUKE! WE CAN DO A LOT MORE GOOD IN THE AIR THAN ON THE GROUND!
WHERE DID THAT COME FROM?
THERE.
GET YOUR MEN INTO THE SHIP.
BUT THAT THING WILL BLOW US OUT OF THE AIR!
NO IT WON'T.

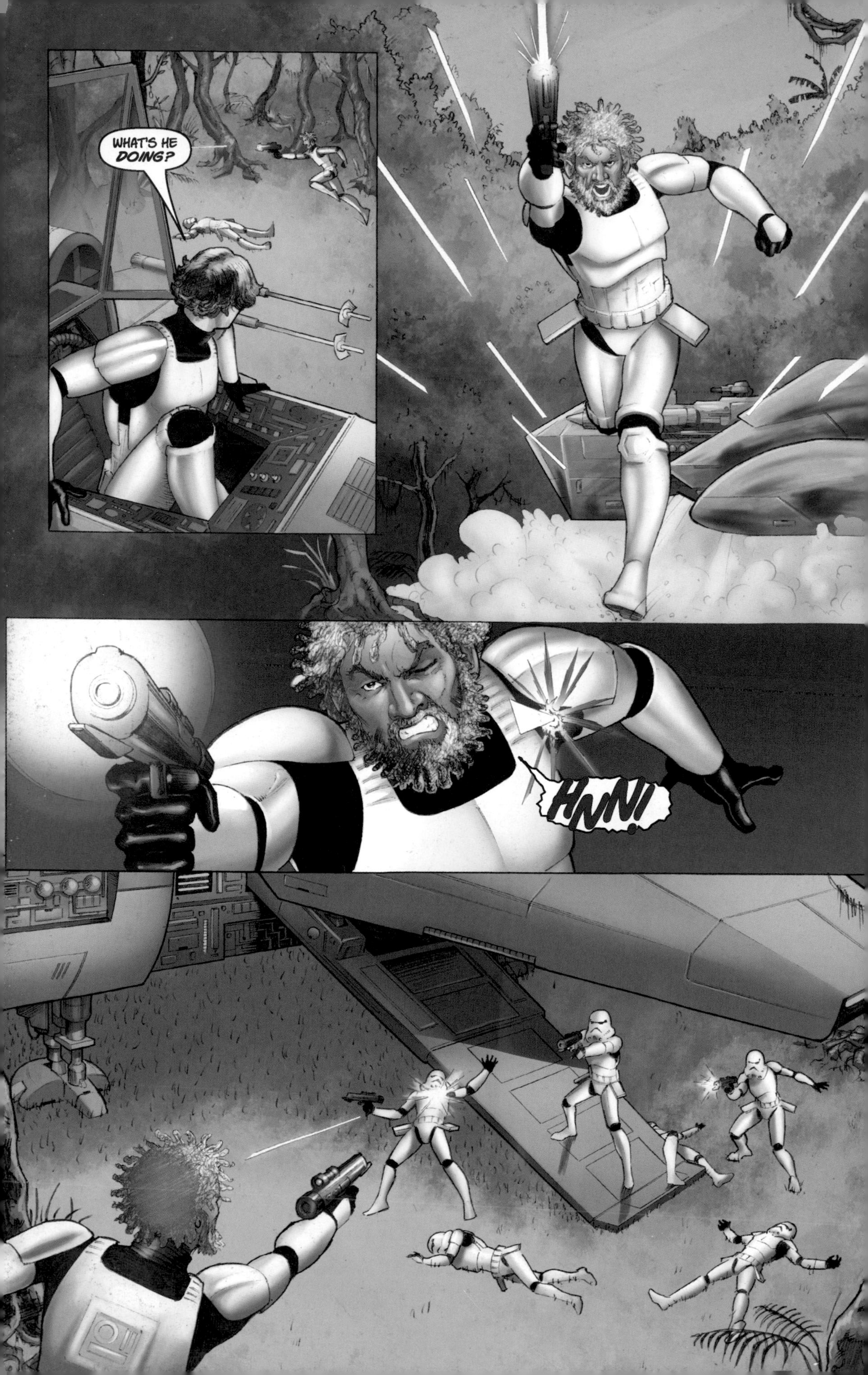
WHAT'S HE DOING?
HNN!

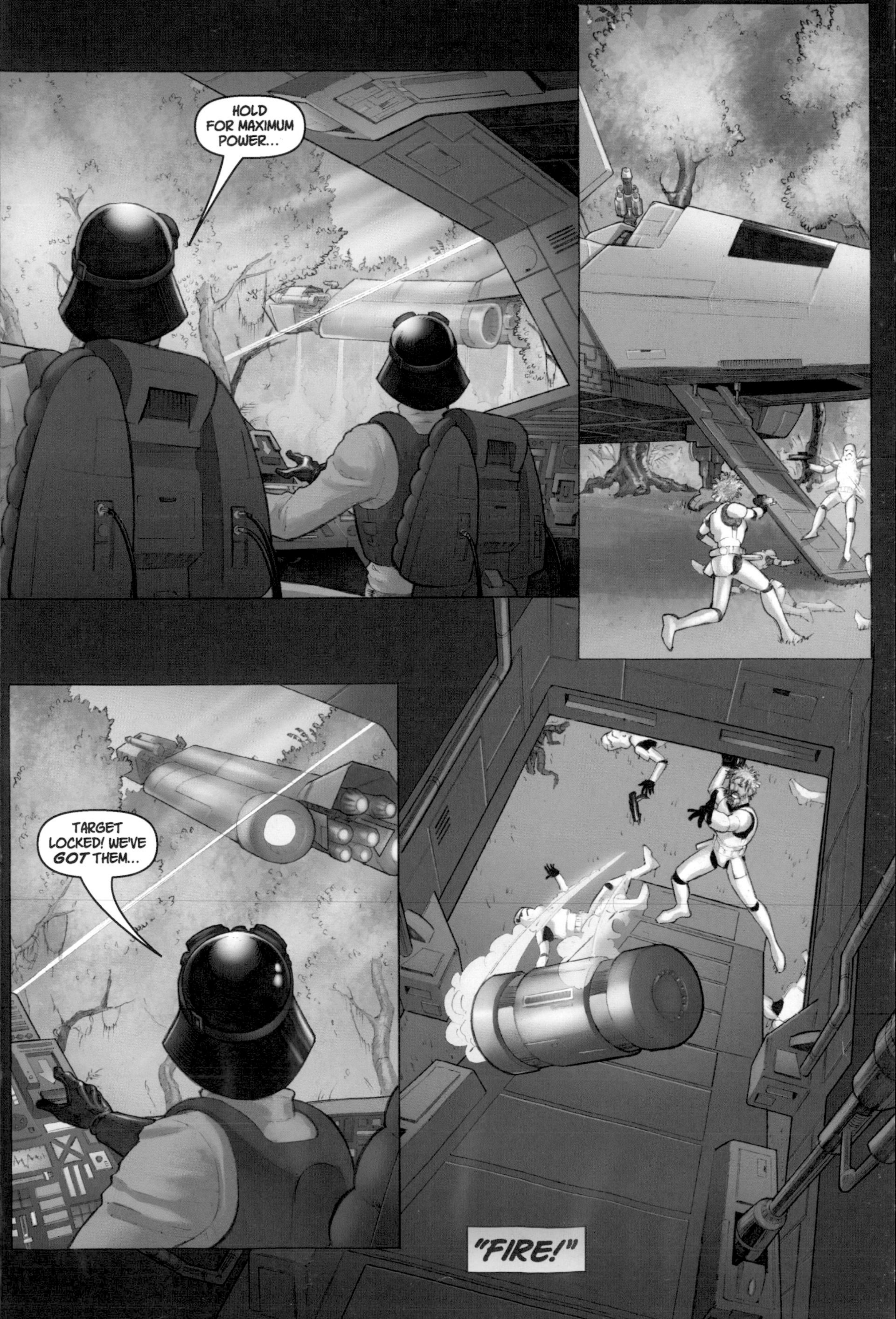
HOLD FOR MAXIMUM POWER...
TARGET LOCKED! WE'VE *GOT* THEM...
"FIRE!"

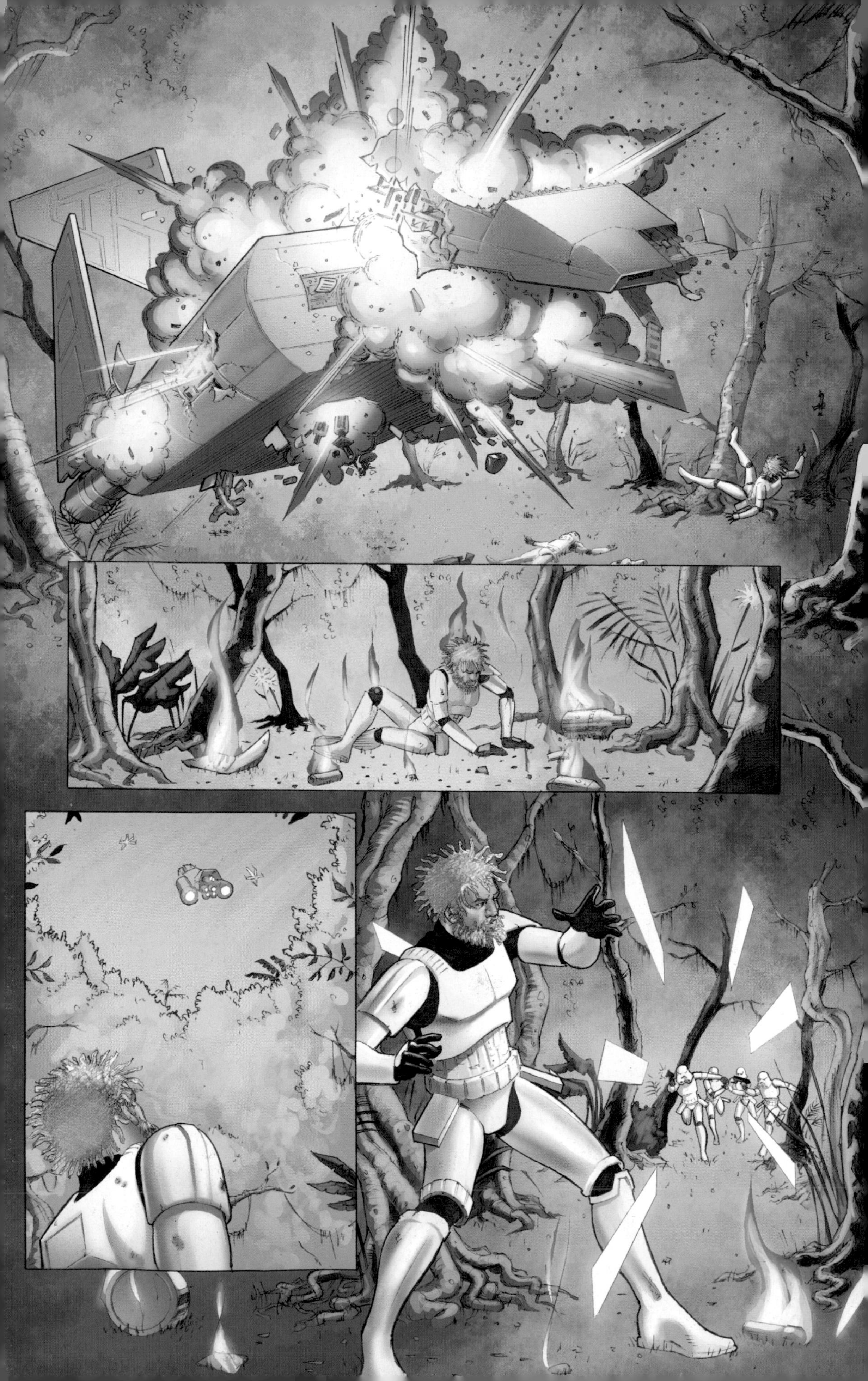

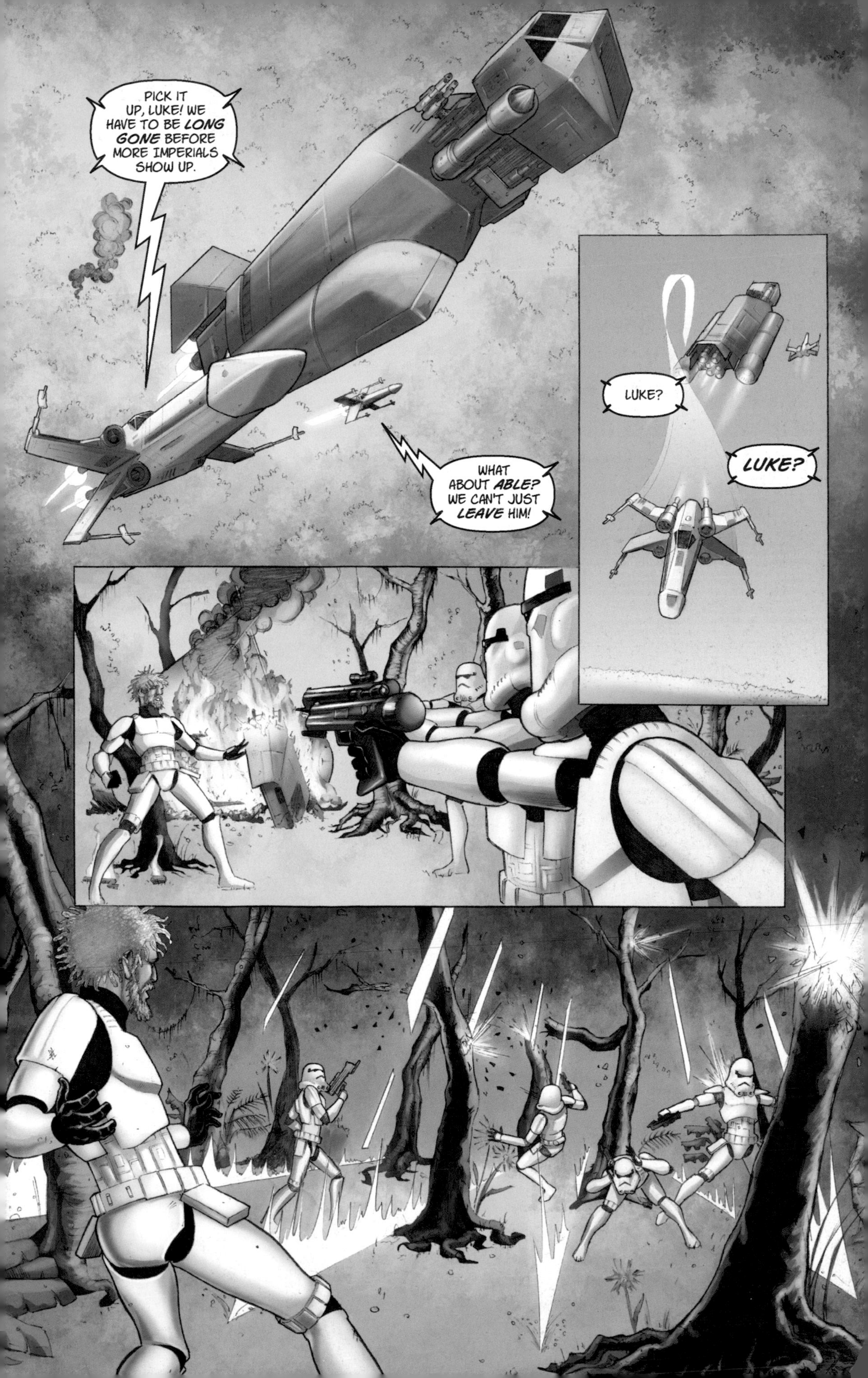
PICK IT UP, LUKE! WE HAVE TO BE LONG GONE BEFORE MORE IMPERIALS SHOW UP.
WHAT ABOUT ABLE? WE CAN'T JUST LEAVE HIM!
LUKE?
LUKE?

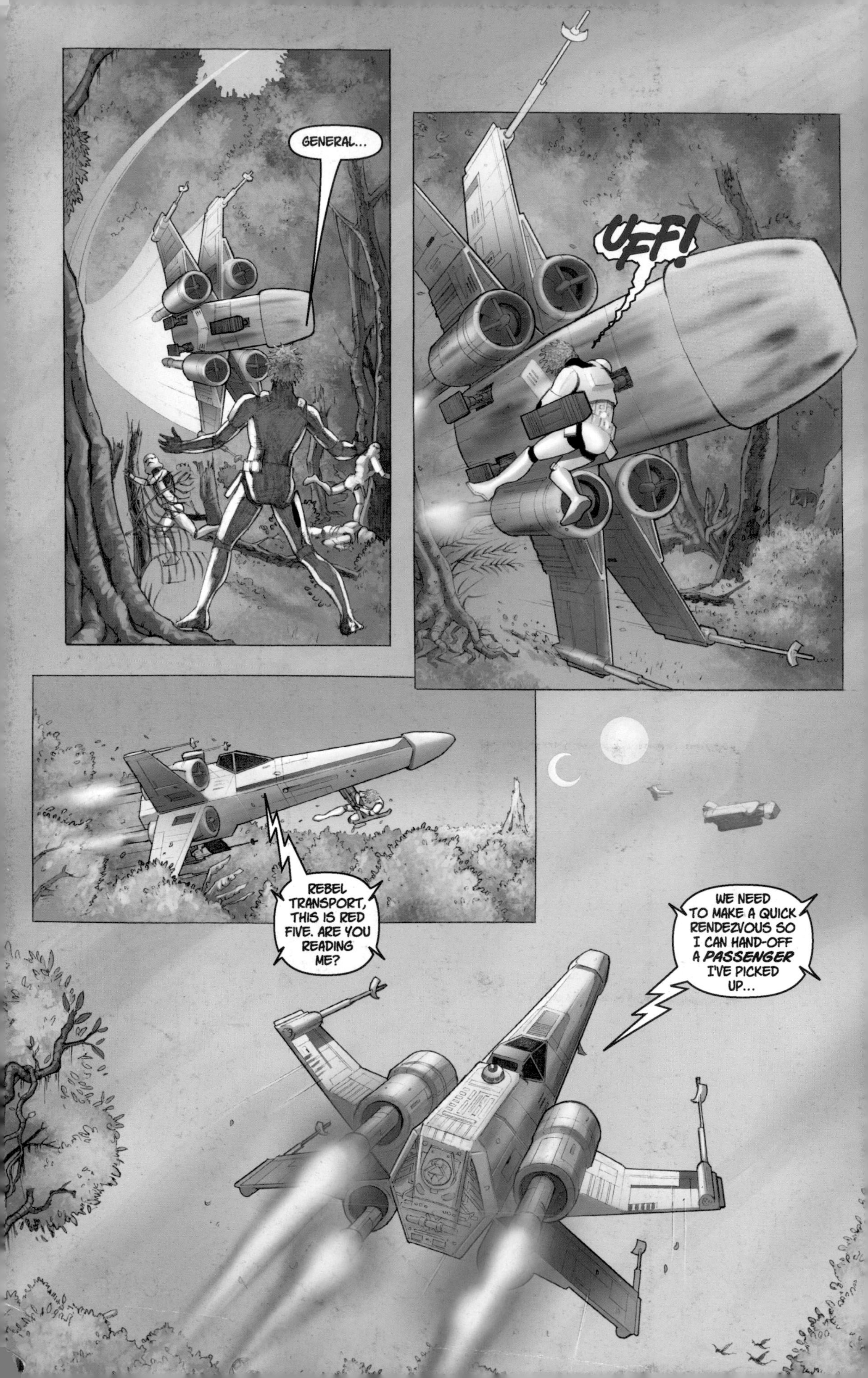
GENERAL...
UFF!
REBEL TRANSPORT, THIS IS RED FIVE. ARE YOU READING ME?
WE NEED TO MAKE A QUICK RENDEZVOUS SO I CAN HAND-OFF A *PASSENGER* I'VE PICKED UP...

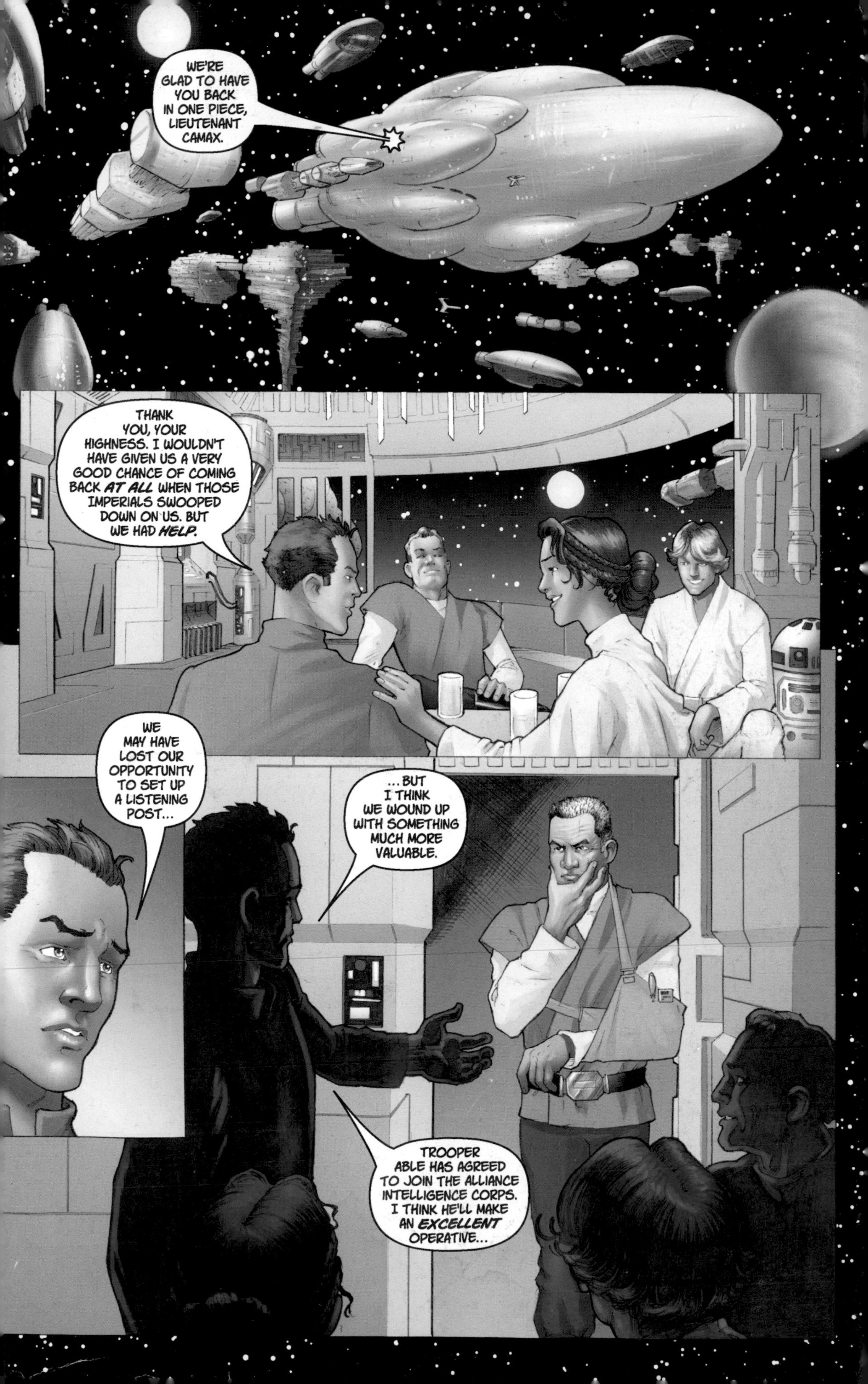
WE'RE GLAD TO HAVE YOU BACK IN ONE PIECE, LIEUTENANT CAMAX.
THANK YOU, YOUR HIGHNESS. I WOULDN'T HAVE GIVEN US A VERY GOOD CHANCE OF COMING BACK AT ALL WHEN THOSE IMPERIALS SWOOPED DOWN ON US. BUT WE HAD HELP.
WE MAY HAVE LOST OUR OPPORTUNITY TO SET UP A LISTENING POST...
...BUT I THINK WE WOUND UP WITH SOMETHING MUCH MORE VALUABLE.
TROOPER ABLE HAS AGREED TO JOIN THE ALLIANCE INTELLIGENCE CORPS. I THINK HE'LL MAKE AN EXCELLENT OPERATIVE...

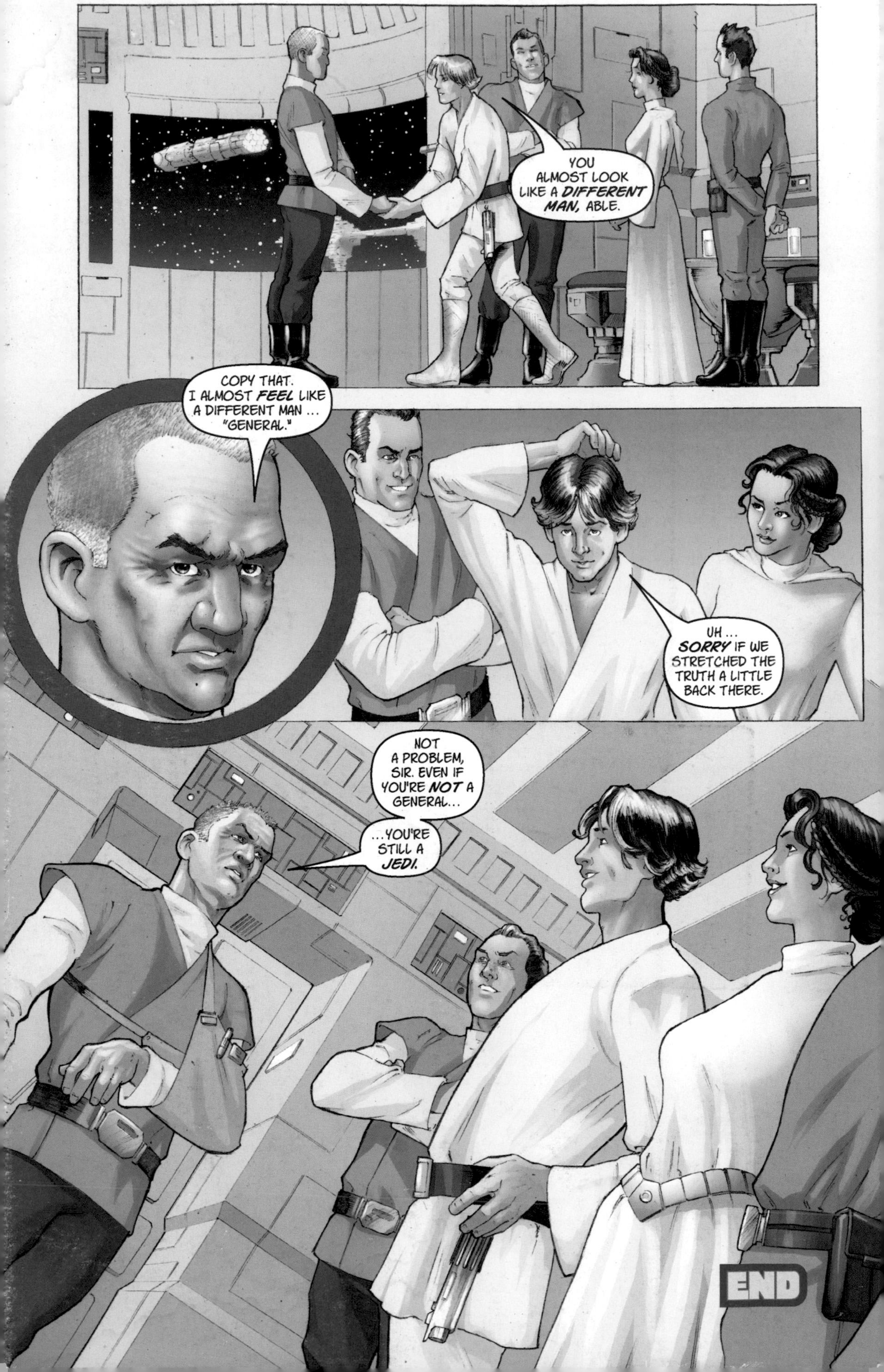
YOU ALMOST LOOK LIKE A *DIFFERENT MAN,* ABLE.
COPY THAT. I ALMOST *FEEL* LIKE A DIFFERENT MAN ... "GENERAL."
UH ... *SORRY* IF WE STRETCHED THE TRUTH A LITTLE BACK THERE.
NOT A PROBLEM, SIR. EVEN IF YOU'RE *NOT* A GENERAL...
...YOU'RE STILL A *JEDI.*
END